The Anglo-American Media Connection

The Anglo-American Media Connection

Jeremy Tunstall
and David Machin

OXFORD
UNIVERSITY PRESS

OXFORD
UNIVERSITY PRESS

Great Clarendon Street, Oxford OX2 6DP

Oxford University Press is a department of the University of Oxford.
It furthers the University's objective of excellence in research, scholarship,
and education by publishing worldwide in

Oxford New York

Athens Auckland Bangkok Bogotá Buenos Aires Calcutta
Cape Town Chennai Dar es Salaam Delhi Florence Hong Kong Istanbul
Karachi Kuala Lumpur Madrid Melbourne Mexico City Mumbai
Nairobi Paris São Paulo Singapore Taipei Tokyo Toronto Warsaw

with associated companies in Berlin Ibadan

Oxford is a trade mark of Oxford University Press
in the UK and in certain other countries

Published in the United States
by Oxford University Press Inc., New York

© Jeremy Tunstall and David Machin 1999
First published 1999

British Library Cataloguing in Publication Data

Data available

Library of Congress Cataloging in Publication Data
Tunstall, Jeremy.
The Anglo-American media connection/Jeremy Tunstall and
David Machin.
Includes bibliographical references and index.
1. Mass media—Great Britain.   2. Mass media—United States—Influence.
3. Mass media—Europe.   I. Machin, David.   II. Title.
P92.G7T857 1999   302.23′0941—dc21   99–32730
ISBN 0–19–871522–6

1 3 5 7 9 10 8 6 4 2

Typeset in Minion
by RefineCatch Limited, Bungay, Suffolk
Printed in Great Britain by
T. J. International, Padstow, Cornwall

Acknowledgements

Thanks to the Economic and Social Research Council (and Simon Frith) for a grant covering the entire twenty-four months of 1996–7; also to my City University colleagues for allowing me to take twelve months research leave during this period.

David Machin worked full time for twelve months on this project during 1996–7. He participated actively in all phases, including planning, interviews, the drafting of several chapters and rewriting and editing of most of my drafts. He focused especially on film, music, the Internet, and Spain.

Thanks also to my colleagues in the Euromedia Research Group; since an initial meeting in Denmark in 1982, we have met once or twice a year in Amsterdam, Arhus, Athens, Barcelona, Bergen, Bordeaux, and numerous other European locations. Special thanks, for active assistance on Austria, Germany, the Netherlands, and Italy to four Euromedia colleagues: Josef Trappel; Hans Kleinsteuber (University of Hamburg), and Diana Luhmann; Kees Brants (University of Amsterdam) and Caroline van der Horst; and Gianpietro Mazzoleni (University of Genoa) and Clothilde Galáno.

Christopher Sterling (The George Washington University) was outstandingly helpful in several ways, including reading the American chapters in draft. Finally to Michael Palmer (University of Paris, III), thanks for much hospitality and help, including manuscript reading; some of the ideas in this book derive from our two co-authored books on French and British policy and on media moguls and Europe.

Finally thanks for helpful and revealing interviews to nearly 150 senior media people, mostly in London, but also in New York, Washington, DC, and Madrid.

J.T.

City University,
London EC1V 0HB

Contents

List of Tables and Figures

Tables

Figures

Introduction

THE rapid advances of globalization in general—and of media, communications and financial globalization in particular—came to be widely regarded as truisms in the 1990s. Much earlier than this, books had been written with titles like *Global Talk* (1981) and *Mass Communications and American Empire* (1969).[1]

The media globalization excitement of the 1990s came 100 years after an early Anglo-American (and French) global media invention, the mass sale popular newspapers of New York, London, and Paris. Further waves of American worldwide media influence appeared at intervals of about twenty years. These included the American silent feature film's world conquest around 1920 and the dominance of American media and popular music in the late 1940s. The 1960s saw the world importing American television series and copying TV genres and formats; subsequently in the 1980s and 1990s the world followed the American lead in deregulation, satellite-to-cable, the multiplication of entertainment channels, and much else.

It was argued in *The Media are American* (1977) that each of the main mass media had been (if not invented) packaged into its definitive shape within the USA, and to fit American conditions and market preferences. However, that 1977 book also carried a subtitle: *Anglo-American Media in the World*.[2] In contrast to the earlier volume, the middle two parts of this book deal with Britain, sandwiched between the United States media (Part I) and the European media (Part IV).

In looking at the British media in this wider international context, we seek to present a case study which will throw some light upon 'global' media questions. Britain itself was a pioneer in worldwide media activity. For example the British news agency, Reuters, was (along with Havas of France) the late nineteenth-century pioneer distributor of fast news around the world. The BBC in the 1940s was the world leader in broadcasting credible radio news in numerous separate language services.

This book argues that Britain has attempted to remain a globally significant player in world media. It has had some success in its attempt to be number two in certain media fields (Part II). But this success has been

---

[1] Joseph Pelton, *Global Talk* (Boston: A.W. Sijthoff, 1981). Herbert I. Schiller, *Mass Communications and American Empire* (New York: Augustus M. Kelley, 1969).

[2] Jeremy Tunstall, *The Media are American: Anglo-American Media in the World* (London: Constable; New York: Columbia University Press, 1977).

achieved at cost of a subservient role in relation to other major elements of US media (Part III).

The Anglo-American media relationship in several respects parallels the Anglo-American political, military, and diplomatic connection. While the 'special relationship' is flattering to Britain it is, of course, less salient for the United States. Nevertheless the Anglo-American relationship—in the media, as in politics—can be convenient, comfortable, and commercially beneficial. The American military know (not least from Vietnam) that it is more comfortable to have the British military (and hence media) alongside. So also on the world media playing field, Disney-ABC and Time-Warner-CNN are happy to compete with the BBC.

The BBC, and the British media generally, are welcome to Hollywood and other US exporters because they typically are not seriously threatening commercial competitors. Indeed in this book, we argue that Britain's 'global' media presence is mainly confined to quite narrow areas, such as news.

The other larger western European countries (France, Germany, Italy, and Spain) have rather modest global media accomplishments. Europe is also a reminder of the importance of the continental, or world regional, level. But Europe has been a significant world media region mainly as a market for US media exports. As a general rule, European countries are successful neither in exporting media to each other, nor in exporting media to the world outside Europe.

Four Out of Six Key US Media Export Markets Feature an Important Anglo/British Involvement

The United States is the only genuinely global exporter across a range of media and into most countries in the world. Even this global presence is strongest only in feature films, music, and top-of-the-range TV series (such as comedy, crime, and documentary); also important is American leadership and influence in terms of genres, formats, fashions, and media policies.

But even the USA, as a media exporter, obtains very little revenue from at least 100 of its smaller export markets (especially in Africa and the Caribbean). Of its six major markets in the world, four have a British media connection:

First, Britain itself has long been a leading market. London played a key role in the American film industry's conquest of the world market from 1910 onwards. London later played a similar role in launching American advertising agencies, television series, and themed satellite-to-cable TV channels onto the world scene.

Second, the 'old' Commonwealth countries, especially Australia and

Canada, have been crucial markets for US media. Throughout the twentieth century both were key markets and early importers of US media innovations. In 1925 Australia, Britain, and Canada together accounted for 48 per cent of Hollywood's movie export earnings.[3] Subsequently these three ABC countries were key innovators in commercial television (mixed with public systems). By 1990 these three countries offered an English-speaking market of 100 million different-but-not-too-different customers. All three countries also played a modest offshore production role for Hollywood.

Third, the 'new' Commonwealth countries especially of South Asia, but also Africa, are important as another massive (if not yet lucrative) market where English is widely spoken and where Anglo-American traditions have a foothold. Some predictions suggest that India's population will eventually exceed that of China. Just six countries (India, Pakistan, Bangladesh, Sri Lanka, Nigeria, and South Africa) together already have about one-quarter of the world's population.

Fourth, Europe is much the most lucrative export market for US media. Britain is, of course, a member of the European Union and provides a convenient base and entrance point for many US media companies.

Fifth, Japan is an important market for certain US media exports, especially top-of-the-line Hollywood feature films. However Japan is unique in both being largely self-sufficient in media and having a substantial media presence in the US market. In recent years Sony in particular has established itself as a major US company both in music and in Hollywood film-and-TV production and distribution.

Sixth, Latin America is a potentially lucrative export market for American media. This export relationship was already strong in the 1920s (Hollywood and news agencies) and 1930s (commercial radio and music). The large and rapidly growing 'Hispanic' population within the United States enables both Los Angeles and Miami to be major media exporting locations into Latin America. However this is also a two-way trade; some high-capacity US satellite and cable systems already offer numerous separate Spanish-language channels.

The special circumstances in both Japan and Latin America suggest that the first four markets—all with an Anglo-or-British involvement—will remain the main source of US media exporting profits at least for the next two decades.

---

[3] Kristin Thompson, *Exporting Entertainment: America in the World Film Market, 1907–1934* (London: British Film Institute, 1985).

United States Media Leadership

The United States media have led the world in the multiplication of the number of video channels available to a typical national household. Other countries tend to look towards the USA where they see both more channels and also more production. Britain was in the lead in Europe in launching a second, third, and fourth TV channel and in hosting satellite-to-cable channels; Britain thus added to the persuasion of the US case another more modest alternative version.

A few increasingly vertical American companies—such as Disney, Time Warner, and News Corporation—are the companies most active as exporters. A standard approach with a new media service, such as a satellite 'themed' offering, has been first to roll it out across the United States and then, if possible, to roll it out across the world.

Typically a country which imports a lot of American media output, subsequently replaces some of the imports with domestic product. Nevertheless current (digital and other) channel multiplication again increases pressures towards more importing.

Where the US population grazes, the rest of the world will snack. US households already have more TV sets, and more TV channels, per household than are found in other countries. Most Americans have already learned to graze across broad acres of media material, nearly all of it made-in-the-USA. The rest of the world also tends to prefer its own domestic product, especially during the high-audience evening hours. However outside the main evening prime-time viewing meal, the rest of the world is snacking heavily on American imports; the US imports are mainly on lesser channels or on the bigger channels outside the main evening hours. As it spends less of its viewing time on the bigger channels in the evening hours, the world audience will be confronted with more and more American breakfast, daytime, and late night snacks.

Washington has broadly seen its role as supporting the US commercial media, encouraging competition and discouraging the sins of monopoly. Washington politicians and regulators are also happy to boost the finances of the media in general as well as those of Hollywood in particular.

Media policy seems to be an area in which national politicians combine fantasy, self-delusion, and high moral purpose, with a fondness for seeking crude short-term political advantage. The Anglo-Americans certainly cannot claim to be free of self-delusion. British policy has for decades been affected by nostalgia and inaccurate recollection of the past. The BBC is often encouraged to carry on where the British empire left off several decades earlier.

Not only London, but also Washington seems to experience difficulty in evolving policy for international mass media. Washington used to see the

American media as a useful tool, for example, in encouraging separatism and nationalism inside the Soviet Union. However, Washington's most successful efforts even here were conducted in partnership with Britain.

But the US media in general and Hollywood in particular have provided, and still provide huge support in other areas of American international leadership. One is the general field of fast-moving consumer goods; America's fast-moving consumer media have promoted and exported the popular culture of which these consumer goods are a central part.

Meanwhile the more weighty Anglo-American news (and financial news) media have supported American international banking, financial services, and commercial deregulation. Hollywood entertainment is part of a wider 'communications' business which incorporates telecommunications, computer software, aerospace, and the Internet. Much of this latter industry has had, and still has, military and intelligence expenditure connections. This wider, both software and hardware, communications industry plays a hard ball game; Hollywood participation in a range of broad communications issues—such as software copyright piracy—adds considerable lobbying advantages in Washington, in Brussels, and around the world.

Historical Phases in the Anglo-American Media Connection

An *imperial era* (1860–1914) saw Britain both building and defending its empire. Britain was the initial world leader in the two main Victorian media forms—namely books and news. In the news field the British agency Reuters was the senior partner in a world news cartel which first started to divide up the world foreign news map in 1859. The main partners here were French and German agencies; Reuters was also in partnership with various United States 'Associated Press' agencies. In this early period, Britain was the international and serious (or elite) news leader. But in domestic national media terms, the United States had already developed the largest newspaper press ever seen. In several respects the period around 1900 was the key period for the invention, or reinvention, of the modern mass media. While more British newspapers took the high road, the popular newspapers in New York and other big US cities developed modern popular journalism, including the popular daily not closely tied to a political party. Also invented mainly in New York was modern advertising, and again 'objective' commercial advertising not closely linked to political party. New York, more than any other city, invented popular recorded music, commercial entertainment, and the flickering pictures which soon moved via Los Angeles to world conquest.

Second, during the *era of world wars* (1914–50) the political establishments in Britain and the USA consistently allowed each others'—and their own— media a degree of freedom available in few other countries. In the case of both world wars, the American authorities allowed substantial leeway to British officials and journalists to conduct pro-British campaigns in the domestic US media, campaigns which did indeed help to bring the USA into both wars on the British side. British politicians and media people in this period regarded most Europeans as politically suspect; certainly the US media were regarded as more democratic, potentially more helpful, and more commercially dynamic.

Hollywood cultivated its British connection, because throughout this period Britain was easily its top market. Unlike Germany, France, Italy, or the USSR, Britain was reluctant to impose peacetime restrictions on Hollywood exports. But Britain was important also as the gatekeeper to its huge empire. In the second war there was an integrated Anglo-American media plan (which reflected the integrated military command). Moreover during 1943–9 the Anglo-American allies 'forced freedom' on the media of Italy, Japan, and Germany. But it was only in Germany that the American and British occupation forces ultimately concocted a democratic media plan which was a genuine mix of British and American elements.

During the *cold war era* (1950–80) various elements of Anglo-American partnership continued. Britain's empire unravelled into the Commonwealth, with United States media again being strategically placed for media exporting. Compared with both the previous and the subsequent eras, the full potential blast of American commercial media competition was held back by cold war inhibitions. Britain was allowed to continue various favourable cartel agreements; Britain also saw itself, and was widely seen, as the leader of European 'public service' broadcasting as well as the still limited use of TV advertising.

The *era of deregulation* (1980 onwards), which is the focus of this book, saw more aggressive United States commercial media efforts. In some respects Britain slipped into a state of media dependency; but Britain continued to see itself as number two to the United States media. While the USA offered the world 'deregulation', Britain had an alternative version called 'privatization'.

Britain as Media Number Two to the USA (Part II)

Anglo-American media intimacy has a long tradition. This tradition already existed in 1750, was strong in 1850, and had further developed by 1950. The 'long tradition' includes the following common components:

- A long period of freedom of the media from government or from party political control. In contrast to other media powers, throughout the twentieth century the USA and British media have not suffered under fascist, communist, or military regimes.

- The media occupations similarly have maintained their non-political independence and a general freedom from commercial bribery.
- US and British media companies are, compared with those of other nations, financially transparent.
- The Anglo-American media have long been, and are today, close to the financial communities of New York and London.

In five specific fields the British mass media can claim to be world players and significant number twos to the US lead:

The flow of news around the world is dominated by two countries, the USA and Britain. Reuters and AP are the leading news suppliers around the world, not only in text (aimed mainly at newspapers), but in still photographs, graphics, and foreign video news for TV. The United States is the world leader in terms of selling its foreign news—its daily world views and news—around the world. Depending upon the criteria adopted, either Britain or the rest of Europe would come second with the other third. Britain's three leading players in world news today are Reuters, the BBC, and the *Financial Times*.

In factual television Britain is a significant world player. This includes the BBC and (British 'public service broadcasting') as well as the news, documentary, and natural history genres.

The *world popular music industry* is in an especially volatile and chaotic state. But Britain has clearly played a prominent supporting role (to US music) in this field in recent decades. Relevant to this have been the English language, EMI, and the BBC's role in pop music on both television and national radio.

Britain's *book publishing companies* play a prominent role in a wider Anglo-American book publishing industry.

In the *advertising agency* business Britain is also prominent; London is the leading advertising business location in Europe. British agencies have been significant in developing (with American companies) 'professional' and transparent practices in advertising; British (and French) companies in recent years have introduced the concept of the specialist media-buying company to the world advertising business.

Britain as Subordinate to, and a Media Dependency of, the United States (Part III)

Across the broad range of entertainment Britain has the negative long tradition of adopting a defensive posture in the face of the Hollywood onslaught. This all began when American film exports first dominated British cinema screens around 1914. American entertainment from Hollywood also posed a huge challenge to British television, especially from 1955 onwards. Here again, the British response was defensive. This defensive posture—in relation to imports of entertainment and fiction from Hollywood—has become ingrained into most kinds of British TV and film entertainment. The defensive posture has been central to latter-day definitions of Public Service Broadcasting. For decades the British commercial television regulator required the ITV companies to limit their American imports and to engage in as much British (and thus virtuous) programming as possible, especially in the expensive fiction areas in which Hollywood specialized. Even when programming formats such as quiz/game shows were imported, these were to be populated with British performers; other undesirable elements—such as large prizes—were also heavily rationed and disapproved of.

One consequence of this defensive-posture-against-Hollywood was that all of British television (and such British film as existed) tended to be inward-looking, parochial, and focused on lovable, somewhat caricatured, British idiosyncrasy and eccentricity. This extremely—or excessively—British material did not make for mass exporting success and meant that, overall, neither British films nor British TV made full use of the potential international advantages of the English language. Such exports as did occur mainly involved a few limited genres—such as costume drama and odd-ball comedy—and mainly small audience markets (Northern Europe, the Commonwealth, and American PBS) which liked the costumes and the comedy.

Between the 1960s and the 1990s some of this changed, but the relationship between British and American entertainment remained broadly the same. One major commercial success of the 1990s was the BSkyB satellite-to-home operation. This ensured that British video entertainment would enter the twenty-first century with four major entertainment entities: the BBC, ITV, BSkyB, and Hollywood.

The BBC has fought its defensive battle skilfully. But its still large audience share is shrinking. Its share of total British TV-and-film finance will shrink more rapidly. The BBC is already a bigger importer from, than exporter to, the USA and it is destined to enter more deeply into various partnerships with American companies.

The ITV network, now dominated by two companies (Granada and Carlton), has continued to operate a highly profitable, and effectively monopolistic control over television advertising in Britain. As this huge advertising share reduces, ITV will seek to exploit the dominant position it has been given in Britain's terrestrial digital TV effort. ITV exports little to, but imports a lot from, the USA.

BSkyB—usually regarded as the creation of Rupert Murdoch—was operated by News Corporation (also its leading owner) through its first decade. Although the common European view of BSkyB as a fully American company is an exaggeration, BSkyB does rely very heavily on Hollywood movies; it also offers over 100,000 hours of American programming per year.

Hollywood companies and product are, then, rather well represented on the British entertainment scene. Although over 80 per cent of British cinema screen time is taken up with American movies, this is not the main source of Hollywood earnings in Britain. Video (purchase and rental) is twice as big as cinema. Moreover, the Hollywood majors are not merely supplying most of the product available in cinemas and video stores; Hollywood companies own a lot of the cinemas and video outlets. Without Hollywood, BSkyB would be missing at least half of its programming, including one of its two main engines, the 'pay' movie channels. Moreover Hollywood is overall providing between 25 per cent and 35 per cent of the programming on all five of Britain's main broadcast TV networks.

The Anglo-American-European Connection (Part IV)

Is Britain a Trojan horse for the American media in Europe? The broad answer is No. The other larger countries in Europe—especially France and Germany—have a media import/export stance very similar to Britain's. All three countries—France, Germany, and Britain—do the following:

- They import very little audio-visual material from each other.
- Each of the three imports large amounts of films and TV series from Hollywood.
- All three countries schedule predominantly domestic programming, especially in prime time on their larger channels.
- All three countries export some films and TV mainly to smaller same-language neighbours (e.g. Belgium, Switzerland, Austria, Ireland).

In this context, western Europe's two biggest errors were first the ludicrous Television without Frontiers policy, which was intended to limit imports from the USA, but achieved the precise opposite. Second, Europe's other big error was the national policies of 'injudicious channel multiplication' or setting up lots of new channels without thinking about what programming might go on those channels. This injudicious bout of TV nationalism was led by Italy with France and Germany following. Only later did Britain make its big injudicious channel multiplication decision—Mrs Thatcher's award of a monopoly to BSkyB in late 1990.

Britain's media industry does differ somewhat from those of France and Germany in the high degree of integrated US–UK ownership. There is some high-profile American investment in British cable, in BSkyB, and in foreign subsidiaries of American film, advertising, book, and music companies.

Slightly less well known is the extensive British media investment in the

United States. This tends to be deliberately low profile, rather like the British ownership of some iconic American hamburger, cigarette, and oil companies. In fact so extensive is US investment in the British media and also British investment in the US media that most sizeable British media companies are either US owned companies or (in more cases) British media companies with significant involvement in the US media. These 'over there and over here' media organizations include most British advertising agencies, the BBC, BSkyB, Cable and Wireless, Carlton, Daily Mail, EMAP, EMI, Flextech, Granada, Oxford University Press, Pearson, Rank, Reed Elsevier, Reuters, W. H. Smith, Telegraph, Telewest, Times Newspapers, Trinity, United News and Media.

Although fewer German and French media companies have owned significant slices of the US media, this is changing quite rapidly. German and French companies are significant owners within the domestic American book, magazine, music, and advertising agency industries. This indicates that it is not only American and British, but also German and French, companies which are increasingly constructing an integrated Euro-American media industry.

PART I

Britain and Other American Media Advantages

1

The USA as Popular Culture Number One

At least since 1914–18 the United States has been the world number one both in popular culture and in mass media. Around 1914–18 the USA acquired leadership of the world film industry. The USA subsequently managed to put the imprint of its own popular culture onto each major media innovation. In the late 1990s American leadership in the multiplication of new video channels was incorporated into new digital versions of television.

In digital satellite-to-home television the USA was clearly established as the initial leader. By December 1997 the USA had 71 per cent of the world's digital satellite TV homes.[1] Equally significant DirecTV (the US leader) was in late 1997 already offering 175 digital channels, while in France (the then number two) both competing systems were each offering only 30 digital channels. Digital direct-to-home TV in the USA still faced an uncertain future due to imminent competition both from cable and from terrestrial digital offerings. But the American experience seemed certain to influence all other countries' digital TV roll-outs. Moreover the American example carried the persuasive implication that the rest of the world should also aim for 200 plus (rather than 30 plus) channels. This American choice, meanwhile, had been powerfully shaped by American market-place conditions and popular culture profusion.

The same American companies are leaders both in media and popular culture as well as both within the USA and on the world scene. Time Warner and the Disney company are major forces within the USA in film, in broadcast television, and in cable television. Their names are almost equally familiar on cinema and TV screens across the world. They are also leading distributors of American popular culture. The two companies, between them, are active in *sports* (CNN and CNNSI, World Championship Wrestling, ESPN, and ESPN-Eurosport); in *children's entertainment* (DC Comics, Cartoon Network, Hanna-Barbera, the Disney Channel); *popular music* (Warner); and *theme parks* (some ten Disney parks including those in Paris and Tokyo, and Warner theme parks).

While the United States is universally recognized as number one in

[1] *Screen Digest* (June 1998).

popular culture, there is no such agreement as to which country is number two. Britain, France, Germany, and Japan all have ambitious popular culture industries. All of these countries look up to—and import from—the United States, but they do very little pop culture importing from each other.

Both the mass media and popular culture are marked by very steep international hierarchies. Each country's position in this hierarchy is established by its patterns of media and pop culture importing and exporting. Each country only imports from countries above it in the hierarchy; for virtually all countries in the world this means importing from the United States and perhaps from a larger country which speaks the same language. Most of the world's countries have no significant media or pop culture exports. A smallish group of larger countries (including Britain, France, Germany, India, Japan, Mexico, and Brazil) are both significant importers from the United States and also exporters mainly to smaller same-language neighbours and to ex-colonies.

Within this steep hierarchy the pre-eminence of the United States is seen in two main ways. First there are direct imports, trading relationships, and franchising; this covers everything from imported films and programmes, through toys and other copyright merchandise to Coca-Cola and McDonald's hamburgers. Second there is much non-copyright copying of general ideas, programming genres, business practices, and commercial approach; other countries may adopt (and change) the TV soap opera or talk show format, or they may copy the commercial practice of syndicating recorded shows for subsequent reuse.

Some features of United States media and culture generate both direct trade and also indirect influence. One example is the American 'star system'; polling organizations report that most of the 100 most-recognized names within the USA belong to current stars of movies, television, music, and sport. Some, but not all, of these US star names are also widely known around the world; in some cases the world does not comprehend the original American context (for example in sport); but most US stars still shine around the world helped by movie advertising or product endorsement or press and TV gossip.

Media moguls are another category of personality with a recognizable image not only within the USA but also around the world. In the 1990s many people around the world who had never watched any CNN news channel still recognized the name of Ted Turner; many people who had never read a Rupert Murdoch publication were still aware of his political views. The US media mogul phenomenon also seems to have other indirect consequences; just as journalists tend to be obsessive news-watchers, so media moguls seem to be obsessive watchers of other media moguls. The media moguls of a century ago—such as the young Northcliffe and the young Hearst—took a strong interest in each other. Today we see media moguls (and media stars) not only in Europe, but also in Mexico or Brazil, modelling themselves after other northern stars and northern media moguls.

Yet another example of direct and indirect influence is the Hollywood Oscars or Academy Awards. The Oscar exercise has a publicity/promotional impact around the world, not least because many TV channels carry all or part of the awards ceremony. But the Oscars have long had another indirect influence because many other countries have set up their own domestic equivalents; however, as each country promotes and celebrates its own entertainment stars, it is also more broadly celebrating showbiz glitz in general and stardom in particular—both areas in which the USA has an acknowledged supremacy.

In popular culture, as in the media, the British have long been low-profile allies of the United States. This is a loose and old alliance based on a long tradition of cultural overlap and common language.

But British media companies are helpful to the United States in other more specific and contemporary ways. Lists of the world's 'Top Fifty Media Companies' vary considerably because their definitions of 'media' and 'company' also vary. But in most such lists the USA holds most of the top ten places; Britain is nowhere to be seen. However among the 'companies' between number eleven and number fifty there may be as many as eight or ten British outfits (such as BBC, BSkyB, Carlton, EMAP, Granada, Pearson, Reed Elsevier, Reuters, United News, and WPP). A very few German or Japanese media companies may be bigger or more visible. Meanwhile Anglo-American (including Australian and Canadian) companies can add up to nearly two-thirds of the world's largest media companies.

2

Brits on the Anglo-American Team

How pleasant to know Patric Knowles
Who is the kindest of souls.
But being handsome and a British swell
Nobody expects him to act very well
Which is why he never gets good roles.

THIS limerick was referring to Patric Knowles (1911–96) who played 'best friend' roles, supporting such leading men as Errol Flynn. Although Patric Knowles never became a big star, he acted in over fifty films between 1936 and 1968. Like many Brits who went to Hollywood, Knowles was neither a big success nor a big failure.

Perhaps the most startling element in the present Hollywood ethnic mix—apart from the very few senior people of African or Hispanic descent—is the size of the British contingent, especially the actors. The Academy Awards are one simple measure of what Hollywood collectively approves; since the Oscars began in 1927, about 25 per cent of all the Best Actor and Actress awards have gone to foreigners, and of these awards to foreigners about three-quarters have gone to British performers.[1] The British also provided a sizeable crop of Best Directors, while in 1996 Emma Thompson became the first woman ever to win both a Screenplay award and the Best Actress award.

Among the ten most Oscar-winning films in Hollywood history are *Lawrence of Arabia* (1962) and *The English Patient* (1997). Both of these had British directors who used mainly British actors; but both films reflected the interest of their American financier-distributors in melodramatic settings and British eccentricity/nostalgia.

Most stars are national stars only; they are big at home, but unknown outside their own country or own language. The English language, obviously, gives both American and British stars a more realistic chance of superstardom. But while many British stars want to take a run at Hollywood, many others prefer to retain the accents, idiosyncrasies, and jokes for which the home audience has learnt to love them.

Music is another area in which the USA has been generous in awarding superstar status to British players. Exactly three decades after their first US

[1] Emmanuel Levy, *And the Winner is . . .* (New York: Frederick Ungar/Continuum, 1990). The same trends have continued since 1988 (when Levy's data end).

tour (1964) the Rolling Stones in 1994 achieved the highest gross ($121 million) ever earned by a music tour. Since the 1960s the US tour has been a standard rite of passage for ambitious British pop groups; meanwhile Andrew Lloyd Webber was a unique force in New York theatre from 1971 when *Jesus Christ, Superstar* opened on Broadway. But there has been so much visiting back and forth for well over 100 years between the London theatre and the New York theatre that they can be regarded as two wings of a single theatrical tradition. This merging of the two theatres took perhaps its most extreme form in the 1980s.

Britain has always had a weak film industry, and London acting—like acting in most places—is generally insecure and low paid. A Hollywood offer of work indicates some certain employment at (by London standards) a high rate of pay; the fleshpots of Los Angeles beckon, the winter climate sounds attractive, the professional experience alone will be a career plus. For several decades there was also the attraction of lower income tax rates. Richard Burton, in 1952, was already a successful actor of big Shakespeare parts, but at age 26 he was hot for Hollywood. He was offered three films at (in latter day equivalent) over $1m per film and he accepted.[2]

Despite sometimes cynical and arrogant British actor assumptions, Hollywood has always welcomed a steady flow of British actors; Hollywood attitudes also involve some cynicism and arrogance. But, as seen from Hollywood, the British actors come from a well-known stable; they have typically performed not only in British repertory theatre and the London West End, but they may already have acted on Broadway as well as in films and/or television. The Brits also tend to be quite cheap, especially when they first arrive. Whilst many American actors prefer to play sympathetic characters or charming villains, the Brits believe that the outright bad guys are often the best roles. The Brits take happily to playing serial killers, Nazis, corrupt politicians, sexual perverts, child molesters, and upper-class idiots. The Brits also relish eccentricity and cameo parts. Some Hollywood directors seem to like British actors, partly because they are more disciplined (in the theatre tradition) and may have slightly smaller egos than do some American actors. Many Hollywood people are Anglophile. Thus Ben Kingsley was enabled to show his acting range as a mobster as well as playing the saintly lead in *Gandhi*. Anthony Hopkins got to play a serial-killer-and-cannibal as well as President Richard Nixon. James Mason played the paedophile lead in *Lolita*, in 1961; and in the remade *Lolita*, which was one of Hollywood's top commercial disasters of 1998, another British actor, Jeremy Irons, took on the paedophile burden.

The Brits are present in substantial numbers in and around north west Los Angeles. BAFTA (the British Academy of Film and Television Arts) long

---

[2] 'Hot for Hollywood', in Melvyn Bragg, *Rich: The Life of Richard Burton* (London: Coronet Books, 1989), 112–31.

had a sizeable separate Hollywood branch. British actors, writers and journalists are especially fond of Santa Monica, which reminds them of Brighton
or Eastbourne, but with added palm trees.

The Occupational Diaspora of Anglo Media

The British actors who star in Hollywood movies, and the American actors
who star in British (usually Hollywood-financed) movies are the most visible element in a much wider occupational diaspora of Anglo media people.
Within this occupational diaspora there are many Americans; since early in
the twentieth century US citizens have been involved in local film and
advertising industries in many countries around the world. There is also a
scattering of British media personnel in the wake of empire, Commonwealth, and English language. Many scattered Anglo media people—whom
Americans may see as 'English'—are more accurately Canadian, Australian,
South African, Jamaican, Indian, Irish, Welsh, or Scottish. Even New
Zealand—despite its small population—has in recent years contributed
generously to this diaspora.

These 57 varieties of non-American Anglos fit well with the needs of
Central Casting in Hollywood for a steady flow of different (but not too
different) actors and actresses who speak English with a different (but not
too different) accent. Many of the best 'English' actors and actresses have
emphasized their Welsh (Richard Burton), Scottish (Sean Connery), and
Irish (Daniel Day Lewis) connections. We may soon see another 'English'
global diaspora of performers who emphasize that they are really neither
'English' nor 'Indian', but Pakistani, Bangladeshi, Sri Lankan, or East
African.

In recent years Hollywood movie packagers have often been looking to
complete the package with a director who may be able to offer the youthful
movie audience that vital but mysterious 'cutting-edge gloss'. Quite often
they reject such obvious choices as music video-makers, 'independent'
movie-makers, advertising commercial directors, and recent film graduates
of the University of Southern California. Instead the movie package may be
completed with a young director who has already made one or two low-
budget films in New Zealand, Sydney, Glasgow, or London. This cheap and
young Anglo film-maker is different, but not too different.

Youngish Anglo directors—because of language and cultural affinity—
are more adept than most (but not all) European equivalents at plugging
into Hollywood circuits. For example Mike Figgis was the director of only
one small-budget film when he enticed two Hollywood name actors (Mela-
nie Griffith and Tommy Lee Jones) to act in *Stormy Monday* (1987), a gritty
crime thriller set in Newcastle, in north-east England. For his next film he
acquired Richard Gere and Andy Garcia. The 'unknown' British director

had the cultural insight to recognize that Hollywood stars are often out of work and happy to accept a low-budget, but 'artistic', offer. The unknown Figgis (in fact with a long acting-directing-music career behind him) went on to direct Nicholas Cage in *Leaving Las Vegas*.

Most British movie stars of 'international' status are represented by one of the three top Hollywood talent agencies. The agency reads scripts for the star and negotiates to obtain for the star more 'authorship' in the final product; the agent aims to 'position' the star in terms of career development. Being represented by a Hollywood agency also makes it more possible for an actor or director or writer to seek work in Los Angeles while continuing to live and work in Britain.

But many other Britons accept work in the USA (and Americans accept work in Britain) without knowing how long they will be staying. The big advertising agencies appoint people between London and New York to occupy senior positions; some of these stay for a shortish tour of duty, such as three years, while others stay much longer.

This open-ended job transfer approach is probably easier for Britons and Americans than for people whose native tongue is not English. The open-ended move is also common in journalism. In British journalism there is a big gap between a few thousand national newspaper and TV/radio jobs and all of the rest; both 'provincial' and magazine jobs rate more lowly. London newspaper journalism thus attracts more aspiring youngish journalists than it is able to accommodate with any but the most lowly jobs. Consequently national journalism (what was 'Fleet Street') sucks hundreds of journalists into London each year, but also blows out hundreds of journalists; some of the latter try their luck in the USA or in Canada or Australia. American east coast publications edited by Brits during periods of the 1990s included the New York *Daily News* and *Post*, the *New Yorker*, *New Republic*, *Vanity Fair*, and *Vogue*.

American tabloid journalism of both the daily and weekly kind has employed large numbers of British and Australian journalists in the major US tabloid locations of New York, Florida, and Los Angeles. Many sleaze and scandal stories about entertainment stars appear either in the American or British tabloids, before being picked up by more respectable journalists on more respectable publications. Many Anglo tabloid journalists have worked for Rupert Murdoch in all three locations of the Oz-UK-US media empire. There is also a parallel echelon of newspaper and television barons and executives who have worked for Murdoch on two, three, or four different continents.

Behind the Occupational Diaspora

Behind the very visible occupational diaspora there has been a, somewhat less visible, Anglo-American media industry connection based on commercial and political self-interest as well as upon elements of shared ideology.

The 1940s began with a British diplomatic and media campaign against United States neutrality; but while many Britons were 'selling war' to Americans, many American east coast journalists and west coast film-makers were quite enthusiastically buying the idea of war. Hollywood produced movies in which the bad guys were German spies. Ed Murrow's radio reports from London included the dramatic sounds of bombs, anti-aircraft gunfire, and footsteps walking (not running) to air raid shelters. The British Embassy in Washington infiltrated numerous areas of the American media, including the currently super-popular Joe Palooka strip cartoon.[3] The American best-seller lists were full of books recounting tales of British heroism under fire.

Even after the United States entered the war in late 1941, it was agreed that the BBC would take the radio propaganda lead in Europe. In 1950 the BBC was still doing more external radio broadcasting than either the USSR or the Voice of America.

Cold war concerns played a big part in US space satellite investment and also in the expansion of international telephony. When in the 1960s Intelsat, the civil space satellite pioneer, was launched it was initially 61 per cent owned by the USA; the second largest owner was Britain with 8.4 per cent. Subsequently, United States efforts to introduce deregulation and competition into international telephone traffic again meant that foreign partners were required; again Britain was the leading foreign partner as British Telecom was 'privatized' and telephone competition introduced. Also during Ronald Reagan's first presidential term the United States left the UN cultural organization, Unesco; and the British (Thatcher) administration soon followed the USA out of Unesco.

The international trend to trade and financial liberalization was already well advanced by the early 1980s. Again the United States was in the lead, but Britain was also a strong advocate of currency convertibility and financial deregulation. These ideas and practices were carried around the world by the International Monetary Fund, the World Bank, and by multinational companies. Also in the vanguard were the international editions and services of the *Wall Street Journal*, AP-Dow Jones, the *New York Times*, *Business Week*, and other publications; no less committed to free trade and deregulation were the British *Financial Times*, Reuters, and *The Economist*.

The United States media industries have always acquired the bulk of their

[3] Nicholas John Cull, *Selling War: The British Propaganda Campaign against American 'Neutrality' in World War II* (New York: Oxford University Press, 1995), 176.

export revenue from a small number of foreign markets. This has continued to be the case with Australia, Britain, Canada, France, Germany, Italy, and Japan still providing the bulk of export revenues. Also important is the Spanish language market which involves Spain and Latin America, as well as the domestic US market. Of these few countries most are either English-speaking or are located in western Europe. Britain is the only country with a foot in each of these two major markets. These few markets are also the only ones which have quite high levels of media wealth and competition and quite low levels of media piracy. China and India, however, pay little and a movie or TV export sale to New Zealand (despite its tiny population) may generate more revenue than either of the Asian giants.

3

Hollywood Genre Menu

HOLLYWOOD, of course, did not invent comedy or melodrama. But it did repackage these traditional forms into movie genres; and it succeeded in transferring these entertainment genres from movies and radio into television and then subsequently into cable-and-satellite 'themed' offerings. The 'situation comedy', for example, was transferred from commercial radio to commercial TV and then exported to the world.

A similar pattern occurred with other Hollywood-defined genres such as the cowboy-western adventure and the game show. Around 1915–20 Hollywood successfully took control of the world's menu of entertainment genres, and it has continued to shape that menu ever since. As each new media era arrives, the Hollywood entertainment industry transfers genres across from older media (such as movies and radio) into the new medium (such as television or cable). This process helps to speed the adoption in the USA of the new medium because the American public recognizes that it is being offered a familiar genre in a fresh media package. This old-genre-in-new-medium is nearly equally acceptable in the main export markets which are broadly familiar with the genre in question. The rest of the world accepts the new offering—such as the TV situation comedy in the late 1950s and early 1960s. The world pays to import the American programming and many countries also copy the genre-format for their domestic productions. This acceptance in turn strengthens Hollywood in two ways. First, the foreign revenue feeds back to the USA and helps to provide generous finance for Hollywood production; second the world—by accepting new US genres—is in effect being trained and prepared for yet further crossovers of old familiar Hollywood genres into future new media offerings.

Luck, Skill, and Genre

Hollywood's business success was based on the familiar combination of skill and luck. The industry pioneers were astute in their recognition that the movie industry was a 'one-off' business with customers needing to be hooked into paying to see each new movie show; the pioneers discovered two key hooking devices—the genre and the star. A familiar genre plus a familiar star (such as Mary Pickford or Charlie Chaplin) were the perfect double hook. But the movie pioneers (most of them born in east or central

Europe) were also lucky to have arrived on the scene as the United States was becoming a world leader in marketing and advertising as well as in commercial entertainment.

A second huge piece of luck for Hollywood was the fact that scale economies took an extreme form in the movies. Most of the production cost went into making the first copy of the film; and, after these costs were covered, subsequent audience numbers were extremely profitable. This meant that the 'natural' market for the movie was the whole world, and these industrial conditions made it likely that a single country would become the dominant movie power.

Yet another major piece of luck was the 1914–18 war, which effectively held back all of the European film industries under wartime controls and censorship. By 1920 Hollywood was successfully established in its new business of selling entertainment genres to the world. This commercial success led Hollywood further to emphasize its own commercial definitions. Hollywood in the 1920s already had a menu of enticing genres which it successfully offered to the world. All other countries in the world sampled the tasty American offerings, while also trying to develop home-cooked alternatives (which typically appealed only to their home audience).

Each time there was a major new electronic media offering—especially TV around 1950—other countries in the world tended to drop their national diet plans and to binge on imports from the USA. These imports were attractive around the world not least because they typically belonged to genres already familiar from the previous medium. Eventually other countries began to make their own TV soap operas, game shows, and talk shows. But in so doing they were sticking to genres which were originally made-in-USA; the other countries were also in effect being prepared for the future crossover of American genres from television into the 'new media' of cable, satellite, and video.

Genre, Hierarchy, and Continuity Across Media Eras

A Hollywood star vehicle movie aimed at big audiences will cost several hundred times as much to produce as a movie about sex with a vacuum cleaner aimed at an 'underground' film festival. Likewise star actors may earn 1,000 times as much as other performers or 'extras' in the same production. Similarly steep hierarchies are present in television; in talk shows, for example, the 'host' salary may account for the bulk of all production costs.

The steep financial hierarchy is linked to genres and subject matter. Expensive forms of output include aliens, animation, movies based on bestsellers, costumes (period), dinosaurs, disasters, helicopter crashes, large casts at multiple locations, new special effects, and war. Cheap forms include daily soap drama, games, pornography, small casts on a parking lot, and talk.

There are also huge inequalities in market strength. The supplier of a major bundle of cable channels will be able to obtain a good price from local cable operators who want the popular channels. But the small supplier of a lone cable channel may well have to pay the cable operator to carry the channel on his local system.

Despite huge changes from the silent movie era to today's 100 plus channel offerings, it can be argued that the film and video genre menu has remained basically the same since around 1900. The dominant offerings are still comedy and melodrama. Sixty years after the birth of the radio sitcom, there were no less than fifty-nine TV sitcoms running on the six main American TV networks at the start of the 1997–8 season. Melodrama today includes not only the crime/police/gangster/noir genres (and sub-genres) but also print comic-originated superheroes, special effects, computer-assisted science fiction, and police-assisted 'reality crime' shows.

Genres have always merged as well as subdivided in a manner which has so far defeated both overall mapping and even agreed definitions of the main genres. Figure 3.1 seeks to trace a few broad trends across five eras in media history. Most important is the pattern by which each new era draws upon the previous period.

When American television began to use Hollywood as its main production base in the early 1950s, it drew heavily not only on feature films but also on commercial radio (much of whose entertainment programming had been produced in Hollywood since the late 1930s). In fact Hollywood-produced television drew less on the high-budget (big cast, big star) 'A feature' tradition and more upon the low-budget 'B features'; these latter included westerns, cheap (often comic-book originated) science fiction and also cinema serials (a silent movie tradition which only gradually succumbed to TV competition).

American television around 1950 was experiencing the formidable problems which start-up TV operations in Europe were to experience a few years later. The key problem was the unrelenting demand for seven days a week programming and the limited revenues initially available from the small audience and tentative early advertising. Neither the New York advertising agencies nor the Hollywood majors could solve this dilemma. Even Hollywood's low-budget 'Poverty Row' studios (such as Columbia and Universal) were unable to meet the super low-budget requirement of TV in 1950. It was actors, not big movie studios, who became the first successful TV innovators and producers of distinctively television programming. Desi Arnaz produced his wife Lucille Ball (and himself) in *I Love Lucy* during 1951–5.

Another successfully innovative actor-director-producer was Jack Webb with his *Dragnet* police show which began on TV in 1951. It was a radio drama show, now transferring into weekly television. *Dragnet* relied heavily

Figure 3.1 US media genre inheritance across five video eras

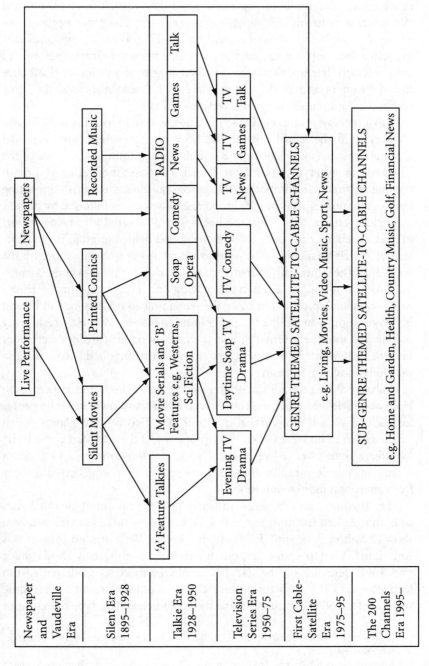

on the cooperation of the Los Angeles Police Department (an earlier version of which was the model for the silent Keystone Kops). The LAPD allowed Webb access to its files, although the names were changed 'to protect the innocent'. Jack Webb was so insistent on quickie production methods that the actors were not even required to learn their lines; the *Dragnet* actors read their lines off TelePromTer, which helped to give the series its distinctive into-the-camera and in-the-viewer's-face look. Webb also used the same scripts for both the TV and radio versions of *Dragnet*.[1]

In 1951 there were still few TV sets in Europe. Britain had much the largest TV service in the world outside the USA and (even with just one BBC channel) was also experiencing the ravenous programming demands of the TV medium. After 1955 (with the launch of its second network) Britain became the first major importer of US programming; this British importing lead—as in most aspects of television around 1955—was followed by the rest of western Europe. This was the beginning of a rapidly growing export market which fed cash back to Hollywood and helped to establish the pattern of 'deficit financing'—the production company spending more on the series than the American TV network was paying for its showings. A common pattern found the US network paying only 60 per cent of the Hollywood company's production costs; the remaining 40 per cent had to be met by 'syndication'—by selling the programming into the domestic reshowing market and into the international market. Thus export earnings were built into the Hollywood TV business, just as export earnings had been built into the Hollywood movie business.

Hollywood's radio tradition not only contributed programming genres to Hollywood television, but the commercial radio tradition of separate genres for each 'day part' also carried over into TV. Two key TV genres which originated in radio were the daily soap opera and the situation comedy. By 1939 there were seventy-five hours a week of afternoon serial soap opera drama on American radio;[2] some of these soap dramas transferred directly from afternoon radio to afternoon TV.[3]

The situation comedy genre similarly transferred, although much less smoothly. At first the most successful TV comedy was the comedian-driven show of Milton Berle on NBC (1948–55); Milton Berle around 1949–51 was American TV's top comic act, but his (initially live) weekly shows made impossible demands on the star. Ultimately the more script-driven sitcom format of the *I Love Lucy* type achieved a more polished result by recording with three linked film cameras and a studio audience. This type of half-hour

[1] Christopher Anderson, *Hollywood TV: The Studio System in the Fifties* (Austin: University of Texas Press, 1994), 67.

[2] Michele Hilmes, *Hollywood and Broadcasting* (Chicago: University of Illinois Press, 1990), 61.

[3] Muriel G. Cantor and Suzanne Pingree, *The Soap Opera* (Beverly Hills, Calif.: Sage, 1983).

comedy continued to dominate the key early prime-time 'day part' across the ensuing decades. The crime/police shows and other more sex-and-violence action material then filled later prime time.

When cable television entered substantial numbers of American homes, from the late 1970s onwards, most of its new offerings were 'themed' channels. This new themed satellite-to-cable programming was really 'genre' programming; the new channels selected from the existing genre menu to provide a specialist (one-genre) alternative. In the next two decades the commercially successful cable channels often had a fairly traditional genre look: ESPN became a sports channel, a genre popular from both radio and the press; QVC—a 'shopping' channel—could also be seen as an 'advertising' channel; CNN was news; Nickelodeon was for children; HBO was mainly newish movies; Discovery was documentary—a movie genre since the earliest days; MTV was a music channel.

During the 1990s, a growing number of American households started to receive over 100 separate channels—in most cases this was a satellite-to-cable service, but from the mid-1990s the 100 plus channel service was also available from satellite direct-to-home. Many new networks were assembled to fill some of the new slots. This new era encouraged the launch of new channels based on a sub-genre. For example in addition to the broad sports offering of ESPN there was the Golf Channel (1995); in addition to the all-news format there were specialized channels covering, for example, just sports news or financial news. In addition to the Lifetime channel there were now such offerings as Home and Garden Television, the TV Food Network, and America's Health Network.

The arrival of the numerous sub-genre networks in the mid-1990s was linked to the arrival of digital television—initially direct-to-home—and its much larger number of separate channels. An increasing number of networks focused on specific hobbies, lifestyles, consumer interests, and animals; and the number of ever more specialized music, news, and documentary offerings also continued to expand.

The Pornography Genre

Pornography is an example of a video genre in which United States producers seem to have maintained an international lead, at least at the 'high end' of the market. There seem to be few reliable facts and very little transparency in the nude video business. But there is little doubt that the US 'adult' video business has an annual retail gross of several billion dollars per year; as with so many other genres this substantial domestic revenue has enabled the US to acquire a reputation for producing highish-quality material and for marketing its output efficiently. Consequently much of the pornography which Europeans (and others) rent and buy from the video store, and see on adult channels or late at night on major TV channels, was produced in Los Angeles.

Most 'new media' have gone through a pornographic phase; since the new medium is unregulated and not yet concerned with brand reputation, more or less anything goes. The non-respectability of the early movie medium derived partly from its what-the-butler-saw pornography. When video rental began—in both the USA and Europe—pornographic titles were prominent. So also with new cable and satellite channels; a high proportion of early Internet, pay-per-view, CD-ROM, DVD, and other 'new media' use has involved pornography.

After the United States and other countries introduced rigid film censorship in the 1920s, pornography reverted to the arena of the printed word—magazines, comics, books—and, of course, the still photograph. There was only a smallish trickle of 'stag films'.

The spirit of the times was very different in 1987 when Steven Hirsch and a partner established Vivid Video in the northern suburbs of Los Angeles. The San Fernando Valley, a few miles to the north of Beverly Hills and Sunset Boulevard, is the location of the world's biggest and most prosperous pornographic film industry. The Valley's porno studios, which produce some 5,000 adult films and videos per year, are surrounded by numerous specialist supplier companies, talent agencies, aspiring talent appearing in live shows, and an active trade press. There are annual Oscar type awards. This is one of a number of genre-specific sub-industries to be found on the fringes of Hollywood. As elsewhere in Hollywood, the industry is both fragmented (anyone can make a porno video) and highly concentrated. The Playboy company, while still producing a magazine is increasingly a naughty video company with a bouquet of cable channels—the softer porn Playboy and the harder porn AdulTVision, plus its acquisitions, the Spice and Adam and Eve channels.

The most highly esteemed supplier of quality porno product to Playboy, after 1987, was Steven Hirsch's Vivid Video. Hirsch himself was born into the Los Angeles porno film business and applied a standard movie business marketing approach. He focused on good-quality (or better than the competitors') product; he even paid as much as $15,000 for a script including some elements of plot. He focused on biggish volume (about 100 films a year); he signed female porno stars to contracts and used them to promote the business. He sold the product through the maximum number of market windows, especially in all available 'new media'. He reused material from old films by re-versioning it into new productions. Vivid Video also offered hard-core and soft-core, alternative versions, of the same film.[4]

---

[4] Adam Sandler, 'Adults only, big business', Variety, 19–25 January 1998. Paul Karon, 'Vivid aims its appeals at John Q. Public', Variety, 9–15 March 1998. 'The Sex Industry', The Economist, 14 February 1998, pp. 23–5. Dominic Schreiber, 'Company Profile: Playboy Entertainment Group', Television Business International (December 1998), 30–3.

The domestic US pornographic video business is huge; its total gross revenue (including video stores, new media, Internet, adult bookstores, gas station outlets, and mail order) is probably not much different from the gross domestic theatrical revenue of 'legitimate' Hollywood. However probably a smaller slice of the retail gross gets back to the producers.

Porno-Hollywood is also an active exporter, especially to Europe. Clearly in Europe it faces competition; in most European countries substantial quantities of pornography are available on cable, in video outlets, and on major TV channels. Countries such as Germany, France, and Italy each have their own idiosyncratic mixes of puritanical regulation and unregulated anything goes. There is little reliable information as to how much video product seen in the rest of the world originates in the USA and Hollywood.

But pornography exports easily because the pictures tell the story. The US porn industry clearly has some advantages similar to those enjoyed by more 'legitimate' US media. Even though (as Hugh Hefner has often said) porn is a 'high margin business', the leading US producers appear hugely to outspend their international porn competitors. Vivid Video claims to be the most highly regarded porno brand in the world. Behind the Santa Monica mountains they're sticking to the high end of a low business.

The USA now only Shares the Lead in Some Genres, but Remains the Dominant Exporter in Most Major Entertainment Genres

Genres in which the USA now has to share the export leadership with others include both 'cheap' and 'expensive' genres. Two cheap ones are soaps and game shows. The United States, of course, invented both the radio and the television soap operas. But by the 1990s the Latin American telenovelas had, arguably, seized leadership of the world soap opera market. Mexico, Brazil, and Venezuela in the late 1990s were producing nearly 200 hours of serial TV fiction each week. The three countries were building on a tradition strongly influenced by the US radio soaps. But the Latin-American soaps had changed several key rules; telenovelas only lasted around 150 episodes; they were scheduled into evening prime time. In the 1990s some European countries imported both United States daytime soaps and Mexican or Brazilian telenovelas. But the telenovelas were more successful in many poorer countries; there were for example telenovela exporting booms in Russia (1992), Indonesia (1994), and the Philippines (1996).

European countries also followed Latin America in making their own distinctive versions of the soap opera. Just as Televisa launched the first Mexican telenovela in 1958, so British ITV created its first soap in the form of *Coronation Street* (1960). By the late 1980s western Europe was still only producing eight soaps—six British, one Irish, and one German. However, the rapid swing towards more commercial television meant that by 1994 there were twenty west European TV soaps and telenovelas; by 1997 there were over fifty soaps in TV production in fourteen different west European countries.[5]

The game show was another American TV genre widely imported and copied, from the 1950s, around the world. One of the last super-successful American game exports was *Wheel of Fortune*, which started in the USA in 1975; the *Wheel* appeared in Australia (1981), Britain (1983), France (1987), and Germany (1988) and subsequently in an additional fifty other national markets. But in the 1990s the American game show genre went into decline, not least because the talk shows—especially in the afternoon—attracted larger audiences. Consequently other European countries including the Netherlands (Endemol) and the British Pearson (Thames, Grundy, and All American Fremantle) and Action Time moved into the game business. A busy trade in game show formats began to operate across Europe, with decreasing American involvement. But again, American game shows did not disappear; other countries continued to import American game shows which, in several cases, had been invented many years earlier.

In video games, the Japanese involvement is clearly very prominent. And in two other factual genres—news (dealt with in a later chapter) and documentary—the British element is substantial. Britain and the USA each produce 100 separate TV documentaries or documentary episodes (30 to 120 minutes) per month. Precise numbers are hard to obtain, not least because 'documentary' has no precise definition. Moreover documentary is a very international genre; indeed many documentaries are jointly US–UK financed.

Another substantial group of genres are ones in which the USA leads as an exporter of 'high-end' or more expensive programming. Pornography, just discussed, is one such genre. Two others are daytime talk and reality crime. For twenty years (1967–87) Phil Donahue was the US ratings leader in daytime talk focused on ever more sensational single topics. Donahue stopped in 1996 by which time Oprah Winfrey was the long-established daytalk ratings leader. These shows—especially Oprah Winfrey—did seem to work successfully as direct exports. The sex-and-sensation topics and the confrontational production style evidently had universal appeal; also outside the USA there was the appeal of 'only in America would people confess to that on television'.

Then there was 'reality crime'. The biggest single portion of this genre appeared on the Murdoch-controlled Fox network from the late 1980s onwards. This cheap format (in several sub-genre variations) may be especially suited to US conditions; compared with other countries, the USA has

---

[5] Hugh O'Donnell, *Good Times, Bad Times: Soap Operas and Society in Western Europe* (London: Leicester University Press, 1999).

more police forces, which are more interested in videotaping their activities and seeing themselves on television. Compared with other countries, the US legal system is extremely tolerant of pre-trial publicity. Some of the US coverage also includes a strong element of Keystone Kops comedy as small town police forces strut their stuff before the 'reality' cameras. Nevertheless some of this programming crossed the Atlantic where both TV producers and police were keen to offer their own localized versions of reality crime.

Children's programming in general and animation in particular are other genre areas in which the USA dominates the expensive end of the output. Individual countries make some of their own children's programming, linked to national traditions, language, culture, and school system. Nevertheless several characteristics of children's programming match with American advantages. Children, when they view television, tend to watch a lot of non-children's programming. Moreover children's dedicated programming needs to be fairly age specific, and a small age range inevitably means a small audience. The type of children's programming which appeals to the widest age range happens to be Animation/Cartoon; this is an expensive product, but a product which travels well across cultures and one in which the USA is the leader. Four of the largest US companies have developed strong basic cable channels for children; Nickelodeon (Viacom), the Disney Channel, Cartoon (Time Warner), and Fox Family are formidable competition for producers of children's television in Europe and around the world.

Finally there are several other genres in which the USA remains the dominant exporter. These include the high-budget movie business and the television situation comedy; both of these genres in the late 1990s generated some single projects which eventually grossed over one billion dollars in the US domestic market. The super-popular sitcom seems to have more repeat stamina than any other TV genre; but the TV melodrama series—crime, police, hospital, science fiction—is still popular, and is also strong in many export markets.

And finally. The biggest American genre resource remains the movie. These come at several budget levels. The thirty most commercially successful movies each year gross about as much money as the next 200 or 250. But the USA offers the world at least 700 movies a year—if major distributor releases, the leading 'independent' movies, and also the output of made-for-TV movies are included. Almost all of these 700 will have had budgets of at least a few million dollars each. Since 1995 over half of these movies' total revenue has come from outside the USA.

4
Multiplication of Video Channels and Programming

THE typical US household has had access to a much greater number of TV channels and networks than has the representative European household. For example in 1975 the median household in the USA had eight channels of TV against an average of two or three in Europe.

Whenever a fresh TV channel has appeared in Europe (or elsewhere in the world), it has been able to acquire batches of entertainment from Hollywood to fill up the gaping holes in its schedule. Since the new channel is initially short of both finance and audience, the Hollywood seller typically demands only a modest price. Because of the much greater amounts of programming generated in the USA, with its bigger number of (more competitive) channels, there are usually plenty of TV series which have not yet been sold to any network in that particular European country.

Table 4.1 shows that the United States expanded the average number of channels per household as follows:

- During 1955–75 US households went from 2 to 8 channels.
- During 1975–95 US households went from 8 to about 40 channels.
- Starting around 1995 US households were entering another period in which those 40 channels would again be multiplied several times, quite probably up to an average of over 200 channels.

This channel multiplication phenomenon meant that at any point in time the USA had more TV channels than did any other part of the world. The rest of the world followed the US lead; proposals (in Europe and elsewhere) to increase channels often claimed that such increases were not only inevitable but desirable, and would still 'leave us well behind the USA'.

Because it was always stretching the channel numbers, the USA developed the rerun 'syndication' business more than did other countries; this meant that the USA not only had big backlogs of recorded programming, but it already had this programming neatly copyright-cleared, packaged, and bundled (often into runs of 100 to 200 episodes) and ready to be shipped abroad. In most countries the price paid for American TV series was less than 1 per cent of the original cost of production.

In 1970s Europe (and most of the world) it seemed natural, or at least

Table 4.1 Three phases of US video channel multiplication

Number of channels in median US households	Dates	Precipitating events	Extra video market windows
From 2 to 8 channels	1955–1975	1952: End of freeze on new TV stations 1955: 64% of US households have TV sets	• Movies reshown on TV • Evening TV reshown on daytime TV
From 8 to 40 channels	1975–1995	By 1975: Cable is in 13% of US households as HBO is first satellite fed cable channel. 1976: WTBS (Atlanta) as first 'super station' Basic Cable Services • 1979: ESPN, C-SPAN • 1980: CNN, USA. • 1981: MTV	Genre themed TV channels • Basic cable • Pay cable (movie channels) • Sports and movies on 'super stations' Video • Rental • Purchase
From 40 to 200+ channels	1995–2015(?)	1994–6 • Take-off of DBS offering 100+ channels • 1996 Telecoms act • 1995 Disney/Cap Cities, ABC merger	Sub-genre themed channels Direct-to-home satellite CD-ROMs Internet/WWW, Data, Movies-on-demand, Other interactive offerings

reasonable, to stick with just two or three channels. In many countries television was mainly funded by a 'public service' licence fee, so there was a good financial reason to stick to two or three channels in the 1970s; additional channels would not generate enough additional public finance.

In the USA in the mid-1970s it seemed equally natural that the typical household was already receiving about eight channels. These US channels were made up of three national TV networks (NBC, CBS, ABC) and typically an additional three local ('independent' and 'public') stations. In big cities there were additional independent channels; and many households could pick up other network-affiliated and independent stations from other nearby cities.

Radio provided another reason why video channel multiplication seemed normal and inevitable in the USA. Whilst most Europeans in the 1970s received around four or five radio choices, the forty largest US cities in 1975 each averaged 27 radio stations, while the few biggest cities had substantially more. Moreover US radio had decided to face the challenge of television by becoming predominantly local and split up into a number of distinctive 'formats', based mainly on music. In 1975, for example, about 20 per cent of all larger-city US radio stations played 'middle of the road' (MOR) music and another 20 per cent played 'Top 40/contemporary'; other popular and widely available radio formats were Beautiful Music, Country and Western, Soul, Progressive Rock, News and Talk, and Classical Music.[1] Since US television had already followed radio in many ways, it again seemed unsurprising in 1975 that television was beginning to follow the radio path of channels themed to specific formats or genres.

Channel Multiplication Two (1975–1995)—From 8 to 40 Channels—Creates 'Window' Sequences

It was satellite-to-cable channels which took the representative US household from eight channels in 1975 to about forty channels by 1995. There were also other major changes, including an increase in the number of conventional TV networks and a huge growth in home video.

As late as 1978–9 each of the three networks (NBC, CBS, ABC) had an average prime-time share of almost 30 per cent of the viewing audience. Twenty years later (1998–9) each of these three networks' shares had halved to only 15 per cent of the viewing audience. However by now there was Fox and also two baby networks. With these latter included, the drop looked less steep; three networks had a combined 90 per cent share in 1978–9; two decades later six networks still had a 60 per cent share.

Cable in 1975 had been present in only 13 per cent of homes and then

[1] Christopher H. Sterling and John M. Kittross, *Stay Tuned: A Concise History of American Broadcasting* (Belmont, Calif.: Wadsworth, 1990 edition) 648–9.

mainly just provided better picture quality, plus some additional local stations from nearby cities. Nearly all 'cable' viewing in 1975 was actually of broadcast channels. But by 1995 cable provided numerous extra channels to about two-thirds of all US homes; and in these homes it accounted for about half of all viewing. Nevertheless a broadcast network with 12 per cent or 15 per cent of all viewing across the USA still towered over any single cable channel. The ten most popular cable channels accounted for about as much total viewing as the next fifty, smaller, cable channels. Clearly cable generated a huge multiplication of, mainly very small-audience, new channels. By the year 1995 US cable was generating more (subscription and advertising) gross revenue than was broadcast television.

Also during 1975–95 there was a huge increase in expenditure on video software (sale and rental). In 1995 cable and video total annual revenue was over $500 per household (and rising fast) while greatly expanded revenue was generated by television. Paradoxically, as network TV's audience share declined, its advertising revenue continued to increase; the broadcast networks still provided the only truly mass market service. The four big networks remained profitable with their now larger groups of owned-and-operated stations doing especially well.

For a typical feature movie distributed by a Hollywood major company, there was now a sequence of about eight market windows, of which the theatre showings constituted only the first. By 1995, Hollywood had come to place ever greater emphasis on the first weekend heralded by the big advertising boost in the previous week. This first weekend could generate as much as 25 per cent of entire US theatrical revenue; it was generally agreed that a poor start made a poor total outcome inevitable. Hence the saying that launching a movie is like parachute jumping: 'If it doesn't open, you're dead.' By the later 1980s multiplex theatres were a major aspect of the US exhibition scene. Multiplexes were key to the marketing strategy, because the first (theatre) window established the image and word-of-mouth reputation of a film.

Each million dollars of revenue earned in the theatres was typically multiplied at least four times in the subsequent market windows of video rental and sale, pay-per-view, cable and satellite (pay and basic), and the broadcast network showings. This (changing) window sequence—like other domestic US media practices—transferred, with modifications, to other countries. Thus, as it goes out onto the world scene a single Hollywood movie starts to move sequentially through a series of hundreds of national market windows.

Well before 1995 another distinctive marketing sequence was established for the successful TV series. First the TV series was typically shown twice in prime evening time on a national TV network. After about four years the successful series was sold into 'syndication' for five-days-a-week 'stripping' on network-affiliated or independent stations. Later the series would go to a major basic cable channel; finally it might go to a more specialized or, sub-genre, cable channel.

1995 and After: Another Multiplication Era

While in 1995 the median American household still only had about forty channels, some households already had 100 channels or more. Already a very steep hierarchy was visible between the few big traditional broadcast networks and the numerous small new cable offerings, mostly with audience shares of only a fraction of 1 per cent of total US viewing.

Already in 1995 and the later 1990s there were sharp distinctions between A, B, and C networks.

Just *four 'A' networks* (the old broadcast three plus Fox) still had over half the total US viewing audience.

About *twenty or so 'B' networks*—including the cable Big Basics (such as ESPN, CNN, TBS, USA, MTV)—had about one-fifth of the total US audience. These networks had already established the fact that a 1 per cent share of the audience, supplied with appropriately targeted genre programming, could be very profitable.

Several hundred 'C' networks (national or regional) were also in operation by the end of the 1990s. With a total of one-fifth of the US audience between them, these networks typically had audience shares of the order of 0.1 per cent (or one-thousandth) of the USA total. Some of these were regional sports networks; some were very specialized sub-genre networks (one sport such as golf, or one type of popular music, or one sub-category of old movies); most of these tiny networks were losing money, but were oriented towards the imminent digital future.

But the post-1995 era of channel multiplication quickly challenged several of the key distinctions of the pre-1995 era:

- The old sharp distinction between a big Basic tier and a small Pay tier of channels was being replaced with smaller tiers and combinations oriented towards different viewer categories.
- Increasingly the sharp distinction between a 'big' and a 'small' network was being dissolved, as existing networks (both basic and pay) subdivided into several more specialized offerings.
- The traditional Broadcast/Cable distinction was also starting to disappear; some new networks were constructed out of a mix of local television stations and local cable outlets; both broadcast and cable networks were available on digital satellite direct-to-home. Internet and interactive offerings pointed to a future in which a single network would appear (sometimes in different versions) across broadcast/cable/satellite/internet/and other formats.

- The big vertical audio-visual companies were already positioning themselves to offer bundles or bouquets of a number of related, over-lapping, and cross-promoted networks (see Chapter 6).

These changes pointed to a continuation of the earlier hierarchy of A, B, and C networks; however the digital era will also see much change in the detailed operation of the hierarchy.

The whole US market will follow the digital satellite-to-home pattern in offering a larger and larger number of 'C' channels; many of these will be less than national offerings; many will focus on sub-genres; some will be sub-networks which operate for only part of the twenty-four hours; increasing numbers will be in Spanish and other 'foreign' languages.

At the 'B' network level, competition is likely to be especially fierce. Some networks with a 1 per cent audience share may be losing money, while some networks with perhaps only a 0.2 or 0.3 per cent audience share will be making big profits.

'A' networks seem certain still to exist, although in some cases these may overlap with or be hard to distinguish from the 'B' networks. There will continue to be a scarcity of the most popular top-of-the-line programming, such as the leading live sports, the big-budget movies, the most popular first-run weekly series, and the high-budget mini-series. Only networks with high popularity, high revenue, and high profitability will be able to finance the most attractive output. These networks will employ the currently most popular stars and will have the greatest resources for promotion and cross-promotion between networks and other media.

The USA was One Decade Ahead of Europe in Spreading Cable

In terms of getting multi-channel television into the majority of households, the USA was about one decade ahead of western Europe. In the USA the most rapid growth occurred during 1980–5 with cable advancing from 20 per cent to 48 per cent of households; this was also a period of dramatic growth in new satellite-to-cable networks. During the years 1980–3, at least seventeen new national satellite-to-cable services were launched, and already by 1983 it was possible to see the genre-to-sub-genre path that US channel multiplication would follow. In addition to CNN there was CNN Headline, Dow Jones Cable News, and the Weather Channel; in addition to MTV there were two separate country music channels (both launched in 1983).

In Europe, as in the USA, cable television initially depended upon trans-porting conventional TV signals from bigger population areas into smaller ones. In the USA much early cable growth involved small towns and cities importing conventional TV signals from big cities such as Chicago. In Europe much early cable growth involved smaller population countries, such as Belgium, importing conventional broadcast signals from larger neighbours such as France, Germany, and Britain. In the 1980s, especially, such larger countries as France, Britain, Italy, and Spain saw only very weak growth in cable.

Consequently the multiplication of cable channels in the USA followed the previous broadcast TV pattern in that the USA was well ahead of Europe. Moreover as the number of non-broadcast channels increased in the 1990s, the majority of these channels were, of course, own-country—or at least own-language—channels. The main partial exception, predictably, was the UK, many of whose 125 active cable and satellite channels in 1998 were really foreign (mainly American, European, and Asian) channels.

Most of the American networks which migrated to Europe were the basic channels in general and the actual, or would-be, Big Basics in particular. The possibility of making your new network not just a US-wide but also a Europe-wide phenomenon was one of the motivations lying behind investment in US cable offerings.

Will the same pattern apply to new digital channels and sub-networks? Yes it may, because in the later 1990s more US than European homes had access to new digital channels. However, Europe was only about two years (not a decade) behind the US digital lead. Digital may also fit well with European characteristics such as separate language markets.

Certainly in the late 1990s US digital multiplication was well advanced, with the Nielsen research company in 1998 already measuring more than 250 national and regional cable networks. Europe had a larger total number, but a much higher proportion of these were 'local' (national rather than Europe-wide).

An Era of Digital Uncertainty

The feature film production business can perhaps date its version of the 'digital revolution' from the *Jurassic Park* dinosaurs of 1993. In the next few years larger and larger Computer Generated Imaging (CGI) monsters emerged from space and from the oceans. Some movie budgets escalated dramatically, with post-production itself becoming a monster destroyer of cinematic conventions and business practices of all kinds. With the rising budgets, lengthening production schedules, and the extraordinary inflation of separate CGI scenes, the movie business found itself in a period of heightened uncertainty.

The 'digital revolution' in American TV/cable/satellite provision also generated many uncertainties from the mid-1990s onwards. These included:

- Uncertainty as to the prevailing digital alliances of the future. Clearly there would be competition between satellite direct-to-home, digital cable, and terrestrial (broadcast) digital service. In this contest, which technology would establish the better alliances with telephone companies, with the Internet, and with other service providers?

- Would video rental (and purchase) be transformed by one or more digital recording format?
- Could pay-per-view successfully market anything less sleazy than boxing and pornography?
- Would Spanish, and other languages, be important?
- After golf, financial news, and antiques, how many more networks could target the wealthy?

Amongst the many digital uncertainties, one of the few certainties was that many more networks would appear; the next round of channel multiplication would take place. Another near-certainty was a high rate of churn, with new offerings appearing, merging, disappearing, and reappearing. There is a strong element of dealing oneself into the game. A new sub-genre network may test the market; it may pre-empt the competition; and it may become part of a future merger, bundle, or bouquet. Other uncertainties included the policy paths followed by Washington in general (next chapter) and in particular the size of bouquet and the number of separate networks which would, or legally could, be owned by one vertical company (Chapter 6).

5

Washington as Media Policy Umpire and Commercial Booster

WASHINGTON constitutes another unique advantage for the American media. Washington media policy strongly supports the profitable expansion of the US media both at home and abroad. Washington media policy is also—by international standards—remarkably consensual. Vigorous contention occurs between (and within) the main branches of government. This makes for a slow and gradual evolution of media policy, a gradual changing of the rules to fit what Washington sees as current commercial reality. The American media industry is not subjected to the alarming political mood swings which characterize European media policy. Washington policies consequently suffer from fewer unanticipated consequences than do European media policies.

Some long-term themes in Washington media policy-making include the following:

1. Political lobbying by commercial media associations was pioneered in the nineteenth century by both book publishers and newspaper publishers. The Hollywood lobbying body was established in 1922. But for some forty years (1940–80) war and cold war gave weight to considerations of national security and foreign policy; since 1980, however, the Departments of Defense and State have largely withdrawn. This has left movie, TV, cable, music, telephone, computer, and press lobbies, and the copyright super-lobby (The Intellectual Property Alliance), to exert a commanding influence over US media policy.

2. Imminent 'technological convergence' between previously separate entities has been much touted since the 1970s by legislators, lobbyists, consultants, and forecasters. Some convergence does occur, but usually less and more slowly than predicted. Divergence is also common, as is 'sticking to our knitting'.

3. The broad thrust of Washington policy is slow and consensual. Most of the notorious Washington logjams do eventually clear; the final decision can depend on a 5–4 vote in the US Supreme Court.

4. Congress has passed very little significant communications legislation of any kind. AT&T, the telephone giant, was broken up in 1982–4 without any fresh legislation passing Congress. Even the Telecommunications Act of

1996—generally seen as the biggest piece of communications legislation for six decades—fudged several of the key issues.

5. With Congress largely self-immobilized, and the FCC (the regulatory agency) consequently enfeebled, some of the biggest decisions in recent years have been made by Federal Judges adjudicating merger and anti-monopoly cases.

6. Despite upbeat rhetoric about a digital or electronic superhighway, the Washington policy machine has had enormous difficulty in handling commercially vital information technology while also guiding politically vital mass communications. The Telecommunications Act of 1996 was supposed to encourage competition, especially in the telephone business. Some of its most immediate effects, however, were to encourage mergers between Hollywood producers and TV networks and also mergers within and between the telephone and cable TV networks.

A Separate Regulatory Box for Each US Mass Medium

Each main segment of the American mass media was given its own regulatory regime. Paradoxically perhaps, most of the regulating of these separate regimes was done by the same Federal Communications Commission. The FCC began life in 1934 with the twin tasks of regulating telephones and radio. Subsequently it acquired the tasks of regulating television, cable, and the civilian use of space satellites. Along with the anti-trust people in the Justice Department, the FCC in practice also had some regulatory oversight of Hollywood and over newspaper ownership of TV stations. In addition the computer-and-data business attracted much FCC talk, but little action.

The FCC was traditionally expected by Congress to encourage competition and to protect against potential abuses resulting from telephone 'natural monopoly' and from radio (and later TV) 'spectrum scarcity'. Where there were only a few privileged players (such as three television networks) they were to be prevented from abusing their semi-monopoly.

A crucial Washington media doctrine was that legally licensed semi-monopolists—in particular the TV networks and AT&T—should be confined to their clearly demarcated licensed area. These huge organizations should not be allowed to wander freely into other media.

After the 1945–55 earthquake of television's large-scale arrival, the policy consensus of the 1960s and 1970s saw each of the main media largely confined to its own regulatory box, where its good behaviour was then policed by the FCC (as well as by the Justice Department and the Federal Trade Commission). Their different histories and technologies—and differences in their entrenched political strengths—meant that each mass medium had its own quite distinctive regulatory regime.

- The press had a privileged position awarded in the First Amendment. Their traditional potency in national, state, and local politics ensured that newspapers were subject only to a very modest anti-monopoly regime. A central city dominant newspaper (such as the *Los Angeles Times*) was not allowed to own a TV station or to acquire a suburban newspaper in the same city. Newspapers even had some exemptions ('Newspaper Preservation') from general anti-trust law; and newspapers were also free to buy radio, and TV stations and cable companies outside their major newspaper markets.
- Multiple radio station ownership was severely restricted (until 1985) to a maximum of seven FM and seven AM stations. The radio industry thus lacked dominant companies.
- In television there were (by the 1960s) three dominant TV networks. But the networks were confined to under 25 per cent national coverage by their local owned stations. Washington thus left the networks to share television power with other group owners of local stations and also with the main programming suppliers in Hollywood.
- Cable television came from local roots and established a tradition of local monopoly. As cable grew in the 1950s and 1960s it was increasingly seen as the good small guy. From the late 1960s the FCC held cable back, before further rounds of deregulation and re-regulation.
- Domestic space satellites were opened up to competition in 1972. Fuelled by traditional cold war funding, space satellites were correctly seen by Washington to offer special opportunities for American media exporters.
- AT&T had been tightly regulated up to 1982–4. After 1984 the seven new regional Bell phone companies continued the tradition of regulated local monopoly, while AT&T faced the cold blasts of competition in its long-distance and equipment businesses.
- Washington had wanted to ensure that the computer industry was not monopolized by either AT&T or IBM. AT&T's attempts to enter the computer business after 1984 were painfully unsuccessful. The computer industry continued, after the relative IBM and mainframe declines, to exhibit extremes of both competition and monopoly. The advance of Microsoft and others left computer policy being made by the anti-trust authorities at the Department of Justice and the Federal Trade Commission.

Washington Helps a Self-Doubting Hollywood (1970–1985)

Hollywood went through a rather lean period of industrial self-doubt between 1970 and 1985. Previous to 1970 Hollywood could be regarded as having adjusted well to the post-war realities. Indeed the famous anti-trust

Paramount case, which forced the movie companies to sell their huge theatre chains, was a blessing, rather than the disaster it seemed at the time of the 1948 US Supreme Court decision. The movie companies were able to get out of the theatre business in good time before most of the audience decline (caused by TV) had yet occurred. Moreover Hollywood was not only divorced from the theatres at just about the right moment, it was able in the 1950s gradually to acquire most of the production of the more expensive TV programming. By 1970 Hollywood was also the focus of much of the pop music industry. Hollywood successfully redefined itself as the capital of movie-TV-music production. In addition, the crucial worldwide distribution business was still intact and still linked to the production studios.

Why then did Hollywood not think of itself as more successful? The reason seems to be that Hollywood still looked back to its supposedly golden inter-war years. The huge decline in US theatre audience numbers actually hit bottom around 1970; the early 1970s were a production low point, with feature films released by major companies briefly falling below 100 annually.

There was also a 1970s belief that Hollywood had lost control of its destinies, while the television networks were now the real powers and employers. The New York-based television networks were the wealthy patrons who decided which TV genres and programming would be produced; the network showings of movies also generated a substantial slice of movie revenue. The Washington policy-makers in the early 1970s collectively supported Hollywood against the networks; following an anti-trust consent decree, the FCC introduced its 'Financial Interest/Syndication' rules. These rules restricted the TV networks to acquiring the right to show TV series only twice (once in the winter, with a summer repeat). After that, the rights to the potential gold mine of 'stripping' the series (showing an originally weekly series, now five days a week) reverted back to the Hollywood production house.

Hollywood's crisis of confidence continued right through into the mid-1980s, partly because foreign markets still looked weak, but also because Hollywood felt threatened by cable, satellite, video, and piracy. Several developments in satellite-and-cable were especially disturbing to a Hollywood which had always been suspicious of new technologies—especially television technologies—in their early years. One startling technological change was Washington's 1972 deregulation of civilian space, which led to the first satellite delivery of programming in 1975 by Home Box Office; HBO was threatening to Hollywood because it could deliver premium programming—such as top boxing fights—via satellite-and-cable straight into households. HBO soon seemed even more threatening because it began to transmit new movies on a special 'pay cable' basis; instead of being delighted with this crucially important new business, Hollywood felt humiliated by such an innovation being launched by a non-Hollywood company (Time Inc). Some Hollywood managements may also have felt additionally humiliated, since most of these early profits were being shared between HBO and local cable operators.[1]

Another cable-and-satellite challenge to Hollywood was the appearance of several attractive new offerings (the superstations, ESPN, CNN, MTV, and others) which were provided to almost all cabled households as 'basic tier' channels. Most of these new channels also seemed to be bypassing Hollywood, while delivering entertainment direct into American living rooms.

The Hollywood industry was even more worried about the new home video-recorder. Hollywood feared the VCR would enable the public to record movies off their television screens. The arrival of HBO—which, unlike regular TV, showed movies both uncut and without commercials— was seen as adding to the video threat. This anxiety led two Hollywood companies (MCA and Disney) in late 1976 to launch court action against Sony and its pioneering Betamax VCR system. The case dragged on— through the federal appeal court and the US Supreme Court—for over seven years until January 1984, when Sony-Betamax and domestic copying-off-air were declared innocent and legal.

The Sony-Betamax case—added to the competing video formats—meant that the USA fell behind Japan and some European countries in terms of the spread of VCRs. The familiar new medium early phase of illegality and non-respectability was extended in the case of the VCR by the 1976–84 Sony-Betamax case. The Motion Picture Association of America estimated that in 1977 90 per cent of video retail revenue in the USA came from pornography; this (the MPAA claimed) fell to 13 per cent in 1984.

Throughout this period the MPAA focused overwhelmingly on copyright issues. Abroad they tried to persuade, especially European, governments to update their copyright legislation; in Washington the MPAA struggled to persuade Congress (especially the copyright subcommittees in both Senate and House) that video piracy was theft. Jack Valenti of MPAA impressed Washington's lawyer-politicians with the slogan: 'If what you own cannot be protected, then you own nothing.'

Hollywood's lobbyists around 1980 also had a gloomy view of foreign markets. Foreign video piracy of movies was massive; and Europe's monopoly public service broadcasters controlled networks which still imported only a few Hollywood TV series and paid relatively little for TV showings of movies.[2]

After the mid-1980s, however, Hollywood pessimism became less and less easy to justify. In particular the video market went quickly from piracy and

---

[1] Jeremy Tunstall, *Communications Deregulation* (Oxford: Blackwell, 1986), 165–70.
[2] Author interviews with John Giles, MPAA chief lobbyist in Washington, 28 Feb. 1984; and with Jim Bouras (of MPEA) in New York, 17 July 1984.

pornography into being Hollywood's biggest domestic market. In 1983 only 5.5 per cent of US households had VCRs, but by 1988 VCRs were in 58 per cent of US households. A similar boom in VCRs and Hollywood revenues occurred also in Europe. Britain, and then other European countries, followed MPAA advice and legislated against video piracy. Recording off air was less threatening (or more difficult to accomplish) than Hollywood had feared; there was also a huge boom in 'sell through' (direct sale) of movie videos which Hollywood had neither anticipated nor initially wanted.

But, most important of all, Hollywood benefited from communications deregulation in Washington, in London, and across Europe. As deregulation and new services spread and multiplied across Europe and the world, Hollywood experienced a huge surge in sales, profits, and self-confidence.

From Satellites to Internet: Cold War Technology Assists US Media

It was not initially obvious that US government expenditure on missiles, intended to deliver nuclear warheads, would assist Hollywood's delivery of entertainment. However President John Kennedy's January 1961 inaugural and his 25 May 1961 speech on space did foresee a satellite role for US telephony. Initially the showbiz was to consist of 'Men on the Moon by 1970' (achieved in 1969); Hollywood came later.

American military expenditure and planning played a substantial part not only in the space satellite field but in other Washington communications policy decisions. The US pattern of commercial telecommunications and broadcasting gave leading roles to a few high-technology companies. One of these was the telephone giant, AT&T, which in the cold war provided basic telecommunications services for the US military—including communications links for domestic missile sites. AT&T also invented key technology for the targeting of multiple nuclear warheads. This cold war role was one reason for allowing AT&T to be a telephone monopolist up to 1984. As the US telecoms flag-carrier, AT&T was also given a lead role in the development of Intelsat, which from 1969 became the core of the world telephone system. After lengthy investigations, the FCC opened up the domestic US satellite business to commercial competition.

Under the US system several large companies besides AT&T have had especially intimate involvement with the US federal government in general, and with the US military in particular, as well as with the mass media. One such company was RCA, which, together with AT&T, provided much of the technological base for both radio and TV in the USA. RCA had historically been close to the US Navy; RCA owned NBC, which was the leading early player in radio. Moreover in 1941, just before US entry to the war, RCA was already a key military contractor. Washington assigned post-war television to the VHF spectrum in line with the belligerent lobbying wishes of RCA. These decisions enabled RCA not only to carry over its NBC radio network role into the NBC TV network, but also allowed RCA to dominate the patents for the huge post-1945 expansion of US television.[3]

American creation of the Internet and the World Wide Web was also hugely assisted by cold war funding. The original ARPANET (Advanced Research Project Agency) used packet switching technology to link American computers, research labs, and universities involved in military research work.

Breaking Down the Partitions: Washington's Communications Deregulation Campaigns, One (Early 1980s) and Two (Late 1990s)

Washington's 'deregulation' of American communications had two particularly active phases. The high point of early 1980s deregulation was the break-up of AT&T in January 1984. The high point a decade later was the Telecommunications Act of February 1996 which may in retrospect be seen to have gone a long way towards knocking down barriers between separate industries and their respective regulatory regimes. Both deregulatory campaigns appeared to focus primarily on telecommunications, with only secondary attention given to the mass media.

In 1982–4 AT&T 'consented' to the anti-trust authorities, and its local and regional operations were broken away into seven new (and still monopolistic) regional 'Baby Bell' companies. AT&T itself was cut out of the huge local phone business and forced to face real competition in long distance against lean and hungry insurgents such as MCI and Sprint. AT&T's senior executives thought its true destiny lay in a marriage of computing and telephones. AT&T bought one of the big old computer companies and was further damaged, leading to another major break-up. AT&T also did badly in the equipment business, against fierce domestic and foreign competition.

AT&T around 1980 was misled by then fashionable rhetoric about the 'information' revolution. Much of the rhetoric saluted the 'convergence' of the separate media and communications services. The current Washington consensus increasingly suggested that 'natural monopolies' were now unnatural, and that separately regulated boxes were no longer required. The logic of technology and the spur of competition (it was said) now required that each medium break out of its box and advance fearlessly across a level communications playing field.

From the early 1980s there was some modest deregulatory relaxation of rules. Local television stations became still more secure and even less likely

---

[3] William F. Boddy, 'Launching Television: RCA, the FCC and the Battle for Frequency Allocations, 1940–1947', *Historical Journal of Film, Radio and Television*, 9, No. 1 (1989), 45–57.

to have their licences removed. Informal agreements to limit the amount of TV and radio advertising per hour were removed; the market could now decide, and the market duly decided to have more advertising per hour. Congress had failed to pass a major new communications law; the most important new such law of this period was the Cable Act of 1984.[4] The Cable Act largely removed cable price regulation; the Act also reduced the cable powers of local government and placed this now large mass medium under Washington and FCC regulation. The main consequence of this major piece of 'deregulatory' legislation was a big increase in cable consumer prices, and a big increase in cable unpopularity.

For the next twelve years, 1984–96, there was much continuing deregulatory rhetoric and a strong deregulatory trend (or creep) in FCC and other decisions. But there was little in the way of major new deregulatory initiatives. Indeed in 1992 (the Bush vs. Clinton election year) two pieces of re-regulatory legislation passed the (Democrat-controlled) Congress. One Act was in support of minimal amounts of children's programming on regular 'free' TV. The other Act punished the cable companies, by requiring them to reduce their inflated subscription charges.

The Late 1990s Digital Deregulation: Lower Barriers Between More Communications Boxes

The Telecommunications Act of February 1996 was lauded as the biggest piece of communications legislation since the baseline 1934 Act (which it amended) and also as the boldest deregulatory initiative to date. This major Act was accompanied by some of the protracted legislative trench warfare for which Congress is famous.

The main thrust of the 1996 Telecoms Act was supposedly to lower the partitions between three sets of players—the regional (Baby Bell) phone companies, the long-distance phone companies, and the cable TV companies.[5] The Congressional plan was that a long-distance company like MCI or Sprint should get into the local phone business; the regional Baby Bells should enter long-distance; cable companies should enter the phone business; and the phone companies should provide a competitive cable service. All of this sounded impressively deregulatory and competitive; it was also rather frightening to the phone and cable companies. The companies' initial reaction was to launch some quite small experiments; meanwhile these players all seemed more inclined to stick inside their existing industrial

---

[4] Tunstall, *Communications Deregulation*, 121–41, 240–1.

[5] Christopher Sterling, 'Changing American Telecommunications Law: Assessing the 1996 Amendments', *Telecommunications and Space Journal*, 3 (1996), 1–25. Michael I. Meyerson, 'Ideas of the Marketplace: A Guide to the 1996 Telecommunications Act', *Federal Communications Law Journal*, 49, No. 2 (Feb. 1997), 251–88.

boxes. Competition sounded challenging but risky, while the prospect of attacking big entrenched companies inside their existing businesses did not look like the best way to grow profit.

The Telecoms Act of 1996 obviously looked very different when viewed from different corners of the ever-vaster communications playing field:

1. The digital satellite-to-home television operations were now increasingly seen as the new 'good little guys' (even though the leading company, DirecTV, was in fact owned by the giant General Motors). Satellite-to-home still had small consumer numbers, it offered bigger numbers of channels, and it was 100 per cent committed to digital; it had no option but to compete, especially with cable, but potentially with others. Digital satellite-to-home could also be seen as the virtuous technology innovator, forcing the older media to follow it into digital multi-channel provision.

2. The cable television local operators increasingly saw themselves as having to compete against the companies inside four previously separate regulatory boxes. These competitors included: (1) the old enemy, the conventional TV networks and broadcasters; (2) the insurgent digital satellite-to-home companies; (3) the telephone companies (both long distance and local) which saw the phone-cable combination as one way to future digital success; (4) the computer companies such as Microsoft, seen as eager to bypass cable by providing entertainment on a computer screen. Faced with what they feared was an onslaught of fresh competition, the big cable MSOs (multiple system operators) saw the digital set-top box as the way to provide many more channels, with flexible options, and into an old-style TV receiving set.

3. The telephone companies after 1996 did not rush into each others' businesses. But there was widespread agreement that the 1980s pattern of some eleven big phone companies (seven Baby Bells, AT&T, MCI, Sprint, GTE) was too many. The main focus after 1996 was on mergers between big phone companies and some mergers with cable, teleport, and other companies outside the 'phone box'.

4. Some computer companies saw the explosive growth of the Internet as only the beginning of their involvement in home entertainment. Microsoft and other computer and information technology companies acquired local cable operators and also moved into the provision of digital set-top boxes for upgraded cable. Computer companies were involved in acquiring from the federal government, via auction, large tracts of radio spectrum for various uses. There were also plans for new generations of (high-capacity) low-orbit satellite systems.

Faced with all of this digital uncertainty, digital innovation, and digital competition, the conventional-traditional television stations and networks were also anxious about the future. However, amongst the many ambiguities of 1996 there appeared to be two initial winners—the old TV broadcasters and old Hollywood. Indeed these two were increasingly becoming one merged industry.

Then in 1998 AT&T took a huge step from the phone business into the cable business. AT&T did not itself offer cable service. Instead the still huge phone company was bidding to acquire TCI, the second largest operator of local cable systems. The AT&T/TCI merger received regulatory approval in early 1999 (three years after the 1996 Act). The merger triggered further waves of bids and counter-bids, which promised two further massive increases in concentration.

First, the separate US communications fields previously dominated by some thirty big companies spread across film, TV, telecoms, cable, satellite, computing, and internet, now seemed likely to melt down into a much more converged and concentrated communications industry, perhaps dominated by less than ten leading companies. Second, the AT&T merger with TCI helped to trigger mergers in Europe and also promised to lead to greatly increased US–European communications concentration and convergence.

Lobbyists Lobby, While Washington Sprinkles Holy Water

> Only the broadcast lobby uses the public property of the airwaves to threaten representatives in Congress with significant alterations of the public's perceptions in order to retain their private benefits ... They have a tool that no-one else has, and they use it.
> Reed Hundt, chairman, Federal Communications Commission (1994–7)

To most Europeans—indeed to many Americans—the Washington policy process seems excessively cumbersome, slow, politicized, and dominated by commercial lobbies. The original checks and balances system—as modified by generations of lawyers—produces huge quantities of communications bills, rules, and court cases, with very few completed Acts of law. 'Slow' is perhaps an understatement. It has taken an average of about eight years for each of several major communications policies to be finally put in place. It took the 1974–84 decade to get AT&T broken up, while the Sony-Betamax case spanned eight years. The Telecommunications Reform Act took five years (1991–6). The HDTV/digital TV standard, which was delayed by advances in digital technology, took nine years (1987–96).

Each of the communications industries has both its company and its trade association lobbyists who soldier on through these seven- and eight-year wars of Washington policy-making. Each of several separate communications and media lobbies are claimed, by some people, to be 'one of the most effective lobbying groups in Washington'.

Most successful is the newspaper lobby; all democratic politicians are afraid of newspapers and Washington politicians are especially fearful of the leading one or two newspapers in their district or state. All politicians try to be friendly with their local newspaper publishers and editors. The Washington newspaper lobby has a lot of powerful friends; the newspaper industry, consequently, is one of the most monopolistic and least regulated industries in the USA.

Hollywood's Washington lobby has changed its name several times, but the Motion Picture Association has been adept at lobbying, diplomacy, and imagery. The MPA (with a little side-door manipulation) has acquired the address of '1600 Eye Street', which sounds intimately close to (and is only two blocks from) the White House at 1600 Pennsylvania Avenue. Jack Valenti of the MPA was known in the 1980s as the most flamboyant Washington lobbyist; in the 1990s he was said to be the highest paid (nearly $1 million per annum). Traditionally the White House is supplied with the latest movies by the MPA. Several recent presidents have regularly held screenings in a special White House screening room (refurbished by the Reagans in 1982) which contains about sixty club chairs; cokes and popcorn (both air-popped and oil-popped) are served. The MPA also invites key politicians to its own screenings of new movies.[6] The MPA in recent years has aligned itself—for example on piracy and intellectual property issues—with the computer software, music, and other copyright interests. Hollywood thus presents itself as the icing-on-the-cake of the wider communications industry, America's biggest and best business export success story.

Three other communications lobbies may have to struggle with some belligerence. The Baby Bell regional telephone companies after 1984 built themselves up into hugely successful industries; but Americans still had no effective choice of local (as opposed to long-distance) phone service.

The cable lobby played the brave 'little guy' role brilliantly in the 1970s, but the big multiple system operators (MSOs) who lost out in the 1992 Cable Act are not exactly brave little guys any more.

The National Association of Broadcasters (NAB)[7] is the US media industry's equivalent to the National Rifle Association. While the NRA wields the big stick of the constitutional 'Right to Bear Arms', the NAB's big stick is the First Amendment (and Free Speech). Reed Hundt (FCC chairman, 1994–7) described the NAB as 'the most powerful lobbying group'. The 1996 Act extended TV and radio station licences to eight years and made renewal close to automatic. Station owners were also awarded a completely free and guaranteed entry into HDTV/digital broadcasting. Under the newly fashionable spectrum auction approach, this might have cost the broadcasters about $70 billion. Meanwhile the NAB was belligerently opposed to any legal requirement to screen children's programming for 26 minutes per day; the NAB was equally opposed to any requirement to 'give' free time to

[6] John Brodie, 'DC dreams it wakes up screening', *Variety*, 10–16 July 1995.

[7] Leslie Wayne, 'Broadcast lobby excels at Washington power game', *New York Times*, 5 May 1997. Paige Albiniak, 'NAB: King of the Hill', *Broadcasting and Cable*, 22 Dec. 1997, pp. 16–19.

politicians running for electoral office. The NAB, however, was quite happy with over 15 minutes per hour of advertising and promotions on prime-time television and about 20 minutes per hour out of prime time. Several key Republicans in Congress in the mid and late 1990s were on the same wavelength as the NAB. The Republican Majority Leader in the Senate—Trent Lott of Mississippi—had been a class mate at the University of Mississippi (Ole Miss) with Eddie Fritts, President of the NAB.

In addition to the broadcasters (NAB) and Newspaper Association of America, the other most potent communications lobby of recent times has been the Copyright Lobby; the latter has the impressive official name of the Intellectual Property Alliance and this includes some fairly non-intellectual things such as movies, TV programming, and pop music as well as published works and computer software. The Copyright Lobby claims that since 1996 it has been the United States' biggest export industry, having now surpassed the traditional leaders—agriculture, aerospace, and automobiles. The Copyright Lobby achieved a threefold legislative victory in late 1998, when the 105th Congress was devoting most of its dying days to the federal budget and the Monica Lewinsky–Bill Clinton saga. First, Congress agreed to extend copyright protection from seventy-five to ninety-five years. Second, Congress agreed to US ratification of World Intellectual Property Organization (WIPO) treaties which further strengthened US copyright law. Third, and perhaps most importantly, strong copyright protection was extended to the DVD and to cover all Internet and on-line transactions; it was now illegal to duplicate or distribute copyright material on the Internet without the permission of the copyright holder. This lobbying victory was achieved against the opposition of the electronics and telecommunications lobbies. The victory was achieved in mid-October 1998 and the involvement of the media lobbies—just before the November elections—may have been significant.

It was during the final negotiations on the HDTV/digital standard in late 1996 that Reed Hundt, as FCC chairman, urged the industry lobbies to come to a final technical agreement, thus allowing the FCC 'to sprinkle some regulatory Holy Water' on the agreement.[8] In the case of a decision as to the shape of America's future TV sets and TV technology, its chairman saw the FCC in this ritual 'regulatory holy water' role. The phrase fits not only many FCC decisions; the phrase also matches the general communications policy picture of active commercial lobbies, with a reactive—or umpiring—role for Washington policy-makers. To a very considerable extent not only the regulatory agencies—but also the Congressional committees, the courts, and the administration—umpire the lobbying contest and approve the final agreed consensual lobbying outcome.

[8] Harry A. Jessell, 'Hundt calls for free time', *Broadcasting and Cable*, 30 Sept. 1996, p. 26.

What may be most effective about this policy-making is its strong emphasis on commercialism combined with consensus. US media policy is overwhelmingly commercial. So also the policy process is itself heavily commercial, with relevant industries making substantial annual investments in Washington lobbying and in financial donations to key Congressional leaders and relevant committee members. The Washington policy process is, of course, highly political, but—by European standards—the ideological differences are minimal. The heavy commercial emphasis, in Washington, and the slow inch-by-inch search for consensus, avoids the huge policy reversals between different party governments which tend to make European policy-making so ill-conceived and ineffectual.

6

Bulking up for Digital: The Vertical Imperative

THE 1998–9 merger of AT&T's long-distance phone business with TCI's local cable operations was not precisely what the US Congress had had in mind with its 1996 Act. But this merger did promise to introduce real competition in local telephone service between AT&T/TCI and the local Baby Bell companies.

More generally, this merger focused on cable. It suggested that AT&T/TCI and Time Warner (the largest local cable operator) might become the two leaders across several communications fields and might bring cable and Internet closer together.

Cable had already been through several phases of being loved by Wall Street and hated by Washington, and vice versa. Now cable increasingly looked like the glue which would bind the various communications businesses into a single whole. Cable could aim to become a combined video-audio-Internet pipeline. Cable might become not the rival of television, but the partner or sibling of television. Already TV and cable were seen as one industry by many consumers; already executives who had risen through the ranks at MTV were in senior positions in television. By 1999 local cable systems cost about $4,000 per subscribing household, meaning that a system with one million households could now be purchased for about $4 billion.

Bulking Up: Mouse House Swallows Alphabet Net

The 1995 Disney acquisition of the ABC network and the 1996 Time Warner acquisition of Turner Broadcasting were the two central events in the mid-1990s bulking-up of American media companies.

The Disney (the mouse house) acquisition of Capital Cities/ABC (the alphabet net) would, only a few years previous to 1995, have been completely taboo. But now, in 1995, it was acceptable for a powerful Hollywood company (a producer and distributor of films and TV) also to own one of the traditional television networks and its 'owned and operated' local TV stations. This newly vertical Hollywood colossus thus controlled its own pipeline into all American TV households plus other pipelines into foreign markets. Disney-ABC had a commanding position in sports TV, in children's video entertainment and in theme parks. The ABC network had long been the leading American TV location for sports; and ABC's ESPN cable networks were the cable sports leaders. Second, the company controlled Walt Disney Pictures and the Disney Channel on cable. Third, Disney owned the famous California, Florida, and Tokyo theme parks, plus 39 per cent of Disneyland Paris.

Time Warner (itself the result of a 1989 merger) acquired Turner Broadcasting in 1996. This merger highlighted another form of vertical bulking up. Warner was also a major Hollywood producer and distributor of film and TV programming. Time Warner did not own one of the traditional networks but the merger left Time-Warner-Turner as the leading vertical player in cable. Time Warner itself was the biggest owner of local cable systems; and Turner was the biggest owner of successful cable networks; the Time-Turner cable bouquet included CNN, Cartoon Network, TNT, and TBS (the two leading general entertainment cable offerings), plus two leading movie channels in Home Box Office and Cinemax. In addition Time Warner was the majority owner of WB, the fifth conventional broadcast TV network.

Time Warner was also a dominant American force in certain selected fields. These fields of dominance included magazines (*Time, Fortune, People, Sports Illustrated*); the various CNN offerings gave the company a unique position in television news; Warner was the leading American-owned music company. Finally Time Warner had a special position in movies—as a producer and distributor as well as the leading TV purchaser of Hollywood movies; its HBO network was the pay-TV leader and its TBS and TNT networks were the main competitors to the broadcast networks for the first 'free' television showings of Hollywood movies.

Both Disney and Time Warner had yet other elements to their vertical pipelines. Both, for example, owned sports franchises. Both of these companies also had their own chains of retail stores where they could sell their merchandise direct to the public. Disney has striven to become an Internet leader (Go.com).

Their 1995–6 acquisitions confirmed these two companies as the new vertical giants of American media. Their vertical strength generated enhanced buying and selling power. Each company's multiple (cable and broadcast) networks had the pick of its own company's productions. Because they also had vertical selling power into households (via cable, broadcast, and video) these companies' networks were strong buyers of 'product' from other Hollywood companies. These multi-network companies had unrivalled opportunities for cross-promotion. Both Time Warner and Disney were also among the top ten advertising spenders in the United States. As the joint industry leaders—in paid advertising, in the 'free' self-promotion and in cross-promotion of networks—these two companies had unsurpassed marketing bulk and muscle.

Murdoch and Fox: Pioneering the Hollywood-Network Combination

The Hollywood-TV network combination—which became an established pattern in the mid-1990s—was pioneered a whole decade earlier in the mid-1980s—by Rupert Murdoch. In 1980 the three established TV networks (NBC, CBS, ABC) were still at the height of their dominance. The Washington policy consensus was now moving away from its focus of restricting the networks from dominating their affiliates and the programming suppliers. The policy consensus was, consequently, favourable towards Rupert Murdoch's mid-1980s attempts to launch, not only a new network, but a Hollywood-network Fox-Fox combination.

The pioneer Murdoch operation at first seemed not only unthreatening, but almost laughable. It moved slowly and made mistakes. The first Murdoch move was the acquisition of half of Twentieth Century Fox in 1984. This was followed by his 1985 acquisition of six big city TV stations from Metromedia. In 1986 he announced his intention to launch a new network. Not until 1987 did the 'network' operation begin; even then it was only on Sunday night, only on a rather weak collection of independent stations, and the initial programming was unsuccessful. During 1987–90 the Fox-Fox combination continued to struggle and to experience setbacks. Murdoch continued to seem the 'underdog'—resorting to some rather tabloid tactics, perhaps—but struggling bravely against the Big Three.

Murdoch's dogged determination (and huge cross-subsidies from his British and Australian print operations) was once again rewarded with extraordinary luck. By 1991–2 the Fox operation looked increasingly likely to grow into a real major network; indeed it was a growing super-network allied with a Hollywood production house (plus *TV Guide*). Murdoch's timing was lucky because his Fox-Fox combination grew to significant mass just as the Washington consensus shifted towards restraining the sins of cable; the cable industry was now seen as exemplifying monopolistic sins, whilst Murdoch's fourth conventional network exemplified virtuous competition.

Between the mid-1980s and the mid-1990s the Hollywood-plus-network combination became an established and generally acceptable phenomenon. The door, through which Murdoch had been allowed to squeeze his new combination, was pulled wide open by the Telecommunications Act of early 1996.

The 1996 Act's Digital ABC: Acquisitions, Bouquets, Concentration/Cartel

The mid-1990s media mergers were dwarfed (at least in financial terms) by the mergers of telecommunications companies, which were happening at the same time. The years 1996–7 saw three massive telecoms mergers which seemed to presage a reduction from about ten or twelve big telecoms companies to about four major survivors. The seven regional 'Baby Bells' were melting down to only two or three big regional telecoms players. In the long-distance field a sole rival to AT&T emerged in the form of MCI WorldCom; these two companies also both engaged in an extraordinary multiplication of ocean cable capacity across the Atlantic and Pacific.

The Telecommunications Act of 1996 endorsed the notion that telecoms (and other) companies should be allowed to advance into neighbouring businesses. As seen from the media industry, the prospect of such advances was frightening. From the viewpoint of broadcast television, a number of new technologies looked ever more threatening. Cable television itself was now a huge industry and the much anticipated marriage of cable and telecoms looked imminent; after several false starts, the cable giant TCI did indeed agree in 1998 to merge into AT&T. A second massive threat seemed to be posed by DirecTV and other digital satellite direct-to-home operations; this was a high-capacity pipeline into the home, which bypassed the old broadcasting systems. Third, there was the Internet—a combination of telephone lines and computers—which also occupied a position between the media and telecommunications; the Internet was another way of bypassing the old pipelines and a system which promised a huge range of audio-visual offerings.

Consequently Time Warner, Disney, and other media majors such as News Corporation and Viacom, all embraced the bulking-up orthodoxy; all decided to build vertical strength and vertical pipelines. This involved also embracing the ABC combination of Acquisitions, Bouquet, and Concentration/Cartel.

Acquisition and mergers had not been a significant part of the American network television business for the thirty years up to 1985, because Washington policy and the FCC forbade them. However, acquisitions and mergers did recommence in 1985–6, when all three networks changed ownership. Other group ownerships of TV stations had continued to generate mergers. True, the famous names on the outside of the Hollywood studio complexes had remained much the same over the decades; but while the valuable name-plates stayed in place, most Hollywood companies changed ownership several times between 1920 and 1990. Consequently, in embracing the acquisitions approach, the Hollywood companies were just following their own traditions. Their vertical ambitions of the 1990s merely involved reverting to the vertical shape of Hollywood prior to 1948. Moreover we can expect further mergers of networks (cable and broadcast) and of whole media companies to continue into the future.

The *bouquet* strategy was genuinely new. Basically, Hollywood and the TV networks followed the old adage of 'If you can't beat it, buy it'. Nearly all of the most popular and commercially successful cable networks are now part of the network bouquet (or bundle) of one of the big vertical companies. A major company now aims to embrace all three levels of network: first a conventional broadcast network; second several of the bigger and more popular cable nets; and third a collection of small sub-genre, niche, and specialized premium networks.

Concentration and cartel issues obviously became more salient under such a policy regime. But concentration, cartel, and anti-trust issues are as American as apple pie. Media monopoly court cases affecting the Associated Press go back to the 1890s; the American film industry's first cartel (the Motion Picture Patents' Company) was found to be illegal under the anti-trust laws in 1915.

Some three years after he entered office, President Clinton signed the bipartisan Telecommunications Act into law in February 1996. Straddling the passage of the Act, the years 1994–8 saw a comprehensive reshaping of the ownership of US television, Hollywood, and cable. During this period two new baby TV networks were born—WB and UPN—both aligned with a major Hollywood company. All of the now six networks were part of larger companies which were actively 'bulking up' their media activities during 1994–7.

1. Time Warner acquired Turner and launched the WB baby TV network.
2. Disney acquired the ABC TV network and its cable services.
3. Viacom acquired the Hollywood major, Paramount, and the video retail giant Blockbuster, as well as owning half of the new TV network baby, UPN.
4. News Corporation continued to develop its growing Fox network (and stations), to strengthen its Fox-Fox studio-network combination and to acquire cable services.
5. Westinghouse acquired the CBS TV network and stations, made huge acquisitions in radio, and bought cable services.
6. The NBC network and stations continued to be owned by the giant corporation, General Electric. It strengthened its cable presence, including an alliance with Microsoft in MSNBC and with Dow Jones in CNBC.

The relatively few big basic cable networks were mostly owned by Time Warner, Disney, and the other big companies. Thus the 'fragmentation' caused by cable had already by the late 1990s led to a new concentration. The Big Six companies through their combined broadcast affiliate networks and their cable networks had a 75 per cent share of time spent by Americans in front of their TV screens. The leading six companies were also the leading exporters.

Cash Cows and Loss Leaders

All of the American Big Six (national TV networking) companies were involved in major media acquisitions in the 1990s. Between them they acquired a substantial number of high-profit or cash cow properties.

Leading or dominant media operations in the largest cities have often been exceptionally profitable, especially through their 'owned-and-operated' TV stations. All of the Big Six owned station groups mainly in the largest cities. It was also exceptionally profitable to own a big 'cluster' of local cable systems in a single big city; Time Warner was the dominant cable operator in New York City, while TCI had the same position in Chicago.

The 1996 Act also allowed one company to own several radio stations in a single city; CBS (ex-Westinghouse) demonstrated that ownership of some 150 radio stations could be a cash cow without equal—especially when radio air-time was aggressively sold in a big city like Los Angeles.

Both Hollywood and the TV networks (now joined together in matrimony) have tended to be highly conservative in the face of innovation, especially risky innovations requiring major capital investment. Several of the major pioneering American media efforts of recent years came from far outside. The video game business was dominated by high-spending Japanese companies. An Australian outsider was the builder of the fourth network and the first network/Hollywood combination to get past the Washington regulators. This outsider pattern was especially true of the new applications of digital technology; most of the Internet pioneers came from outside the media. In digital television, while the conventional broadcasters and cable companies held back, the lead was taken by outside companies such as EchoStar and DirecTV (Hughes) which took big risks and made massive initial losses.

Talent Agencies and Star Power Mirror Vertical Concentration

Reflecting the concentration of power in the entertainment industry, the 'talent'—not only the actors, but directors and writers—have chosen to channel talent power through just two or three major Hollywood (and New York) talent agencies. The stars, who see the system from the inside, choose the same few big talent agencies, because they recognize that it takes concentrated talent power effectively to bargain with concentrated corporate power.

Hollywood talent agencies first became prominent in the 1930s; the rise to Hollywood prominence of the William Morris company and of an agent like Myron Selznick mirrored the industrial conditions of those times. Stars were tied down by long contracts. But, at the end of the seven years, the star was free to negotiate a fresh deal. This was where Myron Selznick stepped in, demanding big salary increases for major stars. Selznick established in a court case that he had raised Carole Lombard's salary from $750 to $18,000 per week.[1] Talent agent negotiating belligerence had seriously modified studio power before the 1948 Court anti-trust ruling. Agent negotiating skill had successfully demonstrated that the old seven-year contacts were one of the restrictive devices operated by the Hollywood cartel to control costs and competition.

The first super-agency was MCA, which in the 1940s was a dominant force in American popular music, before it switched its attention to movies and then to television. After MCA moved into TV production, it was required by the Justice Department anti-trust people to give up either agenting or TV production; it decided to drop agenting and, as MCA-Universal, became a TV-and-movie Hollywood major.

After MCA left the agenting scene, the leading Hollywood agency of the 1960s and 1970s was William Morris.[2] Hollywood agenting effectively became a duopoly when in December 1974 the second and third largest agencies merged to become International Creative Management (ICM). Hollywood went through a crisis phase around this time; most of the new managers brought in to reorganize all of the major studios came from either the William Morris, or the ICM, agency.

In the 1980s a new agency came to the fore; called Creative Artists Agency (CAA), its two key personalities were Michael Ovitz[3] and Ron Meyer. CAA combined negotiating belligerence with an intensive pooling and analysis of up-to-the-minute information about impending deals and projects in both TV and movies.[4] The core CAA activities remained client representation and project packaging. Television packaging is especially lucrative because the talent agency role does not end with the assembly of such key TV series ingredients as two actors, a pilot script, and a producer-writer. The agency continues to extract its percentage for each of the episodes in the series; the percentage may rise from 3 per cent of the licence fee (the amount paid by the commissioning network) to 10 per cent in the case of a super-successful series. The huge packaging earnings of the talent agencies have long been a focus of debate.

But an equally remarkable fact is the concentration of this packaging power and profit into a very few agencies. About three-quarters of all the 1997–8 network prime-time series (returning and new) were packaged by

[1] Leo Rosten, *Hollywood: The Movie Colony, the Movie Makers* (New York: Harcourt Brace, 1941), 94.

[2] Frank Rose, *The Agency: William Morris and the Hidden History of Showbusiness* (New York: HarperCollins, 1995).

[3] Robert Slater, *Ovitz* (New York: McGraw-Hill, 1997).

[4] Jeremy Tunstall and David Walker interview with Ron Meyer at CAA, April 1980.

just three agencies (CAA, William Morris and UTA).[5] A large minority of all new prime-time network shows had been packaged by two or more agencies. This type of two-agency combination—in a concentrated sector within a concentrated industry—is yet another significant example of Hollywood's cartel habits.

The heavy concentration into a few talent agencies also occurs because—despite the huge numbers of low-budget movies and lower-budget cable episodes—there are only perhaps 200 big-budget new projects in Hollywood each year; these are primarily the large and mid-budget movies, the new network television series, the main network mini-series, and the increasing number of cable network prestige (or branding) projects.

Some observers claim that the successful talent agent has the best—most secure, well-paid, and satisfying—job in Hollywood. The complexity of the task has increased with the ever expanding number of market windows, new (and future) technologies, and foreign markets. The challenge is greater also because of the newly vertical giants. The agents in recent years have had to compete with talent management firms; one of the largest management firms is itself owned by two of the big vertical companies. Such signs of naked corporate power spur on top agent-talent partnerships to demand ever bigger slices of the cake.

The Big US Vertical Companies are the Leading Media Exporters

Traditionally the world's main audio-visual exporters have been the big Hollywood distributors. In the 1990s those distribution companies bulked up and became more vertical, while they continued to be the dominant media exporters. These leaders were such companies as Disney, Time Warner, Viacom, and Fox-News. Also prominent were Sony, Seagram, and the cable giant, TCI.

Possession of a pre-existing worldwide system of distribution offices—whether for movies or for music—was an enormous advantage. These big companies had a presence in, and corporate knowledge of, the major foreign markets; they employed expert local nationals and had existing business alliances and contracts with local theatre exhibitors and TV networks.

But the relative success of American exporters still varied greatly, not only between countries, but between movies, television, and music. Movies were the one medium of massive Hollywood export dominance—a dominance not only in cinemas, but typically on television and in video stores. From around 1995, Hollywood increasingly recognized that its export earnings would in future be worth more than its domestic American earnings. *Titanic*

---

[5] Ted Johnson and Jenny Hontz, 'TV packages: Agents share joint custody', *Variety*, 9–15 June 1997.

was only one of several big-budget movies which grossed much more abroad than at home. But it was also noted around 1995 that Hollywood would need to take more seriously the ancient business adage: Think global, act local. Sony became especially active in financing more local co-productions, more local musical repertoire, and more local networks around the world.

In recorded music the traditionally dominant US position weakened considerably through the 1990s. The music business was increasingly more international than American, and more local-national than international. All of the music majors developed the policy of local labels in each important national market. BMG (of Germany) claimed in 1998 to own 'over 200 labels in more than 50 countries'.

The situation in television was also highly complex. In contrast to the 1980s, American TV series in the 1990s increasingly disappeared from prime evening slots on the main national networks in Europe and around the world. However out of prime time, and on the smaller audience new satellite and other channels, there were more and more hundreds and thousands of hours of US programming available to the foreign viewer.

Some of the new American satellite-to-cable networks went international. The most successful American satellite roll-outs took about a decade, starting from a domestic US service and ending up as a network in numerous separate country versions and languages. CNN (News), MTV (Music), and ESPN (Sports) were some of the fairly few which successfully completed these steps between the late 1980s and late 1990s.

Some American networks with seemingly obvious universal appeal were international failures. The sun did not shine on the international roll-out of The Weather Channel. Even Dow Jones, with its international network of *Wall Street Journal* offices could not make a success of its European and Asian business channels (which merged with the NBC competition in 1997). Even MTV—one of the most 'global' and most successful roll-outs—found increasing difficulties in the later 1990s. MTV Europe (based in London) was initially a huge success, but through the 1990s it began to fall behind competing national music video offerings in Germany and then in other countries.

The 'Going Global' box indicates some seven stages, through which an American network might pass before it became an international twenty-four-hour service. In many cases a network achieved a partial success by selling branded blocks of a few hours a day to various national markets. In the 1990s the same roll-out procedure was followed by several American Internet services; Yahoo! took four years to set up local versions of itself in fourteen foreign countries.

Some other genres appeared to have fewer problems in not only establishing, but also maintaining, a world presence. Genres which seemed to lose less in translation included the action movie, cartoons, and perhaps

---

Going Global: Phases in the Growth of Themed TV Networks Late 1980s to Late 1990s

1. *Domestic USA service:*
   • engages in some foreign syndication

2. *'International Network' claimed:*
   • typically a US network, still all US programming and still all in (US) English
   • maybe a few local presenters, VJs

3. *Now some regional material is included:*
   • also substantial repackaging, rescheduling
   • typically this starts as a European service only; probably based in London

4. *Continental regionalization:*
   • separate services for Asia and other world regions

5. *Sub-regionalization phase:*
   • services at least partly in several major regional languages: German, Hindi, Japanese, Mandarin, Spanish, Portuguese

6. *Separate national services for additional key countries:*
   • national services may include some national, some continental, and still some, or much, American content
   • more use of more languages
   • some joint venture arrangements, 50/50, 30/70

7. *Increasing national response:*
   • national regulation of international channels, which covers ownership, technology, taxation, content, advertising, and language rules
   • national response also takes the form of new local national offerings, in own language and designed to compete with international offerings

---

especially the documentary series (which lends itself to re-editing, re-versioning, and fresh commentary). Sports networks (such as ESPN) also had broad international appeal and could have strong national appeal based on acquired rights to locally popular sports leagues and contests.

What tended to happen in any world region was first the early arrival of some of the potentially strongest players, led by CNN, ESPN, MTV, and a few others. Then subsequently perhaps another 100 foreign (mostly American) satellite networks would arrive, or at least offer themselves to local cable and satellite operators. In the case of Latin America there were still only about ten networks in 1994 from outside the subcontinent; four years later (1998) there were 120 'international' networks attempting to reach the still quite small Latin American cable and satellite audience.

The newly vertical American companies were not equally successful in exactly the same combination of media export businesses; but typically each had three or four major export businesses or export pipelines through which to sell product into foreign market windows:

- Disney's international activities included movie distribution, theme parks (France and Japan), and major cable networks (ESPN and the 'pay' Disney Channel).
- Time Warner was a movie distributor, a music major, and the leading owner of major cable networks (CNN, Cartoon, TNT).
- Viacom was a movie distributor (Paramount), and had cable networks (Nickelodeon, Paramount, MTV) and Blockbuster Video.
- News Corporation was a movie distributor and had a clutch of international satellite networks under the Fox, Sky, and Star labels.

Hollyweb Cartel Versus European Monopolies

A cartel can be defined as 'an informal association of manufacturers or suppliers to maintain prices at a high level, and control production, marketing arrangements, etc.' (*Concise Oxford Dictionary*).

Despite ritual public abuse between controlling moguls (such as Ted Turner comparing Rupert Murdoch with Hitler) there were many elements of a 1990s club or cartel of big American media companies. This was greatly increased by the 1996 Telecommunications Act and in particular by the legitimation of Hollywood-network mergers. In *Variety*-speak the networks were the 'Webs': The Webs are Dead. Long Live HollyWeb!

American executives visiting Europe are amazed by what they see as the still monopolistic or duopolistic character of the national media within each country. European executives are equally amazed by the still cartel character of the US media businesses. But the general perception is that visitors' cries of Monopoly or Cartel are inadvisable for two reasons. Such cries would hazard badly needed goodwill 'over there'. Moreover cries of Monopoly over there, could lead to your competitors repeating the accusation against you back here at home.

There are today many echoes of the 1930s Hollywood cartel in which each company's theatre chain needed to rely on movies from the other studio-distributors. Under new Hollyweb conditions each of the combined broadcast-and-cable-network bouquets needs 'product'—TV series and movies—from the competing big companies.

As in the 1930s, there were both vertical and horizontal cartel elements. There was substantial 'stretching down' towards the final consumer, as Hollywood companies increasingly owned more local TV stations, more local cable systems, more local movie theatres, and more retail stores stocked with their own branded merchandise. Stretching vertically 'upwards', Hollywood companies were not only distributing and producing movie/cable/ TV entertainment, but were taking on a banking and financing role. Whereas the 1930s movie cartel had depended heavily on east coast banks, the 1990s cartel members themselves increasingly acted as banker/financiers towards 'independents' of various kinds.

The accompanying chart (Figure 6.1) was an attempt by *The Economist* in late 1998 to show some of the main ownership connections between seven leading media companies. The media industry has very unclear borders and definitions, so there are many different possible lists of top companies. The same *Economist* article referred to these seven companies as 'Oligopolists' controlling by 1996 well over half of 'US media industry revenue'. The companies controlling the US media industry, on this analysis, could be divided into three very roughly equal categories in terms of market share:

- *Three all-American vertical* media companies (Time Warner, Disney, and Viacom) had a combined US media market share of nearly one-third.
- *All other American companies* had a somewhat bigger combined market share of about 40 per cent.
- *Foreign companies* (headquartered outside the United States) also had a share of around 30 per cent. The four largest 'foreign' companies— Seagram (Canada), Bertelsmann (Germany), Sony (Japan), and News (Australia)—together had one-quarter of US media industry revenue. Smaller foreign companies (such as Pearson, Reed Elsevier, and Thomson and Hollinger of Canada, and other French and German companies) took this foreign total well above one-quarter. Of course, two of these companies (News and Seagram) were merely head-quartered in Australia and Canada. Both Sony and Bertelsmann also would protest their strong American credentials.

If the US media did constitute a cartel, it was a cartel with an inner and outer membership. The kind of details shown in *The Economist* 1998 chart do not stand still. Joint ventures, an endless sequence of acquisitions, and partial spin-offs, make for a high rate of ownership churn. But five main types of connections existed between larger US media companies:

1. *Cross-ownership* ties such as those between News (Fox) and TCI, or between Seagram and USA networks. Many key Disney assets were co-owned. Cross-ownership relationships were endemic between the leading

Figure 6.1 Ownership patterns, 1998

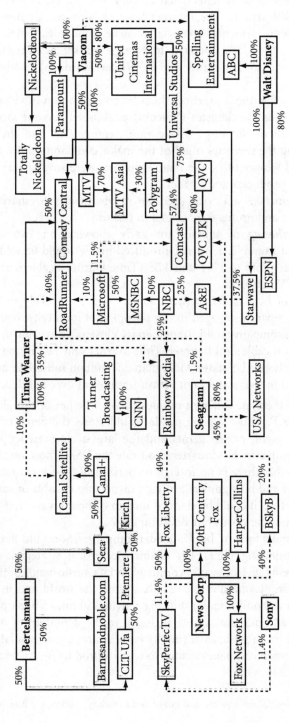

Source: The Economist, 21 Nov. 1998.

owners of local cable systems (such as Time Warner, TCI, Comcast, Media One, and Cablevision). The Internet business also quickly developed big cross-ownership elements. Some cross-ownership deals, which might be illegal within the USA, operated in foreign markets; examples included the UIP movie combine and the ESPN-Star(Murdoch) combination in Asia.

2. *Revenue Sharing*, a practice which became common in video retailing in the late 1990s. Blockbuster (Viacom) established revenue sharing contracts with all of the other Hollywood majors. This had the effect of strengthening the revenues of all of the major companies, from both their stronger and weaker titles; the main casualties were smaller independents, both among producers and retailers.[6]

3. *Co-production*, a device used by movie majors to share the risk. *Titanic*'s risks and profits were shared in this way.

4. *Co-purchasing* of movies for early showing on two competing networks. For example, a Warner-produced movie would be sold in a television contract both to TNT and TBS (Time Warner's cable nets) and to a competing TV network.

5. *Swaps of local outlets between major owners* especially in cable and radio. Big companies engaged in the swapping of local cable operations so that each big company could strengthen its 'clusters' in specific urban areas. One such local cable deal between Time Warner and TCI in 1997 involved properties in twelve US states. More than one million subscriber households were involved in swaps and joint ventures valued at over $2 billion.

Inevitably there are different opinions as to whether or not all this adds up to a 'cartel'. Those on the inside would stress the fierce competition between six, eight, or ten giants and the large-scale presence in the US market of companies headquartered outside the USA. Those on the outside might stress that there is no foreign ownership of broadcast *networks* (US citizens only) and no significant foreign ownership of cable or satellite networks. Therefore, it could be claimed foreign companies are shut out of the key elements of the vertical media company.

The two 'most foreign' big US media companies, Sony and Bertelsmann, were both pursuing their own distinctive vertical strategies. Sony was explicit in seeing its Hollywood company and its music major in the context of Sony electronics hardware strength around the world and in the USA. Bertelsmann was only a major if its big activities in music, book publishing, book clubs, and magazines were included in the definition of media. But Bertelsmann had a traditional (book) vertical strategy; after a late Internet start, the German company decided to rejig its production-to-retail strategy for books and music.

[6] Paul Sweeting, 'Major squeeze ploy put on indie vendors', *Variety*, 3–9 Aug. 1998.

As digitalization spreads, there will continue to be much churn of both owners and customers. As the telecoms, computer, Internet, and satellite companies advance onto the media playing field, they also will be looking for mergers which will enhance their vertical strength.

PART II

Britain as Media Number Two to the USA

7

Britain as Number Two in the Anglo-American Media

LONDON has long been a media entrepôt, a media hub through which media products pass on their way around the world. London (or Britain) was the core of the world's cable system and telegram traffic in the late nineteenth century and well into the twentieth century. In the years 1910–15 London also became the focus of the world trade in films; but here Britain soon became a colonial dependency (of Hollywood), and not a movie major in its own right.

These two separate stories represent two different aspects of Britain's media involvement with the United States; and these separate and contrasting aspects are the subject matter of this Part II and the following Part III. In Part III we explore further the 'colonial' aspect in general and in particular Britain's continuing relationship of dependence on Hollywood.

Here in Part II we deal with the other element of the Anglo-American media relationship. Here we look at a number of fields in which the British media can, or do, claim to be genuine world leaders. While the USA is Number One, Britain can claim to be a meaningful Number Two on the world scene. This kind of claim seems to have validity in the field of international news (Chapter 8). In 'public' broadcasting Britain can claim to have been, and perhaps still to be, the world leader (Chapter 9).

In some other media areas the British industry has to a significant extent been merged with the American industry. In popular music, book publishing, and the advertising agency business, it has become hard to say where the divide can be made between the British and the Americans. Britain—in expenditure terms—is typically (after Japan and Germany) the fourth largest media market. If and when the fourth player is partly merged into an already comfortable number one player, the first plus fourth combination is still further beyond any single challenger.

London continues to be a media entrepôt for reasons partly linked to those of a century ago. The adjoining Box records comments made by the chief executives of the (then) three agencies providing fast video news film on a daily basis to all the leading broadcast networks in the world. These three agencies—Reuters TV, Associated Press TV, and WorldWide TV News (WTN) were all based in London, although the latter two were owned in the

USA. Shortly after these 1997 comments, WTN was merged into APTV, leaving just two agencies.

London has been chosen by most American media organizations as their single most important foreign location for two other reasons. One is the relaxed regulatory (and commercial) regime which has obtained in London for many years, but especially since the 1980s Margaret Thatcher era. The

Why are the Video News Agencies Headquartered in London?

'Language.'

'The five-hour time advantage over New York.'

'London's an obvious consolidation point.'

'London was originally chosen for air-freighting news film; now London is ideal for quick trips to many countries.'

'London is the hub for about one hundred countries in Europe, Africa and the Mid-East.'

'Europe is the biggest market for TV news.'

'With the BBC, ITN and Sky, London is a major location for TV news.'

'It has the best supply of skilled personnel.'

'Britain led Europe in deregulation, especially of satellites, in the 1980s.'

'Lack of trade union problems since the 1980s and the prevalence of multi-skilling.'

'Europe has lots of good TV people, but not so many in one location as does London.'

'London's easy on a light news day. You can do a learned piece with an author or an LSE academic. Also London's unbeatable for the light/whimsical/sexy/tabloid piece.'

Source: April–May 1997 interviews with the three current chief executives
Robey Burke, WTN
Stephen Claypole, APTV
David Feingold, Reuters TV
    David Kogan, formerly Reuters TV
    Terry O'Reilly, WTN, New York
Tony Donovan, Reuters TV (December 1998)

relaxed regulatory regime has led to Britain being the most popular location for American satellite TV offerings aimed at Britain and across Europe. While this is primarily an American presence, London is also chosen by some European-based satellite networks, as well as by Mandarin Chinese, Hindi, Arabic, and other offerings.

London is also commonly used by American and other international media operations as their headquarters location, not merely for western and eastern Europe but for Africa and the Middle East, a total of nearly 100 separate nation states. This is an extremely varied collection of countries, which includes most of the world's wealthiest as well as most of the world's poorest countries. Especially from an American viewpoint, the big advantages of London include time and linked communications convenience. But the division of the world into just three regions—the Americas, Asia-Australasia, and Europe-Africa-Mid-East—also dates back in part to the Victorian news agencies and to silent Hollywood.

In keeping with its role as an international media location, London offers several kinds of specialist media expertise. Over 170 separate trade publications, newsletters, and yearbooks dealing with the media and communications are published in Britain. Many of these are internationally oriented (e.g. *Asia-Pacific Telecoms Analyst, Cable and Satellite Europe, Screen International, World Magazine Trends*). London is also a focus of media law publications (e.g. *Entertainment Law Review, European Intellectual Property Review*) and for consulting companies, and financial analysts, specializing in media and communications businesses.

Long Tradition: The Anglo-American Media Free from Both Government and Political Party Control

Of course, the American and British media never have been fully autonomous and fully independent from government and political party control. The key point here is that the Anglo-American media have historically been more autonomous and independent than the media of any other countries (with perhaps a few exceptions, such as Sweden).

This relative autonomy and independence has a long and, equally important, a largely uninterrupted history going back to perhaps 1855 in Britain and earlier in the USA. The media in nearly all other countries have been subjugated by fascist, communist, or military regimes at some time in the twentieth century. This did not happen in Britain or the USA. Well before 1914, the British press was a power in the land and during 1914–18 press censorship only went as far as the press owners and editors would more or less voluntarily accept. Especially in Britain, the free press actually pre-dated full democracy by a number of decades. Consequently—although American journalists certainly believe their media to have the more admirable history—there is a strong mutual belief that the Americans and the British are together cradled in the arms of a unique media tradition. This unique 'long tradition' can be seen as having several loosely linked components:

- News wholesalers or 'news agencies' in both the USA and Britain circumvented the relative poverty of Victorian newspapers. These agencies supplied domestic and foreign news to newspapers of different party complexions; the agencies thus created the concept of non-partisan or 'neutral' news.
- Britain, especially, invented the 'Elite Press' tradition around the 1840s. *The Times* initially gained its extraordinary strength from a semi-monopoly position. The present-day elite press of the USA also consists of semi-monopoly big city dailies, often controlled by a family. The *New York Times*, from its 1851 birth, emphasized 'objective' reporting.
- The tradition of non-partisan news, invented by the news agencies, with some help from the elite press, went on into non-partisan radio and, later, TV news.
- Britain was not alone in pioneering public service broadcasting; but because other European countries fell under Fascist and Nazi control, the British acquired the longest continuing tradition of this kind.
- The United States developed a different commercial tradition of broadcasting; but this system initially had duopolistic (NBC, CBS) national leadership and the radio/TV news followed the news agency/elite press model.
- Advertising also developed in both the United States and Britain as a largely non-partisan activity. Obviously there was some political bias but—in contrast to common patterns in Europe or Latin America—advertising was broadly separate from politics and committed to 'objective' (non-partisan) commercial choices.

Parallel to the Anglo-American long tradition of independent media is the related long tradition of independent media occupations. American and British journalists, TV producers, and advertising executives are known for, and normally employed for, their perceived professional skills, with their political views being regarded as less important. Of course there are exceptions in the USA and Britain. But the situation is certainly different from, say, Italy or Germany, where political allegiance is much more often a major factor in appointments and promotions.

Financial 'Transparency'

A final common element in the Anglo-American long tradition is the emphasis placed on financial transparency. This has a number of elements. At the simplest level there is the notion that bribes and kickbacks are unacceptable and corrupt. To offer a bribe is to insult the intended recipient's competence and professional or business integrity.

At the company and industry level, most larger media companies in the USA and Britain are public companies whose shares are traded on the stock market. These public companies are legally required to publish a large amount of financial detail. The BBC and the commercial broadcasting regulators in Britain are also required to publish a considerable amount of factual detail.

Advertising agency personnel in the Anglo-American media claim that their businesses are very transparent. Advertising clients of advertising agencies, for example, know what prices the agency is paying (because invoices and other detail are available to be scrutinized). The advertising agencies would also claim that they play an important role in maintaining transparency across the media. The Americans and the British were leaders in, for example, properly audited newspaper and magazine sales figures and also in the generation of detailed television ratings data.

Once more, none of this means that the Anglo-Americans are perfectly objective, non-partisan, transparent, and truthful. They merely tend more in these directions than do their equivalents in most other countries. But these more-or-less commonly held values and practices do partly explain why when American media people first move abroad they tend to go to London; and when British media companies look for a foreign acquisition they tend to look westward across the Atlantic.

The Anglo-American Media are Close to the Financial Communities of New York and London

Another common element of the 'long tradition' of the Anglo-American media has been their proximity to the financial and banking industries of London and New York. *The Times* of London in the 1840s already carried substantial amounts of both financial news and financial advertising; and it was located within a few minutes' walk of the Bank of England and the Stock Exchange. Similarly the *New York Times* and the rest of the New York newspaper industry were located on Manhattan Island, close to Wall Street. This proximity of finance and media developed and expanded through the twentieth century. Many present-day pioneering Internet and Online media companies are located in Silicon Alley—the same lower Broadway area once known as Tin Pan Alley—which lies between the main media area and Wall Street.

Broadly those aspects of the media which are dealt with in Part II—news, public service broadcasting, music, books, and advertising—are the areas in which the London–New York connection is strongest, and in which the British media are credible partners to the US media. The more 'colonial' relationship, dealt with in the chapters of Part III, are mainly the areas in which Hollywood (not New York) is dominant, and in which Britain is subordinate.

During the 1980s the connection between the media and finance strengthened in several ways. 'Globalization', even in the media and finance, was more limited than many enthusiasts claimed. But there were indeed significant trends towards globalization in the spread of free markets and free exchange rates, the spread of international banking, and the advance of cheaper and better telecommunications. All of this went alongside the rapid growth of new television channels, of satellite and cable operations, and the growth of extra market 'windows' for Hollywood products. One of the linking elements was the international growth after 1980 both of financial data and news services; indeed organizations such as Reuters (of London) and AP-Dow Jones (of New York) illustrated the common origins of financial information for both consumers and businesses.

Another element of this increased post-1980 finance-and-media intimacy was that the financial community came to see media and communications as a fast-growing industrial sector, worthy of serious investment and of serious bank loan activity. In the previous chapter we considered the vertical bulking up of American media companies. These trends meant in effect that the media changed from being a middling business to being a big business with an increasing number of companies well up the Fortune 500 league table. This trend was, of course, not confined to New York and London. Observers in Japan, Germany, and France also drew similar conclusions.

8
World News Duopoly

THE flow of news around the world is dominated by two countries, the USA and Britain, and in particular by the US Associated Press and the British Reuters. This is only a partial change from the period 1870–1910, when the British Reuters and the French Havas were the dominant providers of world news. Reuters and AP are the leading news suppliers around the world, not only in text (aimed mainly at newspapers), but in still photographs, graphics, and foreign video news for TV.

The United States is the world leader in terms of selling its foreign news— its daily world views and news—around the world. Depending upon the criteria adopted, either Britain or the rest of Europe would come second with the other third. There is no important candidate for fourth place; although the Japanese media are big gatherers of foreign news, they have few foreign customers for their world view.

Leading players in the US world news team include Associated Press and Cable News Network (CNN) but the special strength of the USA lies in its major newspapers, which also sell and syndicate news to other news organizations. These include the *Wall Street Journal*, the *New York Times* service (which includes Cox and *Boston Globe* news), and the Los Angeles Times– Washington Post service (including *Newsday* and *Baltimore Sun* material). Also jointly owned (by the New York Times and Washington Post) is the *International Herald Tribune*. Finally, the steady growth of *USA Today* has added a significant extra element to this international newspaper team effort.

Britain has three world leaders in specific foreign news categories: Reuters (the largest of all foreign news operations), the BBC (probably the leading conventional broadcaster of foreign news), and the *Financial Times* (which claims the world's largest newspaper foreign correspondent team). On a lower level Britain has another four or five press groupings with some foreign news significance.

Western Europe is even more difficult to score. But it has in Eurovision the world's largest daily video news exchange—which spreads beyond Europe into Africa and Asia. No other continent has a collection of news agencies comparable to the worldwide Agence France-Presse (AFP), the German DPA, and the Spanish EFE (widely rated as first or first equal across all of Latin America). Western Europe is also unique in its high number of both newspapers and broadcast networks which each employ more than token numbers of foreign correspondents; Germany, France, Italy, Spain, and the Netherlands have some of the world's best foreign news, but very little of this foreign news is sold even to other European countries' media. Nevertheless, if western Europe is defined—in the most obvious way—as including Britain, then western Europe offers serious competition to the USA for the title of world news leader.[1]

All three leading British news players—Reuters, BBC, *Financial Times*—have increasingly oriented themselves towards Europe. Since the break-up of the USSR, Europe (west and east) is the world's leading news market, and, although AP has long offered a domestic German–language text service, AP is outgunned within Europe by Reuters.

However, only the US and British news operators are genuinely world players. It is also evident that Agence France-Presse is really a French flag-carrier (subsidized by the French government); but all of the Anglo-American world news players are the flag-carriers of larger media organizations. Reuters news carries the flag for Reuters financial data; BBC news carries the flag for BBC entertainment, the *Financial Times* carries the flag for the Pearson company.

In the United States this news flag-carrying for bigger commercial media operations has grown more pronounced. Along with the old newspapers and their owning families, we now see substantial elements of the Hollywood/network combines using major news operations as corporate flag-carriers. CNN is the proud prestige news operation of Time Warner. CNBC's business news channel is a flag-carrier for NBC (and General Electric). Fox News in the USA and Sky News in Britain are prestige networks within the News-Murdoch bouquets.

This prestige view of news is only one of several elements in common between the leading American and British news players. There is a tendency, for example, to employ each others' citizens. London-based Reuters employs numerous Americans. Stephen Hess reports that of 400 American media foreign correspondents in 1992, some 32 were actually British citizens. John Chancellor even complained that 'American broadcast English is becoming a British-New Zealand-Aussie-Irish patois.' Britain also seemed to be the only foreign country from which American media would accept foreign news. Stephen Hess found that in 1992 four large American dailies (average 323,000 circulation) took about 60 per cent of their longer foreign stories from AP, 20 per cent from the *New York Times*, and 10 per cent from Reuters; all other sources (including their own correspondents) made up the final 10 per cent.[2]

---

[1] Jeremy Tunstall, 'Europe as World News Leader', *Journal of Communication*, 42 (Summer 1992), 84–99.

[2] Stephen Hess, *International News and Foreign Correspondents* (Washington: The Brookings Institution, 1996), 55, 93.

When in the field, journalists tend to work in cooperation with colleagues from other news organizations. Because *New York Times* correspondents regard the Associated Press as a competitor, they often 'work with' Reuters correspondents in the field; in the past the *NYT* and other US newspapers actually transmitted their stories back home over Reuters facilities. This was the situation at the height of the Vietnam war in 1968. The *New York Times* correspondents had previously shared an office with Reuters in downtown Saigon; the *NYT* team had subsequently moved to its own office three blocks away, but the correspondents still used the Reuters office for transmission purposes and to get an early look at Reuters' current stories. *NYT* and Reuters correspondents sometimes also worked together covering military action outside Saigon. During the Tet offensive in 1968, American news-paper correspondents in general—and *New York Times* journalists in particular—used the Reuters office as a base for covering the street fighting in Saigon.[3]

The *NYT*'s previous Saigon correspondent, David Halberstam, had been critical of the US military's conduct of the Vietnam war.[4] Senior *NYT* jour-nalists had subsequently encouraged continued scepticism. In 1968 the *NYT* was also the only US client of Agence France-Presse (while Reuters had forty-five US newspaper clients at the time); AFP was itself sceptical of the US Army's chances of succeeding where the French Army had previously failed. AFP, at the time, had the only western news correspondent in Hanoi. Much of the coverage of the Vietnam war around the world was highly critical of the US military; a substantial proportion of this critical coverage must have derived from Agence France-Presse and from the loose alliance of Reuters and the *New York Times* and its international syndication service.

British Strength in Elite World News

Modern journalism was an Anglo-American invention.[5] France also played some part in this invention, especially through its news agency, Havas. But France lagged behind in the development of the elite newspaper; well into the twentieth century the leading French newspapers accepted corrupt subsidies from commercial interests and even from foreign governments.[6]

Elite journalism involved monitoring national and international politics and finance, and doing so without subsidy from government, from political party, or from special interest. This pattern of elite journalism was largely

---

[3] Peter Braestrup, *The Big Story* (Boulder, Colo.: Westview Press, 1977), i. 9–14, 47–51, 69–72, 104–117.

[4] Halberstam in his book on Vietnam frequently refers to British journalists: David Halber-stam, *The Making of a Quagmire* (London: Bodley Head, 1965).

[5] Tunstall, *The Media are American*, 13–37.

[6] Jean K. Chalaby, 'Journalism as an Anglo-American Invention', *European Journal of Communication*, 11.2 (Sept. 1996), 303–26.

invented by *The Times* of London in and around the 1840s. Some American newspapers after 1865 increasingly carried foreign news, although they initially did so in a more popular manner, for example by focusing on wars and somewhat fanciful accounts of heroic explorers.[7] Gradually, however, the *New York Times* drew level with *The Times* of London. Certainly by 1940 the USA was the clear leader in world news.

Reuters used its position as the semi-official news agency of the British empire to become the world news leader between 1870 and 1914. But from 1914 right through to the 1960s Reuters struggled to compete with the American agencies; Reuters lacked the huge media home base of AP and its then domestic competitors (UP and INS). In 1942 Reuters and Associated Press signed a wartime news swapping agreement which effectively created a fresh news cartel controlled by the USA and Britain.[8] Reuters, in fact, in both world wars was embarrassingly dependent on the British government; well into the 1960s an effective subsidy was fed by the British government into Reuters via the BBC world service.[9] Reuters management in the 1960s decided to seek a new source of revenue; Reuters entered into computerized financial data, arguing that a big news event (such as the Kennedy assassination of 1963) was both a financial, and a general news, story. Reuters' computerized data activities were spectacularly successful especially in Europe, but also around the world.

The BBC is Britain's second world player in elite news. Like Reuters, BBC news has established a world reputation as perhaps the least biased and most reliable international news service in its field. Previous to the late 1980s the BBC had wastefully operated three largely separate networks of foreign correspondents—one set of foreign correspondents for domestic radio, one for domestic television, and a third different team of foreign correspondents for the external radio service.

By 1998–9 the 'vernacular' (reporting in forty languages other than English) correspondents of BBC world service radio were still largely a separate force. But the correspondents working for the English language services (including the two all-news networks) now consisted of a single radio-and-TV team of seventy foreign correspondents based in forty-two overseas bureaux. Seven of these were 'hub' bureaux (Brussels, Delhi, Hong Kong, Jerusalem, Johannesburg, Moscow, Washington), each with several journalists and producers.

---

[7] Beau Riffenburgh, *The Myth of the Explorer: The Press, Sensationalism and Geographical Discovery* (Oxford: Oxford University Press, 1993).

[8] Kent Cooper (of AP), having long complained about the European news cartel, seemed quite happy to become a founding member of the fresh 1942 cartel. See Kent Cooper, *Barriers Down* (New York: Farrar and Rinehart, 1942), 300–14.

[9] Donald Read, *The Power of News: The History of Reuters* (Oxford: Oxford University Press, 1992), 329–31.

The third British-based news player is the *Financial Times*, which now has much the largest British newspaper team of foreign correspondents. The *Wall Street Journal* is certainly the world's leading financial daily, but the *Financial Times* substantially outsells it on the continent of Europe. The *Wall Street Journal* prints each day in four European locations and four Asian locations. The *Financial Times* prints each day in five European locations outside Britain, in two Asian locations, and in three US locations. These two financial dailies have quite a lot in common; both grew rapidly after 1950 with the expansion of the New York and London financial markets. The *Wall Street Journal* became the biggest selling US daily by printing in many locations across the continent. Both the *WSJ* and the *FT* were effective monopolies, growing, making profits, and well aware of their power in their respective financial worlds. Both papers observed the electronic explosion of news agency activity from the 1960s. Both newspapers were cautious about jumping into the international market; then the *Wall Street Journal* suggested a combined *WSJ-FT* European financial daily. When these negotiations broke down, the *Wall Street Journal* initially avoided taking on the *FT* in Europe and launched a Hong Kong printed Asian *Wall Street Journal* in 1976, taking advantage of the US civilianization of space. The *Financial Times* began its first foreign printing in Frankfurt in 1979, initially flying copies from Frankfurt to the USA each night.[10] Both papers found that additional local printings were relatively cheap to launch; the main requirements for a new print were to generate some significant additional advertising and also to have some prospect of selling an extra 10,000 daily copies.

Anglo-American Video News for the Global Mass Audience

Most of the foreign video news shown on the world's TV screens comes from two video news agencies—one British-owned, one US-owned—both based in London. Probably well over one billion people each week around the world see at least a few minutes of these agencies' foreign news stories. This is the truly global, and truly mass market, TV foreign news service. While these two agencies—Reuters TV, and APTN—deliver each week at least a few minutes of video stories to over one billion people, CNN delivers bigger hunks (hours, not minutes) of news around the world to a much smaller audience. BBC World reaches a still smaller audience than does CNN.

After 1991 the United States domestic TV audience was watching less and less foreign news on the main TV networks. By 1996 each of the big three US

---

[10] David Kynaston, *The Financial Times* (London: Viking, 1988). Jerry Rosenberg, *Inside the Wall Street Journal* (New York: Macmillan, 1982). Lloyd Wendt, *The Wall Street Journal* (Chicago: Rand, McNally, 1982).

networks' supposedly half-hour evening news shows averaged just one foreign item per day or some 87 seconds of material 'filed by reporters with a
foreign deadline' (*The Tyndall Report*). This amount had roughly halved
since the big foreign news (1988–91) days of the Soviet break-up and the
Gulf war. NBC, the most popular network in this period, was showing the
least foreign news; and nearly half of all US adults seldom or never watched
TV network news. However, the decline of the audience for major network
news was partly balanced by the success of news magazine programmes in
network prime time. The local TV stations showed more national news and
of course CNN made news available around the clock. Both of these outlets
depended heavily on the video news agencies.

Each of the two 'global' video news services is in fact a relatively small
news operation based in London, and attached to a larger media organization. Reuters TV generates only about 2 per cent of the total revenue of
Reuters; this agency has newsreel, British Commonwealth, and BBC elements in its history and was called Visnews previous to being absorbed into
Reuters. APTN is the video news operation of the other giant news agency,
Associated Press of New York. A third video agency, WTN (Worldwide TV
News) was in the past linked to the UPI news agency and was called UPITN;
it was subsequently controlled by the ABC TV part of the Disney-ABC
merged company. This latter connection led competitors to express surprise
at Mickey Mouse's new-found enthusiasm for world news; such scepticism
was shown to be valid, when in 1998 Disney-ABC gave up on WTN, which
was merged into a new APTN combination.

Foreign news for television is costly to collect. Even the big American
networks now have few foreign bureaux, because one TV bureau involves
several people, high rents and living expenses, travel, extensive equipment,
satellite links back home, and so on. Consequently all significant TV networks in the world (including the main US and European ones) rely upon
the video agencies to supply a basic foreign news service. A London video
agency typically supplies more than one TV network in each of the main
country markets; this is why viewers, switching between channels, can see
the identical foreign material, edited in slightly different ways. Even a TV
network which has its own correspondent and camera on the ground in
the war zone will still mix its own material together with video agency
footage.

A middle-rank receiving TV network might be paying $100,000 for a
year's supply of about 100 hours of foreign news film. As seen by the video
agency this is an absurdly low price, but a traditional news agency dilemma
is evident here. Networks (like newspapers) are accustomed to getting
agency news cheap.

These agencies do acquire some coverage, under contract, from major TV
networks. Reuters uses the news resources of the American NBC network;

Reuters TV, 1998–1999

- Reuters TV has contracts with about 300 national television networks around the world.

- Some 15 contracts—with US, UK, Japanese, and German networks—generate 20 per cent of the revenue. The other higher paying customers are mainly in Europe and Latin America.

- There are 16 major general Reuters feeds by satellite each day; these are partly affected by time of day and which world region has upcoming TV news deadlines. Each feed lasts 30 minutes and includes about 12 separate stories (from perhaps 9 or 10 different countries).

- Each 24 hours sees an additional 25 more specialized feeds, including financial, showbusiness and sports news feeds.
- Most Reuters TV feeds are from London, but there are Asian feeds from Singapore; and North American feeds from Washington; Latin American feeds from Miami-Washington.

- A Reuters news-feed does not include voice commentary, but is accompanied on satellite by script material, which includes a shot list, a brief summary, and a longer version of the story. The customer network is free to edit and to voice the pictures in any way it wishes. A major US network might use 30 seconds, while an African network might use 15 minutes.

- Reuters Financial Television is a specialized service sold to banks and the financial services industry. It specializes in press conferences and similar events as well as analysis presented on screen alongside data.

- *Yahoo!* has made Reuters more widely known to the US public. Reuters sees the Internet as an increasingly important market for video news.

WTN used the news output both of its ABC corporate parent and also the BBC. But Reuters TV and APTN originate the great bulk of their own video output; video journalists, operating from Reuters and AP offices around the world, generate video coverage which is passed back to London by satellite. In London the news receives substantial editing before being included in one or more world region feeds.

This international video news agency business is now in its third historical phase. In the first phase, up to the late 1970s, the news film travelled by air and Visnews was located in west London near to Heathrow airport and photographic laboratory back-up; in that air freight era news film often took two or three days to reach its final destination. From the late 1970s there was a new era of videotape and satellite transmission, which allowed much quicker and more complex patterns of distribution.

Until the mid-1990s the video news agency business was a relatively tranquil duopoly. There were numerous new network customers—many new commercial TV channels and a post-communist TV boom in eastern Europe and Central Asia. All of this was good for the then two dominant companies, Reuters (Visnews) and WTN. However in 1994–5 a third player—Associated Press—entered the business; APTV brought significant competitive turbulence, because it initially charged low prices. It was accused by its competitors of predatory pricing, or of 'buying market share by giving the service away for free'. Associated Press (with its newspaper roots and cooperative ownership) had left its entry to a surprisingly late date. AP was finally convinced that the new digital and Internet era would 'need multimedia services'.

APTN followed the Reuters approach of dividing the world into three regions—the Americas, Asia, and Europe-Africa. London was chosen as the base location for what was intended to be a more international AP. Indeed the AP service was centralized to an extreme degree, with even Latin American news being routed through, and edited in, London.

All-News TV Networks: for the News Addict and from the Large Media Organization

The non-stop all-news TV network is a prestige niche offering for the smallish numbers of all-news addicts. Consequently only the largest and most determined media organizations can be serious players of the all-news TV game.

All-news television was made possible by the explosion of channel capacity in the USA around 1980. It was driven by the apparent success of Ted Turner's CNN; and it was subsequently sustained by big media companies' organizational urge to include all-news offerings in their emerging portfolios (or bouquets) of programming streams.

CNN was modelled in part on the established all-news radio format. Ted Turner borrowed the radio concept of repeating the news frequently during the day. Some people saw this as really a breakfast news show warmed up and served at all times in the twenty-four hours. But CNN (and CNN Headline) gradually became the prestige item within a bigger Turner package of entertainment offerings, including TBS and TNT. Turner (who in 1980 knew little about TV news) offered local cable companies discounts for taking CNN with the entertainment channels. He also exploited the Atlanta location, and the weakness of local trade unions, to pay much lower than New York salary levels. His timing was lucky in technology terms; satellite capacity was getting cheaper, the television newsroom computer system (essential for organizing big amounts of material each twenty-four hours) was just coming on stream, and there were cheaper and quicker new ways of getting reporters' video material back to base.

CNN could not have happened without the video agency service from WTN (initially in its UPITN days). Much of CNN's early news thus came from the American ABC network and from the British ITN; some of the reporting from Nicaragua in the early 1980s, for instance, came from British ITN reporters whose reports had a much less pro-Reagan slant than did CNN reports from Washington.

When Ted Turner got into bad financial difficulty in the mid-1980s, he was rescued by other bigger players in the cable industry. TCI and Time wanted to keep CNN in operation, because this all-news network earned the whole cable industry legitimacy in Washington and with the advertising industry. The CNN service was also increasingly present in press and TV newsrooms around the USA, thus helping to keep cable, as a medium, in the news.

CNN by the later 1980s was in nearly all cable-subscribing American homes. But CNN remained the sole all-news TV channel in the world for most of the 1980s. Europe's first all-news TV was Sky News, launched in 1989 as part of Rupert Murdoch's Sky package in Britain. Sky News also lost money, and was heavily subsidized both in its Sky form and then in its BSkyB form (after the late 1990 merger). Sky News was hugely dependent on WTN ABC news; ABC's 8 a.m. breakfast news was served 'live' but five hours late to British viewers at 1 p.m. each day.

CNN followed the common subdivision strategy, leading to CNN, CNN Headline, CNNfn (financial news), and CNNSI (sports news). Meanwhile after its Gulf war (1990–1) ratings success, CNN found ratings falling, while its best audiences tended to be attracted by sensational murder trials (such as O. J. Simpson's in 1995).

Nevertheless Time Warner (and Ted Turner) were clearly determined to maintain the genre lead and to put extra pressure on their competitors by strong promotion of CNN International. Very soon after its 1980 launch, CNN began feeding its service to foreign broadcasters and to 'international' hotel rooms. CNN International formally launched as a separate entity in 1985. In part CNNI was simply building up the foreign bureaux which a credible domestic CNN news service needed. CNNI also relied heavily on Visnews/Reuters TV, on CBC (Canada), and ITN (Britain).

Gradually during the 1990s CNN built up its European audiences and became (along with MTV and Eurosport) one of only three profitable pan-European networks. Nevertheless CNNI still faced a hard struggle in seeking to become a genuinely global operation. For example after six years of Spanish-language newscasts, and an increasing Latin American effort (including Cartoon and TNT), CNNI and CNN Español in 1998 were in only about 6 million Latin American homes.[11] Moreover CNN was only obtaining about five dollars per year (including advertising revenue) from each of these Latin American homes.

The BBC is the leading non-American example of a media organization which is providing all-news both nationally and on a worldwide basis. By 1997–8 the BBC was carrying some news on each of twelve radio and TV networks:

- The radio (music) networks—BBC 1, 2, and 3—carried brief news summaries.
- Two radio networks (Radio 4, and BBC local radio) and three TV networks (BBC1, BBC2, and BBC Interactive) carried substantial amounts of news and comment.
- The BBC already had no less than four all-news networks. These were Radio Five (news and sport), BBC World Service radio, BBC News 24 (the domestic TV all news service), and its international TV partner, BBC World.

This array of radio and TV as well as domestic and international networks meant that—across these entire twelve networks—a single news story could be used and reused several dozen times. By possessing so many networks, including its BBC1 and BBC2 domestic TV channels, the BBC had an unusual degree of flexibility; exceptional news events could receive the all-news treatment on one of the two domestic TV nets.

There is, of course, a continuing evolution in both the competitive and partnership relations between these news entities. The world players have numerous connections, contracts, and deals with national and regional operations. Numerous connections also exist between the Anglo-American news players. The BBC in the 1990s was on close terms with ABC-WTN, which included their camera crews working together on war coverage and other complex foreign assignments. The BBC also had a close relationship with Associated Press which was the supplier in 1997 of the BBC's 'next generation' Electronic News Production System (ENPS).

The Financialization of News

Financial news has, since the end of the cold war, become more and more central to news and journalism. This trend plays to the strengths of the dozen leading international news suppliers. Three of these (Reuters, *Wall Street Journal, Financial Times*) specialize in financial news; a fourth, Associated Press, is involved with Dow Jones (owner of the *WSJ*) in the AP-Dow Jones financial service. In addition, most leading newspapers today

[11] 'Turner Latin America at 10', *Variety*, 23–9 Mar. 1998, pp. 59–69. 'Global Media', *Advertising Age International* 9 Feb. 1998.

follow the *New York Times* in devoting a substantial fraction of their pages to financial and business news.[12]

But the biggest changes have occurred at Reuters, at AP-Dow Jones, at NBC, and with the insurgent Bloomberg company. Reuters in the 1970s and 1980s changed from being a news agency into an electronic financial data company. News (text, pictures, video) now generates about 7 per cent of Reuters' $5 billion annual revenue.

Michael Bloomberg launched his on-screen financial data company in 1982; the London office opened in 1987, with other offices following in most European countries. Bloomberg revenue passed $1 billion in 1997. The core of this company's business is the Bloomberg terminal on the desk of the financial market trader or analyst. The book *Bloomberg by Bloomberg*[13] was a financial mogul demonstrating his bravura skills as a self-publicist; we also saw a fully qualified own-and-operate media mogul with a highly personal and belligerent management style. He explained why he decided also to enter the media—Bloomberg radio and television news, magazines, a financial pages service for newspapers, a news wire service, book publishing, and, of course, the Bloomberg website. His reason for going into media was publicity. The media publicity, the eternal media repetition of the Bloomberg name, would help to sell terminals. The few per cent tip of the Bloomberg iceberg was media news; the iceberg itself was financial data.

Previous to Bloomberg's arrival, the financial data business had been dominated by Dow Jones and by Reuters. The main casualty of Bloomberg's arrival was the Dow Jones Telerate service. Clearly Dow Jones, as the owner of the enormously successful *Wall Street Journal*, had been reluctant to drop the values of journalism and to commit itself 100 per cent to selling endless streams of numbers on screens. Dow Jones also (in 1997) gave up its European Business News and Asia Business News financial video news services, which were merged into CNBC's international service.

Following two decades of rapid and profitable growth, Reuters also was somewhat shaken by the appearance of new competitors in general and of Bloomberg in particular. In some respects the News vs. Data dilemma was easier for Reuters because of its huge bias towards data. Did Reuters need to stay in news, including world video news? News was worrying, uncertain, and unprofitable. But Reuters needed to stay in news for the same reason that Michael Bloomberg had wanted to get into news. However as Reuters considered all kinds of fresh data markets (such as on-line medical data) which it might enter, it did not consider going into the financial newspaper business.

[12] For more detail on Britain, see Jeremy Tunstall, *Newspaper Power* (Oxford; Oxford University Press, 1996), 354–73.

[13] *Bloomberg by Bloomberg* (New York: John Wiley, 1997).

Reuters' commitment to data had caused uneasiness among some Reuters journalists for at least two decades. The financialization of news has many strange consequences. Marxist-sounding phrases such as the 'commodification of news' are uttered by financial journalists with otherwise impeccably right-wing and free market views. There do seem to be genuine conflicts of interest. For example, Reuters makes much of its revenue from large-scale trading in shares and currencies; the more movement and insecurity in the financial markets, the more Reuters is taking commissions from (literally) hundreds of billions of dollars of weekly currency hedging and trading.[14] But isn't it financial news (often from Reuters) which causes the markets to move? Another possible conflict of interest: since Reuters and Dow Jones earn much of their revenue from banking clients, does this make them slow to report banking scandals or to critique bank mergers?

Dominating the World News: But For What?

Why are they doing all this? Senior people deny any complex non-profit motivation: 'When I hear the word Synergy I reach for my wallet', and 'Nobody does anything for prestige any more.' One reason for a certain vagueness on these matters is that the video news operations (in particular) may be losing modest sums of money.

Another source of vagueness was the strong tendency towards Anglo-American duopoly. Associated Press and Reuters bestride the news agendas and news flows of the world. Each can be quietly happy about the other. Associated Press exerts a degree of dominance over domestic United States news which would not be tolerated in the cement business or even the movie business. But AP can happily point out that, in Reuters, it has a formidable competitor.

As the duopolistic wielders of a unique political force—'the power of news' around the world and in multiple fast news formats—the American AP and the British Reuters are almost entirely unregulated. Even if they normally behave with self-restraint, and normally justify their reputation for accuracy, AP and Reuters inevitably sometimes act out of narrow self-interest. One major blemish on their records was their treatment of Unesco around 1976–82. The leaders of AP and Reuters helped to orchestrate an international media campaign which soon led to the USA, plus Britain and Singapore, leaving Unesco. The AP and Reuters leaders accused Unesco of supporting the kind of restrictive anti-media measures common under repressive third world regimes. As an account of the main report in question—chaired by

[14] Michael Palmer, 'The Political Economy of News Flow within Europe: News Agencies, Foreign Exchange Dealing and the European Monetary Crisis of September 1992', in Farrell Corcoran and Paschal Preston (eds.), *Democracy and Communication in the New Europe* (Cresskill, NJ: Hampton Press, 1995), 143–55.

Sean MacBride, a former Foreign Minister of Ireland—this was a travesty; the MacBride committee included a former Editor of *Le Monde* and several other distinguished journalists and authors. The report's main thrust, much more French than third world, reflected common European-style centrist views.[15] Moreover much of the criticism of the Reagan/Thatcher decisions to punish Unesco came from American, not third world, commentators.[16]

Even the brave new world of international all news video networks seems likely to be dominated by big American players with some less than lethal competition from BBC World. The *Financial Times*'s attempt to emulate its half-brother *The Economist* (50 per cent Pearson-owned)—by selling more copies in the USA—will not damage the huge domestic US sale of the *Wall Street Journal*. In fact the *Financial Times* and Dow Jones are cooperating against their joint enemy, Reuters, in several specialized financial TV news and database offerings. Meanwhile the US domestic daily market remains a *WSJ* preserve.

The *Financial Times* now owns leading financial dailies in Paris and Madrid and co-owns (with Bertelsmann) a German financial daily in Hamburg; Europe has been tacitly agreed to be a *Financial Times*/Pearson financial daily preserve. The real benefits of the stronger *Financial Times* effort in the USA are that the *FT* can build its general international strength, can obtain more advertising from Wall Street, and can especially consolidate its status as the leading financial newspaper voice of Europe. In addition the *Financial Times* also owns a flotilla of specialist financial weeklies, newsletters, trade publications, and web services.

There is, then, much calculated vagueness about this domination of world news. Some of the vagueness is a defensive reluctance to admit duopoly. Some of it derives from waiting to see if the interactive future actually arrives, although Reuters and AP-Dow Jones have been profitably mining some of the digital and data 'future' since the 1970s. One thing is certain: this low-key vagueness is very Anglo-American.

AP and Reuters will doubtless survive for many more decades, but the same cannot be said for the dozen or so American, British, and European organizations which in the 1990s staked a claim to being serious players in world news. However, several of these players will be very reluctant to give up. In most cases this news operation is the prestige tip of a very large, very profitable, and extremely determined media organization. The news service is often intended as one offering within a portfolio or bouquet of satellite-and-cable services. The big media organisation will not want to drop the

[15] Sean MacBride (chairman) *Many Voices, One World* (London: Kogan Page/UNESCO, 1980).
[16] This included the (Conservative) Freedom Forum of New York. See also Mark D. Alleyne, *News Revolution* (New York: St Martin's Press, 1997), 64–88.

prestige news service because this may look like an admission that the wider bouquet lacks market appeal.

As increasing numbers of households acquire capacity for 200 or more channels, there will be room for a substantial number of news offerings. Within any particular country these channels could belong to as many as four categories:

- National all-news channels, some of them offered by the traditional broadcasters.
- Regional or continental all-news TV on the model of Euronews— available across Europe with a selection of separate language versions.
- The truly international, or globally, oriented service such as CNN, BBC World, and CNBC.
- Particular countries will also import, into their high-channel capacity systems, foreign national all-news channels for the benefit of significant minorities (such as Hispanics or Koreans in the USA, or Turks in Germany).

Meanwhile it seems safe to predict that the truly international all-news offerings will be predominantly American or British.

9

Public Service Broadcasting

IN public service broadcasting, many people would agree, Britain has been number one. Other leaders in public broadcasting since 1945 have been Germany and Japan. The United States Public Broadcasting Service (PBS), National Public Radio (NPR), and associated organizations are often derided for their small audience share against the dominance of com-mercialism. Nevertheless public broadcasting is an important card in the Anglo-American hand on the world scene. Even if the BBC and British broadcasting generate most of the Anglo-American public broadcasting effort, it remains true that the Anglo-Americans have both the leading example of commercial broadcasting and also the leading example of public broadcasting in the world.

Along with the major newspapers, CNN and the old networks, PBS is followed by the Washington and national political elite. More broadly also the public broadcasting system is one of several elements (including the elite newspapers) which are not merely for profit. PBS is completely not-for-profit and shares this status with the dominant Associated Press news machine. In the late 1990s PBS's prime-time rating—about 2 per cent of US households viewing PBS—looked quite respectable. Its audience rating and share figures made PBS the biggest of the small serious networks; PBS had a larger audience than the CNN, Discovery, or Arts and Entertainment networks.

'Public' broadcasting in both Britain and the United States has had an easier time than in some other countries because there were already familiar notions of the public good and the public sphere. In Britain, especially, public service broadcasting was to a considerable degree the creation of Post Office civil servants; some of the non-partisan principles of the British civil service were adopted within, and around, the BBC.

Public broadcasting in Britain, but also in the USA had a relatively easy time because there was already a dominant and accepted definition of national identity. 'Public' broadcasting was inevitably more controversial in countries which were more divided in terms of national language and cul-ture; in such countries the public broadcaster had to make controversial decisions, for example, about which languages, and which versions of those languages, should be used for national broadcasting.

Partisanship: A European Weakness and a British Secret Weapon

British-style 'Public Service Broadcasting' experienced significant challenges in the 1980s, but these were modest compared with what happened in most other European countries. West European public broadcasting suffered severe blows, not least because it had failed to consolidate a tradition of political neutrality. In France public broadcasting for decades did the bidding of mainly Conservative governments. RAI, the Italian public broadcaster, was too close to the Roman Catholic church and to a succession of corrupt Christian Democrat governments; in Germany the system was too close to politicians in general and, ultimately, to the leftist SPD in particular.

Each of these countries was operating within a much shorter (post-1945) tradition than was the BBC in Britain. The BBC moreover had a secret weapon or formula. This was the (often forgotten) fact that the BBC tradition of political neutrality was really a news agency tradition; in both the 1920s and 1930s BBC (radio) news largely relied on news agencies, which themselves had their own long tradition of domestic political neutrality. Consequently complaints about lack of objectivity in the BBC news seldom went beyond particular stories to any sustained questioning of the neutrality of the news operation overall. This strength of the BBC (and later of ITV's ITN) was not actually secret; but it was not widely understood partly because, from 1939 onwards, the BBC emphasized its news as its own product. Also the great British public was always a trifle confused by the distinction between its international agency, with the non-British sounding name (Reuters) and domestic agencies with such unmemorable names as Press Association, Central News, and Exchange Telegraph.

Once you have a partisan public broadcasting tradition, it tends to be self-perpetuating. Partisan decisions by one government lead to partisan reversals by rival political parties, when they come to power. But similarly, a non-partisan, consensual tradition also tends to perpetuate itself. Of course in the British system, government was involved, but so was the official opposition. The tradition also involved the civil service, regulatory bodies, and a tradition of committees and commissions (again usually fairly non-partisan). Under this tradition there were few attempts, for example, at quick *faits accomplis* designed to realign the system just before the next general election.

A consensual or bi-partisan system invites both government and opposition politicians to appear on its programming on a daily and weekly basis; before each such appearance there are phone calls, brief discussions, and tacit bargaining. This continuing contact becomes a self-adjusting mechanism. The relevant broadcast producers and journalists who are in continuing contact with the full spectrum of politicians usually have little difficulty in locating a central consensual 'neutral' path. Disputes and conflicts between broadcast journalists and politicians do, of course, occur; but most of these disputes blow away quite quickly.

American PBS and the British Connection

The US public broadcasting service has suffered from a number of weak-nesses,[1] one of which may have been its dependence on the British connec-tion. PBS has never fully succeeded in establishing its non-partisan char-acter. The system really dates from the Public Broadcasting Act of 1967, which provided for Washington funding through the Corporation for Pub-lic Broadcasting (CPB). This rather late launch (or relaunch) permanently marked PBS as a product of the left-liberal 1960s, the Lyndon Johnson presidency, and the Democrats. Conservative politicians such as Richard Nixon, Ronald Reagan, and Newt Gingrich continued to label PBS as an inappropriate leftist intrusion into the broadcasting market place.

Despite its name, the Public Broadcasting Service has suffered from not being a single service, supported by a coherent consensus. Rather PBS has been several overlapping and weakly coordinated services. In particular there has been no central network, but instead a large number of local stations. Despite a broad doctrine of localism, there has not been much local programming. The bulk of programming for many years was produced by ten or eleven local stations such as WGBH (Boston), WNET (New York), and KQED (San Francisco). Without a strong national schedule, there has been a rather inefficient public version of commercial syndication. Local stations have always constructed their own schedules, making effective national promotion difficult. However, in the 1990s PBS did nationally net-work (and nationally promote) more of its programming. There are parallel systems of TV and of National Public Radio.

PBS is, by international standards, not badly funded. There is, of course, no general licence fee of the European type, although some local stations collect voluntary membership 'subscriptions'. Funding also comes from the federal government, state government, big business, local government, universities, and foundations. PBS is criticized for failing to produce either popular or quality programming. Clearly, with a 2 per cent prime-time rating, it was never super popular. Previous to 1967 there were numerous 'educational' TV and radio stations and some programming still comes from University-linked stations. PBS has been unable to match the normal European public network's traditional supplies of sport, entertainment, and comedy. The centrality of the ten key stations has led to emphasis on the

[1] Sydney W. Head, Christopher H. Sterling and Lemuel B. Schofield, *Broadcasting in America* (Boston: Houghton Mifflin, 1994), 264–301.

mini-series—as a prestigious offering within the financial grasp of a single station. But PBS has been relatively unsuccessful (outside children's programming) at generating those lengthy series on which most successful networks around the world depend.

Failing to generate adequate programming of its own—the critics claim—PBS relied upon the British connection for programming which was both prestigious and (by PBS standards) popular. In fact over a period of years foreign-produced or co-produced programming only accounted for about 14 per cent of PBS TV output, a modest level for a TV network by international standards.

British programming was attractive to PBS from 1970 onwards because it was popular, prestigious, and absurdly cheap to purchase. The first 39 hours of *Masterpiece Theatre* (from the BBC via Time-Life TV) cost WGBH only $10,000 an hour. A steady flow followed of *Upstairs, Downstairs* (ITV, not BBC) and many other costume dramas. Also popular were natural history programming and something completely different, *Monty Python's Flying Circus*. This author discovered in 1978–9—when teaching at the University of California (San Diego)—that to 20-year-old California students the initials BBC spelt Monty Python. In addition to *Monty Python, Masterpiece Theatre*, and *Mystery!*, WGBH leaned heavily on British imports (and production personnel) for its science series, *Nova*.[2] The PBS late-1990s ratings success, *Antiques Roadshow* was based on a BBC Bristol format of the 1970s.

But in the 1990s British and American factual programming came closer together. The BBC found that several categories of programming—including sport, drama, and comedy—were becoming expensive; there was much to be said for factual genres, such as documentary and natural history. These two factual genres were still popular, still not too expensive to make, and about the most suitable of all BBC programming for co-production and export finance.

In the USA both documentary and natural history programming boomed in the 1990s. The strongest emerging player in this game was the *Discovery* network with its younger sibling, *Animal Planet*. By the late 1990s about half of all natural history programming hours available for world sales came from the USA—mainly from Discovery/Animal Planet, National Geographic, PBS, and Turner. About a quarter came from Britain—mainly from the BBC and the two ITV specialists (Anglia and Harlech).[3]

The Anglo-American cooperative element in these types of programming was strengthened by the emerging BBC alliance with TCI/Discovery/Flextech. In both Britain and the USA, of course, there are high- and low-priced products within each genre. Some of the highest-cost products are

[2] Laurence Jarvik, *PBS: Behind the Screen* (Rocklin, Calif.: Prima, Forum, 1997), 207–13, 237–74.
[3] 'Wildlife Programming', *Television Business International* (July/August 1997), 18–27.

the most Anglo-American—for example the 26-episode *World at War* series produced by Jeremy Isaacs in 1975 and the *Cold War* series co-produced by Jeremy Isaacs for Turner in 1998.

Many mid-budget natural history series are very Anglo-American in conception and finance. But the American preference is usually for British series filmed in more exotic places than Britain. The BBC natural history producers have become accustomed to obtaining about a quarter or a third of their budgets from the USA; together with other foreign funding (from Australia, Japan, Germany, Canada, and elsewhere) this US funding has become a key ingredient of British 'quality' in factual programming.

Many British documentaries are less acceptable in the USA because they deal with 'parochial' subjects such as poverty or low life in London.[4] During the 1990s British producers developed a cheapish new documentary subgenre, which included elements of both TV comedy and soap opera. These docu-soaps dealt with 'real life' on the hoof in hotels, hospitals, airports, the Army, factories, and football clubs. This sub-genre leant heavily on the British liking for whimsical eccentricity; the narrative was too slow and banal for an American audience but attracted large audiences (at a modest cost) in Britain.

Public Service Broadcasting: Decline and Fall

Michael Tracey's book, *The Decline and Fall of Public Service Broadcasting* (1998)[5] is heavy with nostalgia and pessimism. It exaggerates the triumphs and pays insufficient attention to just how boring and partisan much PSB was. But when Tracey's book was published, the public channels still had about 40 per cent of the West European audience.

Public broadcasting in Britain began as a monopoly and the early history of the BBC neatly paralleled that of *The Times* newspaper in London one century earlier. Following a great war (ending 1815) *The Times* developed a powerful voice, which benefited from a government conferred (penal taxation) effective monopoly; this was altered by another government decision—in 1855—to allow fresh competition. Following another great war (ending 1918) the BBC evolved a powerful independent voice, which depended upon a government-conferred (licence fee) effective monopoly; this was altered by another government decision—in 1955—to allow fresh competition. It could hardly be expected that in the twentieth century a government-conferred monopoly-broadcasting system could retain its monopoly into an era of channel multiplication.

The inevitable consequences of channel multiplication in Britain were in

---

[4] Jeremy Tunstall, *Television Producers* (London: Routledge, 1993), 27–46.
[5] Oxford University Press.

fact obscured and delayed by the 'accident' of the 1939–45 war. The war conferred on the BBC a degree of consensus and prestige which it would not otherwise have achieved. Moreover after the war, not only the British, but also the Americans, effectively chose the BBC model for conquered Japan, Germany, and (to a lesser extent) Italy.[6]

Pessimistic accounts of British public service broadcasting seem to imply that channel multiplication—at least in the 1990s—led to the decline and fall of PSB. This approach does justice neither to the inevitability of channel multiplication, nor to the gradual adjustments towards channel multiplication made within the British system. In particular Britain, as early as 1982, had effectively made a big change within its public tradition by introducing a second 'minority' channel in the form of Channel Four. This in practice led to a division of labour in relation to the old John Reith trinity of public broadcasting goals. After 1982 Britain had two big channels—ITV and BBC1—each with a 30 per cent plus audience share and a predominant focus on *entertainment* (but with some more 'public' material).

The big innovation, however, was that after 1982 Britain had two channels—BBC2 and Channel Four—which largely took on the two more public service goals of *education* and *information*. Each of the two channels (by the end of the 1980s) had a roughly 10 per cent audience share. This represented an important redefinition (but not revolution) in public service; it did combine entertainment with the information and education, while at the same time (in a very PSB way) glossing over the issue of what was pill and what was sugar. These channels were not monopolies; indeed they competed not only with each other, but with the big channels as well.

The two smaller, 10 per cent share, channels were also encouraged (especially by Channel Four's legal establishment and regulatory regime) to search out largish 'minorities'. A minority could be an ethnic minority; but it could also be an age group, or an interest group like sports fans, or some other 'broad niche' audience. However there was not much attention for the difficult and expensive task of local or regional television. Within a strongly national approach both BBC2 and Channel Four were adequately funded for their biggish-minority focus.

Of course, what will happen to these channels in the future is another question (to which we return in Chapter 17). But in the meanwhile the more gloomy observations about the death of British PSB fail to notice that the 10 per cent channels have strengths and flexibilities for the multi-channel future which are less available to channels trying to hold a 30 per cent audience share. BBC2 and Channel Four are full of extremely vigorous life; so, consequently, is British public service broadcasting.

[6] Tunstall, *The Media are American.*

10
British Popular Music and the BBC

WHY has Britain—traditionally seen as one of Europe's least musical nations—been able to play such a big part in international music? One reason is EMI. Another is the English language. Related to the language is the success of British performers in picking up (often black) American sounds and playing them back to the mass (white) American domestic audience. Also helpful to British music has been the American music industry's use of London as its European base.

However we believe that the BBC—and British public service broadcasting approaches—have, ever since the 1920s, also played a key role. BBC music policy has always been to play 'the best' of current American music, but to focus more strongly on the best of current British music. BBC pop music policy has not ignored popularity (as expressed in sales charts) but it has also tried to be ahead of current taste—to play what will be (or should or could be) popular next month and next year. The BBC has thus been an unrivalled launcher, or breaker, of new acts and new sounds. Behind the BBC has been a concentrated music industry ready to sell and to exploit new sounds, and new acts, once successfully launched. Behind Oasis and the Spice Girls, as behind the Beatles (and many others) was a massive early push from repeated play on the BBC playlist and on Britain's nationally dominant radio networks. Britain's small number of big networks also made for much less genre fragmentation than in the USA. In Britain a relatively small spread of sounds was given a relatively big promotional push on radio.

Popular music is another example of a media field which has a dominant Anglo-American long tradition. The English language is unusually important because of the emotional significance of the words. The American musical tradition of the first half of the century was dominant; one of its expressions was an Anglo-American led music marketing cartel. Then in the 1960s and 1970s British musicians played themselves into an increasingly prominent role within the Anglo-American musical enterprise.

Although often compared with the movies, the music business is more fragmented; there is a closer industrial similarity to the book business. Large book or music companies have a number of imprints or labels which specialize in different genres. The big music companies aim for a small number of big sellers because big sellers are more profitable per unit sold; the second million sales generate more profits than the first million. But even in the US domestic market the ten top-selling albums each year still only account for about 5 per cent of the total. The market is fragmented in terms of musical genre and thousands of competing artists. Against this fragmented background British artists have been successful in featuring among each year's Top Acts, both across the world and in the USA.

Popular music is an especially volatile part of the mass media. Sales revenue depends heavily on one-off purchases by young adults; music is similar, in this regard, to movies, but music has a shorter sequence of subsequent market windows than does the movie industry. The music business is also very dependent on radio play and, in recent times, on video music play. Changing technologies are another source of volatility; the Internet and a range of potentially dominant new audio technologies create especially great uncertainty as to future sales, piracy, and industrial profitability.

The music business has evolved a number of industrial strategies with which to handle the endemic volatility. In the 1990s the growth of the CD (compact disc) made for strong sales. A traditional emphasis has been on recording stars; and music stars (and their advisers) developed their own sequence of market windows designed for the star, not just the music. Thus Madonna could appear in various audio and video formats, but also in movies, in books, in personal appearances, and on her own recording label (Maverick). Another trend enabled music stars to become deeply involved in advertising campaigns, without, it seemed, compromising their rebellious or individual authenticity as seen by their fans.

But another big change, especially in the mid and late 1990s, was a swing towards 'local repertoire'. The extraordinary commercial dominance of Anglo-American music entered a period of relative decline from about 1994 onwards. Several European countries which had previously only produced about one-third of their musical intake now advanced to a domestically produced share of half or more. Italy, France, and Germany all swung quite decisively in this 'local repertoire' direction.

The music industry has consequently become a leading example of combined local and global tendencies. There is a strong trend around the world for consumers to buy, and for new radio stations to play, local-national music. At the same time the six major music companies have become more and more part of vertical media companies which operate through subsidiary companies—each with its own labels—on all of the continents and within all of the larger media markets. Much of the 'local' music appears on labels owned by the 'global' companies.

The BBC and Popular Music

The BBC's traditional music policy of preferring British popular music, alongside a substantial (informal) quota of American music, has been remarkably successful. The BBC, despite its committee bureaucracy and its middle-aged and middle-class absurdities, did have considerable success in assisting four separate crossovers vital to the emergence of modern British popular music. These were the crossovers from recorded music and radio into the visual media; from local to national and international music; from black to white music; and from working class to middle class. With the active help of the BBC, the Beatles made all of these crossovers more smoothly in Britain than did Elvis Presley a few years earlier in the USA.

The first major challenge to the BBC's reliance on British big bands and light orchestra music came in the late 1930s from commercial radio stations in northern France and Luxembourg. These stations were mainly taking advantage of the lack of British radio advertising, but those Britons who heard them enjoyed the fact that they did not regard Sunday as a day for religious music. Then in 1939–40 the BBC recognized that many of the British soldiers, who were in France until the defeat at Dunkirk in June 1940, preferred the American music which they heard on the French commercial stations.

During 1940–5 the BBC responded to audience demand and established a new set of music policies. The BBC's main wartime radio offerings were the 'Home' network and a 'Forces' network which—through written 'requests' and similar devices—tried genuinely to reflect the taste of the young conscripts in the armed forces. The 'Forces' network was also hugely popular with the civilian population. The network placed emphasis on British acts such as Gracie Fields along with new patriotic, sentimental, and comic songs[1] and also on the new and hugely popular American music. After sizeable numbers of American military personnel arrived in Britain in early 1942, more and more American music was played on the BBC; American music also appeared in large doses on the American Forces Network (AFN) which pumped out an all-US programming format from very low power local transmitters on Air Force and other military bases. At the same time there were many Hollywood musical films in British cinemas.

The American soldiers went home in 1945, but the US musical invasion broadly stayed in place and during 1945–55 the BBC's rationing policy for American music came close to collapse. Compared with Britain, the United States in the 1940s was already far more saturated with popular music, jukeboxes, and radio stations playing the top twenty. In industrial terms the British music industry in 1950 had still not caught up to where the American industry had been in 1940.

Late 1940s British popular music existed only on a very modest scale. There were British shortages of most key ingredients from musical instruments to radio airtime. Pop music in Britain was found mainly only on the

[1] Steven Seidenberg, Maurice Sellar, and Lou Jones, *You Must Remember This . . . Songs at the Heart of the War* (London: Boxtree, 1995).

BBC Light network which it had to share with other non-music programming. EMI, the British record company, found that its imports from the USA outnumbered its exports to the USA by about three to one. The BBC in 1947 transmitted relatively little completely British popular music. Even as late as 1954–5 British music was taking up only 44 per cent of BBC popular musical output.[2]

BBC senior executives were again on the musical defensive, as 1955–6 seemed to bring two new massive threats. One was the 1955 launch of advertising-financed ITV, and the other was Elvis Presley, whose records monopolized the US number one spot in August–December 1956 and whose first movie, *Love Me Tender*, was also released in 1956. Presley's first British hit record was 'Heartbreak Hotel' in May 1956. But the challenge of Presley and Rock'n Roll plus the challenge of ITV led the BBC to compete effectively in both radio and television.

The BBC had experimented with TV shows such as *Hit Parade* (a 1952 copy of a current American show) and *Off the Record* in May 1955. With the arrival of ITV, the BBC saw youth programming as one possible area of strength with teen-music offerings such as *Music Shop, Cool for Cats* (1957–9), *Oh Boy!* (1958), *Juke Box Jury* (1959), and in 1963, *Top of the Pops*.[3]

The Beatles, who with perfect lucky timing had their first British top twenty records in winter 1962–3, were able to use this BBC commitment to both radio and *television* music programming. The Beatles were also lucky that EMI—having lost its big import deals with Columbia (1952) and RCA (1953)—were specializing in the first wave of British rock music; EMI was also worried about Capitol, its sickly US company. Both the BBC and EMI gave big pushes to the Beatles who, with apparently effortless ease, made all of the crucial crossovers. Starting with their first hit record in late 1962, they moved quickly to BBC radio, to both BBC and ITV television, and to their first feature film, *A Hard Day's Night* (1964). Their jump from local stardom in Liverpool to London and to US touring was equally rapid. The Beatles also made the black–white crossover, by drawing on Rhythm'n Blues, Gospel, and Motown music as well as on white rockers like Buddy Holly and Elvis Presley. Finally, the Beatles were making the social class crossover, coming from very modest Liverpool backgrounds.

Elvis Presley himself had had a much less smooth crossover experience in the USA. Presley did follow the record-radio-visual path; but his main visual output was his bland Hollywood films; the US television networks in the late 1950s were not ready to give Presley a big splash (although, of course, he did appear on TV). To the then New York advertising agency TV producers,

---

[2] Asa Briggs *Sound and Vision* (Oxford: Oxford University Press, 1979), 756–8.
[3] Asa Briggs, *Competition 1955–1974* (Oxford: Oxford University Press, 1995), 457–64, 508–15. John Hill, 'Television and Pop: The Case of the 1950s', in John Corner and Sylvia Harvey (eds.), *Television Times* (London: Arnold, 1996), 55–6.

Elvis Presley looked too working class, too raunchy, and too down South provincial.

Even the British Musicians' Union played its part in the emergence of acts like the Beatles, Cliff Richard, and the Rolling Stones. The Union's insistence on live performance, and its rationing of 'needle time', strengthened the long London tradition of live performance. The London advertising and film industries also helped.

Britain and the World Record Industry

With its smallish number of loud pop music voices, London looked aggressively out across the Atlantic and also across the water to Europe. The British music industry in the 1990s was still a much bigger exporter than importer. This London musical success, based on an Anglo-American rooted industry, locked the British industry into the world music industry in general and into the American music industry in particular.

Elton John, Rod Stewart, the Rolling Stones, the Beatles, Pink Floyd, Queen, and Led Zeppelin were hugely popular in the USA; but this success led to complacency and lack of forward thinking in the British record companies. In the US album charts the main British features of the 1990s were acts like the highly Americanized Phil Collins, and with less success, Simply Red and George Michael. It is unlikely that there will be a new Beatles or Rolling Stones due both to an increasing fragmentation of musical tastes and genres and an increase in the number of albums on sale at any one time.[4]

British music was prominent in the 1981 launch of MTV on US cable stations and the subsequent evolution of video music. British electronic bands such as Duran Duran, the Thompson Twins, Wham!, and the Human League, were already marketing themselves through video and could thus offer the new MTV a ready supply of material.

Britain and America are without challenge at the top of the pop music cultural hierarchy. These two countries have all the history and legends that young hopeful bands aspire to, such as the Beatles, the Stones, Jimi Hendrix, Woodstock, and many more throughout the decades. While many countries may have their own famous names, and possibly the odd international sensation like Abba or INXS, it is the Anglo-American acts which literally are the history and culture of popular music. They are also ever more important as the core of 'back catalogue' exploitation, and of the music publishing business, in which EMI is a leader.

---

[4] S. A. Pandit, *From Making to Music: The History of Thorn EMI* (London: Hodder and Stoughton, 1996), 199.

British Radio and BBC Radio One

Since the 1960s British radio has increasingly taken on American characteristics, such as the use of jingles, voice-overs, ad styles, promotions, and
'Selector' computer-generated playlists. Most of the sounds and textures of
British radio were imported from America in the 1960s and 1970s. Many
jingles and promotions are imports which have just had the words changed.
Anecdotes recounted by senior British radio programmers indicate the
strong impact of their first tour of American radio stations.

Commercial radio began in Britain in 1973. But BBC Radio One was the
network largely responsible for the development of new acts. For some years
after its 1967 birth BBC Radio One was listened to each week by 25 million
people or about half the British population aged 5 or older. As late as June
1993 Radio One still had a weekly 'reach' of 19 million people:

It puts out live gigs, pioneers unsigned bands and carries a repertoire that stretches
from zouk to techno and beyond, taking in rap, dance, soul, metal, grunge, garage,
new jack, swing and more along the way. No commercial station would risk all this.
John Peel alone has launched more bands than he could shake a stick at. Alongside
this, the station runs documentaries, comedy, and 'social action' campaigns—
homelessness, racism, etc.[5]

But by 1993 Radio One was dominated by a team of middle-aged DJs,
some of whom had been there for most of the years since 1967. The audience
also was getting older and starting to crowd into the middle-aged territory
supposedly occupied by the BBC's Radio Two. The Director-General, John
Birt, and the BBC high command were worried by suggestions (from Conservative politicians) that Radios One and Two could be privatized, sold off
as commercial radio. John Birt wanted to confirm the BBC's status as a
broad service for everyone; this meant retaining Radio One. A need was seen
to 'reposition' and 'rebrand' Radio One as oriented towards the 16–24 age
group.

The 'rebranding' of Radio One involved kicking out most of the middle-
aged DJs and their music; it also involved deliberately losing most of the
thirty-something members of the audience. Within less than a year nearly
one-quarter of the audience departed. In five years, 1993–8, the audience
reach and share fell by about a half. However the BBC could claim that, with
the huge 1990s increase in commercial radio competition, a big fall in the
total audience was inevitable. Even after this massive drop, and the commercial radio onslaught, BBC Radios One and Two together had 22 per cent
of all British radio listening in 1998–9.

The people at Radio One would claim that in a market of more numerous

[5] Malcolm MacAlister Hall, 'The End of the Road Show', *Observer* magazine section, 18
July 1993, pp. 17–24.

stations their weekly audience reach of 9 or 10 million was still impressive, not least because Radio One policy was to avoid simply playing the chart-toppers; there was an absolute ban on playing golden oldies and a total commitment to new music for a young audience. Radio One was consequently still committed to a 'public service' role within popular music. It focused heavily on new British music. Radio One was in the vanguard in giving mass airplay to the Britpop music of the mid-1990s. Radio One's policy involved proactive selection of new music which was not, or not yet, in the charts. This meant selecting a Radio One playlist (with seven categories of play frequency) partly based on the fresh offerings of the music companies' pluggers; but it also meant taking music straight out of live performances in clubs and venues. Radio One and its personnel at BBC Broadcasting House were centrally positioned in London's pop music belt which stretches from Capital Radio in the West End to MTV at Camden Town, 2 miles to the north.

Radio One in the 1990s also repositioned itself into the heartland not only of British pop music, but of British pop culture. There was a very close affinity between on the one hand the large-sale tabloid daily newspapers and on the other hand the leading DJs and the currently most popular musicians. Radio One could be accused of reflecting and enhancing London (rather than British) pop music and pop culture.

Britain has a few highly localized 'ethnic' radio stations. But these hardly add up to anything like the increase in choice originally envisaged for 'Independent Local Radio'. Ironically it is still left to the ancient BBC to break new acts and to provide something different. ILR's best manifestations have been in London and a few other large cities where there has been some increase in variety. London offers most choice although apart from dance and jazz this involves local stations such as Melody, Heart, and Virgin having different, but not too different, playlists.

Broadly the 1996 Broadcasting Act left the British provinces with a still very limited choice of 'local'—but not very local—radios. Radio policy in Britain is still skewed towards a strong national BBC radio effort. The BBC was allowed to retain the cream of the national FM frequencies (four BBC against only one commercial).

Meanwhile the musical poverty of the British provinces leaves London to focus on national and international musical concerns. London has a very extensive music club activity; it has much the best collection of local and ethnic radio stations. And it is the home of the BBC, which—through its TV and world service radio, as well as its domestic radio—continues to seek out, to support, and to play, the best of British pop. Within this public service effort the BBC's Radio One remains the core, because it focuses on new, young, and British music. BBC Radio Two increasingly presents the now long tradition of glorious Anglo-American pop. John Reith—the BBC's

---

BBC Radio One

'This is Radio 1, for God's sake, the best radio station to work at in the world. The licence fee-payer can be happy with the knowledge that none of their fee has been squandered on wasteful things such as paint or nice furniture.'

Chris Moyles, BBC Radio One DJ

'The thing that most struck me was to learn that the average age of the Radio 1 audience [in 1993] was thirty-one years old. . . . it was a group of people that had grown old together.'

John Birt, BBC Director-General

'. . . Radio 1 is the most important radio station in the world for breaking new music. . . . I try not to think too much about the implications for the music industry on the decisions we make for the playlist, but clearly they are huge.'

Jeff Smith, Head of Radio 1 music policy

'Each week about thirty pluggers—record promotions people—enter Smith's small office for five or ten minutes and sit on a fat chair to flog him their latest greatest new thing. . . . they give Smith two or three songs to play on the CD player behind him. They get a pretty instant response. It's a nervous thing to watch.'

Simon Garfield

Source: Simon Garfield, *The Nation's Favourite: The True Adventures of Radio 1* (London: Faber and Faber, 1998).

---

founding father—would not have approved, but it was BBC Radio One which developed for itself this latter-day public broadcasting role of educating the great British public to appreciate the best new musical entertainment.

11
Book Publishing: US–UK Merger

DESPITE its much-predicted imminent demise, the book is still with us. Ink-on-paper seems to offer an, as yet unbeaten, combination of browsability, portability, clarity of definition, and cheapness.[1]

Book publishing provides yet another example of media 'one-way flow'. Even in a major book publishing country, such as Germany, more than one-third of all books published each year are translations, predominantly of American, but also of British titles.[2] Britain is similar to other European countries in that it imports a lot of book titles; but Britain's imports are of untranslated American books. Only about 2 per cent of the 100,000 new titles published in Britain each year are translations.

Anglo-American Publishing: Intimacy at a Distance, 1830–1960

The American–British publishing relationship has had three distinct historical phases: an era of *piracy* (until 1890); a *gentlemen's cartel* era (1890–1960); and finally (since 1960) an era of *commercial integration*. In recent decades British book publishing has been commercially integrated into a combined Anglo-American English language commercial enterprise.

The period up to 1890 was an era of piracy, because only in 1891 did the US Congress legislate to protect international copyright. Until then, many American publishers reprinted London-published books and periodicals without permission and without payment. In some cases voluntary payments were made, but several American publishers competed to bring out the quickest pirated copy of the latest London novels. Charles Dickens, on his American travels in 1842, was shocked both by popular American newspaper sensationalism and by American book publishing piracy. Proposed copyright legislation was repeatedly defeated by the aggressive publishing lobby in Washington until Congress eventually enacted an effective copyright law in 1891. Piracy also affected periodicals—both the high-minded elite Reviews and more popular London magazines of the mid-Victorian period.[3] However, the traffic was not all in one direction. As early as 1841–6,

[1] Felix Dennis, quoted in *Media Week*, 21 June 1996.
[2] Information from Gordon Fielden, the Society of Authors (London), Jan. 1999.
[3] James L. Barnes, *Authors, Publishers and Politicians* (London: Routledge, 1974).

at least sixty American books per year were reprinted in England, mostly without payment or permission.[4]

The era of gentleman's cartel began in 1891 and among its early beneficiaries were celebrity British authors such as Rudyard Kipling and H. G. Wells who were now assured of substantial American earnings. Kipling's popularity reached its peak in 1899 when he became ill, apparently near death, in New York; hourly health bulletins were issued to the press by his doctors. But Kipling got well and returned home; subsequently his books were never quite so popular again, and Kipling complained that his American public never forgave him for not dying in New York.

Throughout the 1890–1960 period, both American and British book publishers were relatively small businesses; the American publishers focused on their rapidly expanding home market, while the British publishers monopolized the British Empire market. British authors' books did sell in the USA, and US authors' books did sell in Britain, but there was often a significant time lag. Typically the New York publisher sold the British Empire (or Commonwealth) rights to a London publisher, who—after a delay of months or years—would publish the American book in what was effectively a protected British Commonwealth market. Similarly an American publisher would acquire the US rights to a British book and—after a significant delay—would produce an American edition. These arrangements paralleled the practice of the recorded music business. There was an Anglo-American book cartel, just as there was an Anglo-American recorded music cartel. In the 1930s depression this seemed a prudent and sensible way to do business.

These comfortable cartel arrangements were especially comfortable for the British book publishers. After 1940 the British and Commonwealth markets became even more sealed off from outside competition. This partly came about through the same paper rationing which between 1940 and 1956 reduced the size of British newspapers. Newsprint was rationed so as to minimize the importing of paper by sea. During 1940–5 this meant a severe rationing of new book production, and paper rationing continued for a decade after 1945. As the paper rationing was gradually reduced, there remained a policy of restricting 'dollar imports'. Consequently during 1945–56 the importing of US-published books into Britain was restricted; the entire range of American fiction was very severely rationed. The main weight of American media influence on Europe after 1945 was confined to the audio-visual media.

[4] John Tebbel, *The Media in America* (New York: Thomas Y. Crowell, 1974).

US Mega Publishing Arrives

Especially during 1945–60 the advance of American book publishing onto the world scene was quite hesitant. While Hollywood films dominated European cinema screens in the late 1940s, American books largely stayed at home. Official occupation policy in Germany emphasized the regeneration of good (non-Nazi) German publishing, although in the 1945–55 decade some 1,400 American novels were published in German translation.[5] But the traditionally strong book publishing industries of Germany, France, and Italy all returned to vigorous existence.

In Britain also, during 1945–60, American books were fairly scarce. There were considerable delays even in the arrival of major American fictional writing of the 1930s. British paper rationing policy also involved a reluctance during the 1940s to import American 'pulp fiction'—the cheapest paperback range of crime, western, science fiction, sex, and horror. There was, however, a pent-up demand for these types of fiction, generated mainly by the buoyant imports of Hollywood films. Established British publishers, operating in a seller's market, deliberately avoided this low-prestige (and low-profit) market. The consequence was a rapid rise of new British publishers to fill the demand for pulp fiction. A remarkable aspect of this sudden boom of 'American' pulp fiction was that not only the publishers, but also the authors, were British. The most celebrated of these authors was 'Hank Janson' who authored dozens of books with such titles as *This Dame Dies Soon* and *Broads Don't Scare Easy*.[6]

British publishers focused heavily on both the 'old' and (later) the 'new' Commonwealth countries, where in many cases the school textbooks were still locally printed editions of London publications. The US publishing business saw another huge expansion in its home market. A predominant export pattern was the sale of translation rights, which allowed the German, French, Italian, or other publisher to take the risk.

A new phase began around 1960. Indirectly significant was the Soviet Union's successful 1957 launch of the first space vehicle ('Sputnik'), which induced much soul-searching as to the failures of the American educational system. One consequence was the fashionable expectation of an imminent 1960s 'convergence' between book publishing and computerized learning. The big American companies which now bought book-publishing companies included IBM, ITT, Litton, RCA, CBS, Raytheon, Xerox, GE, and GTE. After some years these commercial giants recognized their mistake and sold the book companies, but the buyings-and-sellings of companies

---

[5]   Ralph Willett, *The Americanization of Germany, 1945–1949* (London: Routledge, 1989), 54–60.
[6]   Steve Holland, *The Mushroom Jungle: A History of Postwar Paperback Publishing* (Westbury: Zeon Books, 1993).

constituted merely one among many rounds of publishing mergers and 'convergence' yet to come.

While the ambitious convergence with electronics failed to happen, a more pedestrian magazine-book convergence was successful. Over the years 1960–85 a number of American book publishers moved onto the world scene. Several were magazine publishers which already published export editions. Time Inc successfully used the international arm of its magazine business to move into international book publishing; many Time books had expensive illustrations, a publishing genre which lends itself to foreign sales and translation. Another magazines-and-books international major of this era was the technical and educational publisher McGraw-Hill; by 1985 McGraw-Hill had established significant publishing operations in Britain, Canada and Australia and was active in fourteen other countries, publishing books in thirteen languages.[7] Also successful was the Reader's Digest company which used its mammoth circulation monthly magazine as the flagship of a book publishing business whose European sales equalled its sales in the US home market.

Random House, another American publisher of both magazines and books, exemplifies the series of steps through which a number of American publishers went on their way to international book publishing. It was in 1959 that the two founders of Random House decided to sell 30 per cent of the company. Random House was already in general 'trade' as well as educational publishing; it now began to acquire other prestigious hardback companies such as Pantheon and Knopf. In 1965 Random House was itself bought (for $40 million) by the huge RCA electronics company, owner of the NBC TV network. But RCA soon became bored with Random House and eventually gave up in 1980. The next owner was the Newhouse family-controlled Advance magazine and newspaper company—now in a phase of aggressive growth. Random House became a major paperback owner (Ballantine Books) and therefore capable of a vertically integrated hardback–and–mass-paperback operation.[8] Subsequently Advance followed its previous Condé Nast magazine strategy, by taking Random House down the international route; a batch of well-known London imprints were acquired—including Jonathan Cape, Chatto and Windus, The Bodley Head, and Hutchinson.

From the mid-1980s onwards, British publishing was exposed to radical commercial changes which had occurred more gradually in the United States in the 1960s and 1970s. Like book publishers, book retailers got bigger and stronger. The book retail chains began to insist on 'sale or return' and bargained fiercely with publishers over bulk discounts. The chain bookstores also made quite big cuts in the prices charged to customers for hardback

---

[7]   Peter Curwen, *The World Book Industry* (London: Euromonitor, 1986), 44.

[8]   Thomas Maier, *Newhouse* (Boulder, Colo.: Johnson Books, 1997 edition).

best-sellers, which in turn further stoked up the number of copies a 'hard-back best-seller' could sell. By the late 1990s two US companies each owned over 1,000 retail bookshops.

The years 1984–8 were especially active for American book publishing mergers and by 1993 nine of the ten largest US publishers were part of larger media companies. Three became part of Hollywood/Network Big Six companies—Simon and Schuster (Viacom), Warner (Time Warner), and HarperCollins (News Corp). Another three were part of major print companies; and a further three were part of non-US companies. The top ten publishers accounted for 60 per cent of total US book sales.[9]

The simplest big publisher strategy is to build up a portfolio of big authors. This can include the crossover into movies; there has also been the adoption of Hollywood and show business publicity to promote best-selling authors. The big publisher with its team of big authors comes to specialize in the big book promotion exercise; in the USA this means the establishment of close ties with those TV and radio talk shows (both national and local) which specialize in celebrity interviews, including interviews with celebrity crime, cooking, sex and investment advice, showbiz biography, and travel writers.

Big authors, in addition to having big publishers, have big agents. Back in the 1950s and 1960s the Anglo-American gentlemen's cartel in publishing included 'professionally correct' relationships between New York and London agencies; the British agencies still called themselves 'Literary Agents'. In subsequent decades the London agents tended to drop the 'Literary'. However these British writers' agents now found themselves at a disadvantage in relation to their New York opposite numbers. The New York agents who handle big US authors are more attuned to television promotion; there is a much bigger focus on film rights, because even if only thirty or forty Hollywood studio movies each year are book based, the number of preliminary 'option' rights acquired is probably several hundred books per year.

Increasingly, the biggest US book publishers make sounds very like those of Hollywood and the music industry. The book world has its own superstars and its own book superstores; the New York publisher, like the Hollywood studio, has its few carefully scheduled big 'Event' offerings each year. Publishers who spent too much (in author advance) also hope to 'make it up on the back end'. The complaint is heard that star author payments are growing faster than sales and 'it just can't go on much longer'. One or two wealthy authors, it is said, have attempted to manipulate the best-seller lists by strategic multiple purchases of their own books, just like music companies seeking to manipulate the music sales charts. Increasingly—also as in

---

[9]   Albert N. Greco, *The Book Publishing Industry* (Boston: Allyn and Bacon, 1997), 48–58.

Hollywood—there is a fierce struggle as to whether publisher or author/agent will retain the subsequent electronic-multimedia rights. Like the Hollywood company with its various subsidiaries and 'independents', or the music company with its scattering of record labels, so also the book company has numerous hardback and paperback imprints spanning its main publishing genres.

The US-ABC-European Book Publishing Merger

When in 1998 the American Random House was acquired by the German Bertelsmann, it could no longer be denied that several of the largest US publishers—somewhere between one–third and a half, according to different definitions—were now foreign owned. Bertelsmann now had two of what had been the ten largest US publishers—not only Random House, but also Bantam, Doubleday, Dell. The English-speaking ABC countries still controlled an even larger slice including the Canadian Thomson and the US-Australian-British (News Corp) HarperCollins. When the British Pearson company (Longman, Penguin, and Addison, Wesley) acquired a big slice of Simon and Schuster in 1998, Pearson's resulting share of US educational publishing was sufficiently large as to require anti-trust approval.

There were some differences of emphasis between the German and the British investments in US publishing. Bertelsmann's presence was indeed primarily an investment, although seen also as a possible stepping stone towards additional acquisitions in the US media. The British presence was somewhat different because it was two-way; it also involved a larger number of US publishers in Britain, and at least a dozen British publishers doing a substantial slice of their business inside the USA.

As seen from New York, Britain's role in book publishing resembles its role in pop music. Britain performs four main functions. First, it is the best market (along with Canada and Australia) for sales of untranslated American books. Second, the British editions of US books also make additional export sales (typically about half that of the British sale). Third, Britain is a location for 'picking up' local talent and product (as it is for movies and music); many British authors are published simultaneously by both the UK and US arms of an American publisher. Fourth, London is important as a location for selling translation rights into Europe.

Although the American book industry was not directly mentioned in the Telecommunications Act of 1996, the book industry was nevertheless strongly influenced by the regulatory relaxation and the 'digital revolution' encompassed by the 1996 Act. The reverberations in the book business include these:

- The 1996 Act's relaxations of 'vertical' constraints suggested additional international activity and implied further struggles between book publishers and retailers in discounting prices and in the share-out of retail revenue.

- 'Amazon.com' of Seattle dramatized the possibilities of books-on-demand via the Internet. Like previous 'new technology' offerings, the Internet book business depended upon several linked elements of technologies, old and new. In some respects this was merely a new form of mail order shopping. However an important element was the enhanced ability to locate the volume in question via a huge computer-ized cataloguing system. Another key ingredient was heavy discount-ing, applied to a much larger list of books than previously. But the competitive response by the 'traditional' book industry suggests that online book retailing may become another high-volume/low profit book business.

- 'Internationalization' in books seemed to come in several different forms. Books could become more international, while also remaining highly local. One form of internationalization was the merger of the UK book business into a wider US-UK industry. This might follow a familiarish pattern by which US companies owned 35–40 per cent of the British business, while British companies owned 7 or 8 per cent of the US business.

- But internationalization could also take the form of a German com-pany buying US book companies, while (like Sony in movies and music) keeping most of the American activity still very American.

- In an era of big investment, big debt, and big risk in search of the big vertical profit, there was a tendency to regard books as a commercially somewhat unexciting area. Ease of market entry continues to keep profit levels in book publishing well below the levels of profit earned by local TV stations, local cable systems, and other more obviously attract-ive investment areas. The owners of a big book company may be in no hurry to sell; but they may be willing to sell to the right buyer at the right price.

- Foreign buyers seem willing to 'pay too much' for American book companies as a relatively low-risk (even if low-profit) entry to the US media market.

What the Book Business may Say about Anglo-American Media

To vertically inclined Hollywood-and-network American companies the vertical 'synergy' benefits of owning book publishing labels may seem min-imal or negligible. There may, of course, be other benefits. Ownership of a prestigious book publishing company may have some 'flagship' benefits; such ownership may even confer some political lobbying benefits, although—as Rupert Murdoch learned—the publishing of political memoirs can lead to awkward questions about censorship, conflict of interest, and the payment of excessive advances to highly placed politicians.

Does a movie or TV company need to own sizeable book companies? Although there are many sceptics, it seems likely that at least some future sub-genre, narrow niche, digital TV channels will often operate in harness, of some kind, with book and magazine publishers. Even if only for defensive reasons, the gardening or sports network may also want to be in the gardening or sports books-and-magazines business.

Book, magazine, and music companies may collectively constitute a soft entry area into the US media; German, French, Japanese, and British companies are likely to remain interested in these areas. In contrast to the ownership of American TV stations, there are no legal prohibitions against foreigners. Nor is the situation like newspapers, where in practice few of the really desirable properties are ever available for sale to foreigners. Books, magazines, and music may join a longer list of media areas, such as game shows and soap operas, which United States companies define as undesirable (or unprofitable), or as business opportunities mainly suitable for foreigners.

The impact of the Internet Bookstore concept came in addition to the previous big impact of computerization within the book business and its many hundreds of thousands of separate titles. The Internet Bookstore appears to strengthen the forces of verticalization. The conventional bookstore chains (like Barnes and Noble) and the conventional book club operators (especially Bertelsmann) saw the need around 1997–8 to respond to Amazon.com. The book industry overall seemed to be moving towards concentration in publishing and in retailing, while at the same time the Internet Bookstore could offer a more intimate service to the final consumer; the computer record of the customer's previous purchases enables the Internet Bookstore to offer finely targeted suggestions, reviews, and other 'personal' attention. At the same time the Internet Bookstore (while still dependent on parcel services) does tend to break down some previous barriers. In the future a book may need to be published on the same day in both New York and London.

In all of this the Anglo-American book business will probably remain—whoever owns it—strong and distinct. Books (as yet) lend themselves neither to dubbing nor subtitling. It will be interesting to see how successful computers will be as book translators. Most books will never be translated, because translation into another language generates fresh publication costs and fresh author/translator costs. Consequently book publishing is probably one of the segments of the Anglo-American media most closely tied to the English language. So long as English remains the leading international and second language, so also will Anglo-American publishing (regardless of owners) remain the leader in international book publishing.

12
Advertising Agencies

THE advertising agency is a key media mechanism; and it is a key mechanism of the Anglo-American mass media in particular. We see the advertising itself all around us, and occupying an apparently ever more prominent place in much media output. But besides the very visible presence of advertising as consumer sales operation, there is the less visible strategic role of advertising in media finance, and in the life and death of both old media and new media. The survival of particular Internet companies, like the survival of particular newspaper and TV enterprises, depends heavily upon decisions about advertising 'spend'.

American advertising expenditure is five times Germany's and six times Britain's expenditure. The familiar Anglo countries, the USA, Britain, Australia, Canada, are all in the top ten of the world's advertising spenders. Britain, we will argue, has had a prominent role in assisting the USA to develop modern advertising practice; in particular there has developed an Anglo-American way of doing advertising in a commercially objective, non-political, and transparent way.

Advertising expenditure, since at least the eighteenth century, has had a skewing impact on the media, originally by supporting some newspapers and not others. In more recent times advertising plays a big part in the 'youth' focus of most media, because most advertisers are seeking younger rather than older consumers. Similarly the 'up-market' skew of the media overall—including the ability of elite media to survive with smaller audiences—depends heavily on advertising. Elements of advertising have increasingly also entered the individual aura of the entertainment star, the sports explosion, and much else.

Advertising has political biases, both negative and positive. Advertisers and their agencies tend to dislike heavily partisan media, and to prefer relatively 'neutral' media. Consequently advertisers, and even more so advertising agencies, broadly prefer television; this is especially the case in Latin countries, like Mexico, Brazil, and Italy where (as seen by the advertising agencies) newspapers have never escaped from the high partisan mode. Newspaper industries of that kind are largely ignored by advertisers, which turns those newspapers back to rely upon their fellow political zealots and upon the ownership of newspapers for political (and industrial) reasons.

In the Anglo-American countries and in the non-Latin north, the press is less partisan, has strong data about its readership, and still attracts big slices of advertising expenditure. Paradoxically, however, although advertising takes a (relatively) objective view of the Anglo-American type of newspaper, advertising still has a distorting and skewing impact on politics. Especially in Washington, money remains what it has long been, the mother's milk of politics; and political money is advertising money. This incidentally is not the doing of the hard-headed men and women of Madison Avenue; this is the doing mainly of the broadcasters and their National Association of Broadcasters with its gun-lobby style tactics. American politicians, having given the airwaves away for free to the broadcasters, have to buy back 30-second lots, funded by lobbying 'donations'. Moreover while the leading examples of politics-and-advertising are American, advertising finance and advertising techniques are basic to the Americanization of electioneering in many, perhaps most, other countries.

Advertising, more generally, is where the media system is anchored to the economy, to the market, and to social life. This is where the business of fast-moving consumer goods overlaps with the fast-moving consumer media, which together follow us around in our fast-moving modern existence, and as we work, eat, talk, relax, and fall asleep.

Quietly coordinating all of this advertising activity is the advertising agency, which has also evolved as one of the most effectively combined global-and-local entities within the mass media. The same advertising agency which buys time on the local radio station, or space in the local newspaper, can also swing into global action with its '100 offices in 70 countries'. If you so wish, these 100 offices will each advertise your product in exactly the same way, but the completely standardized global campaign remains extremely rare. Also uncommon would be a completely separate advertising approach in each of many countries. More common would be to use several different approaches across several groups of countries. One of the standard service advantages of the international advertising agency is its ability to advise on, and to deliver, different approaches within different markets.

The Concentration of Advertising Agencies into Large Groups

Concentration of ownership has been a feature of advertising agencies in recent decades. Separate agencies (and related specialist marketing companies) have come together into about ten leading international groupings, which place about half of the world's advertising expenditure; over one-quarter of all world advertising expenditure is placed by just three of these agency groupings, Omnicom and Interpublic (both based in New York) and WPP (London). This is an extraordinary level of concentration, because a substantial fraction of all advertising is very local or specialist advertising which the big agencies choose not to handle. These giant agencies focus most heavily on television; and the top ten agency groups place about two-thirds of all world television advertising expenditure.

Martin Sorrell (of WPP) defines as 'international' any advertising agency operating in at least forty countries. In 1997 there were only sixteen such agencies, controlled by only nine major groups.[1] All of the biggest 'agency groups' include at least two quite separate agencies, each operating in at least forty countries.

The combination of two or more separate agencies into one 'Agency Group' originated (in 1960) with Marion Harper, who managed the McCann-Erickson agency in New York. A traditional rule of 'no competing accounts' meant that each American advertising agency could only work for one car company, one airline, one soap company, one cigarette company, and one soft drink company. Marion Harper saw this as a limitation on McCann-Erickson growth and he devised the notion of a holding company which owned two or three quite separate advertising agency networks; the sharp separation would allow each of the two or three agencies to handle its own car, soap, and soft drink company or brand. Consequently we find today:

- The WPP Group, owning J. Walter Thompson as well as Ogilvy and Mather.
- Omnicom owning three agency networks: BBDO; DDB Needham; and TBWA.
- Interpublic owning three agency networks: McCann-Erickson, Lintas, and Lowe.

The biggest advertisers tend to move only between the biggest advertising agencies; when there is an account shift by one airline or car company, the move is usually only to another big agency which has previously held an airline or car company account. Nevertheless the typical stay of a major US consumer account with an agency is reported to have reduced from an average of seven, to a new average of only five, years. Corporate mergers bring conflicts, new ideas, and agency changes. Advertising agencies themselves initially were partnerships, but most of the larger ones went public into stock exchange quotation. Thus ownership is widely spread, there are few big individual mogul owners, and the stock market wants to see rising profits and dividends.

Advertising agency managements show evidence of considerable insecurity. They are anxious that others—such as management consultants and even Hollywood talent agencies—may be usurping some of their more strategic marketing functions. The WPP Group,[2] as one example, has bought

---

[1] Martin Sorrell 'Beyond the millennium', *Admap* (Jan. 1997), 24–6.
[2] *WPP Group plc, Annual Report and Accounts 1995*, 28–9.

minority stakes in small high-technology and niche marketing companies in the hope that this will provide guidance for the digital future.

Radical questions can be asked about the 'creative' people; these artists, design experts, TV directors, and copywriters tend to have a dominant 'creative' orientation without much interest in the central financial, marketing, and media-buying thrust of the business. Why does a hard-headed international business need to employ hundreds of full-time artists in what amounts to a chain of high-rent art and design studios in perhaps fifty capital cities around the world? Why not turn them into freelances like so many actors and non-staff journalists?

The New York agencies came to London in substantial numbers to take advantage of Britain's launch in 1955 of a fully advertising financed national television channel; they were also attracted by Britain's proximity to Europe and to Brussels. The big New York agencies adopted the obvious practice of buying existing British agencies (often from the individuals who had launched them in the 1920s). By 1962 seven of the sixteen largest London agencies were already owned by New York agencies,[3] and this trend went still further through the 1960s.

But some New York agencies had had London offices much earlier than this. One of the most venerable New York agencies, J. Walter Thompson, had had a small London office (to service US clients only) early in the century; in 1925–6 JWT opened up a full service agency in London. One of its first London clients—Kraft—was still with JWT seventy years later.

J. Walter Thompson's American offices were deeply involved in the 1930s not only in advertising on radio, but in producing advertising-sponsored radio shows for the new radio networks. American agencies encouraged their late 1930s London clients to use the commercial radio stations in France and Luxembourg. Not surprisingly, these advertising agencies subsequently argued in favour of Britain having TV advertising in the early 1950s, and seven months before the start of ITV 'the J. Walter Thompson company decided to advise its advertisers to switch from Radio Luxembourg to British commercial television, and reorganized their staff with this in mind.'[4]

Another pioneering US agency on the world scene was McCann-Erickson, which specialized in taking domestic hard-sell US advertising campaigns and projecting them—with only minimal modification—around the world. For decades it drilled into the consciousness of hundreds of millions of Europeans images of Black and Decker tools, Coca-Cola, Exxon fuel, General Motors cars, and R. J. Reynolds cigarettes. But the pursuit of a monolithic, unaltered, worldwide advertising campaign was followed by only a small number of companies, some of which subsequently changed their

---

[3] Jeremy Tunstall, *The Advertising Man* (London: Chapman and Hall, 1964).
[4] Briggs, *Sound and Vision*, 1019.

minds. Even Coca-Cola relented somewhat and also marketed additional 'national brands' unique to specific national markets.

With big advertisers selling some products in many countries and some in one only, the advertising agency has to be extremely flexible. For example in 1997 McCann-Erickson agencies were handling both Coca-Cola and Nestlé in eighty-seven separate countries; McCann was also handling Boots Healthcare and Cathay-Pacific in some thirty countries, but it was advertising Canon in only five countries (all in Europe) and also the BBC in five countries (all in Africa).[5]

The advertising agency may be required to be more flexible than the product. Often a standard product is sold and advertised differently not only in countries with different languages but in countries with different levels of wealth, as well as with different cultures, dietary habits, drug legislation, notions of appropriate behaviour for men and women, and so on. It is (probably) true to say that more advertisers are now trying a semi-global, or continent-wide appeal; but this standard appeal could be a vague promise of sober teenage fun, or a 'convenience food' appeal. Local advertising agencies across numerous countries may then be told to express this broad theme with appropriate local-national creative and cultural detail. Moreover in each country the competitive situation is different, so, even if the product is the same, its competitive marketing task (and hence claims) will differ.

London and Paris are widely regarded as the two most important advertising cities in Europe. London is salient for familiar-sounding reasons. London is the entry point for American multinational consumer goods companies selling into Europe. Since Germany has lacked a single media capital, London has the biggest and most competitive advertising industry of any city in Europe. It is also a convenient transport hub. It is regarded within the advertising world as being a leader in the 'creative' side of advertising.

While London 'creative' prizewinners are often located in American-owned agencies, the everyday reality of London-based international advertising work in general—and creative work in particular—is often far from glamorous. A very common creative problem is that 'the client', typically a large American (or perhaps Japanese, German, or Italian) company wants the same American or British TV commercial to be used with minor local and language changes. This may well mean that an expensive piece of filming—perhaps a car disappearing into the clouds or down a cliff—is to be reused, while ten seconds of film showing natives of the relevant country on the streets of that country are to be inserted for each of a number of national markets. This kind of splicing of a cheap ten seconds' worth onto

---

[5] The information provided covered 116 countries. See *Advertising Age International* (Sept. 1997), 20–1.

the expensive 'artistic' main sequence is not popular with the local 'creatives', but it is essential:

The agency has separate 'international' people. It's costly; they are highly paid, and they use expensive hotels and flights. There's a lot of confusion and conflict. Nearly always the client insists on a muscle power result. The creative people love it when their work is used in other countries. They hate it when other countries' work is forced on them. If you just get given a complete commercial, that's no problem. You just run it. More often it's a matter of splicing up and putting fresh film shots before and after. There's constant friction as advertising moves around the world. That's one reason why people have to accompany it. Our people often go to somewhere in Europe and say 'You've got to do it this way!' Meetings involve people from several countries. The conflict is not only about creative Ego. The country which had the idea (that the others are following) also wants to take most of the money. So there are financial disputes. It's painful, but also profitable, so management likes it. Everyone knows international is difficult, so clients appreciate it when the agency does well. (Winston Fletcher)

International advertising people do a lot of flying around Europe and beyond: 'Although my job is here in London, my home is in Amsterdam and I return there each weekend, if I'm not in Latin America or Asia. Some weeks I go through Amsterdam a couple of times in midweek before returning again at the weekend.'

Advertising as an Anglo-American Profession and the Saatchi Challenge

When American advertising agencies moved into London in substantial force around 1955, and then into continental Europe, they were offering what seemed an impressively 'professional', expert, and transparently honest operational package. Since the patent medicine sleaze of the late Victorian period, these US advertising agencies had been consolidating a 'long tradition' of professional integrity. But around 1959 the New York advertising agencies became embroiled in the television 'Quiz Scandals'. Ironically, perhaps, this involved corruptly fixing the quiz programming, not the advertising. But from 1960 there was a new effort to re-emphasize the professional integrity of advertising, and some conveniently available imagery of British uprightness and old-fashioned integrity was incorporated. There was a sustained public campaign by the leading agencies to internationalize an Anglo-American concept of 'professional' advertising integrity. One central figure in this Anglo-American 'profession' was David Ogilvy, a British advertising man whose highly successful Ogilvy and Mather (New York) agency proclaimed a gospel of 'intelligent' advertising. Paradoxically the most effective subsequent challenge to this professionalizing urge also came from Britain in the form of the Saatchi brothers.

Three key rules of 'professional' advertising as presented by the Madison Avenue agencies to the world in the 1960s were as follow: first, there would be a standard 15 per cent commission; this made the business relationship relatively transparent and, when the American agencies started to go public, their broad financial picture became still more transparent in their published annual reports. Second, professional advertising agencies did not tout for new business or engage in 'speculative' bidding for accounts. Third, agencies would not handle competing accounts and hence would not be vulnerable to conflicts of interest between competing clients. All of this was well established in New York before the 'Quiz Scandals' of 1959.[6]

Between 1960 and 1975 American international advertising strength continued to grow, especially in Britain and Germany but across western Europe and the world. The American agencies established the standard 15 per cent agency commission and the other accepted New York practices. However after 1975 some of the practices were challenged especially by a new London agency, Saatchi and Saatchi. The Saatchi company took just under two decades (the 1970s and 1980s) to go from nothing to being (briefly) the largest advertising agency in the world. From the outset the Saatchi brothers presented themselves and their agency as highly creative, youthful, original, and very different from normal safe advertising 'professional' practice. The Saatchis contrasted themselves with the major American-owned London advertising agencies which they denounced as formulaic, uncreative, bureaucratic, branch plants.

To the young Saatchi brothers in 1970s London, the 1959 American Quiz Scandals meant nothing. Indeed British advertising had shaken off its earlier lack of respectability; in four different surveys between 1966 and 1976 an average 72 per cent of Britons said they 'approved a lot', or 'approved a little' of advertising. The Saatchis were soon breaking most of the professionalizing constraints approved by the various industry bodies. The Saatchis did not insist on 15 per cent commission; the level of commission or fee could be negotiated. The Saatchis also specialized in original 'creative' advertising and utterly rejected the no-touting rule; indeed they pursued any and all advertisers with considerable determination.

The Saatchis also acquired other advertising agencies with a zeal never seen before in New York or London. In some cases they bought agencies larger than Saatchi and Saatchi. In 1981–2 their turnover more than doubled; it more than doubled again in 1982–3; it also doubled in 1983–5; and it nearly doubled yet again in 1986–7, when they bought the American Ted Bates agency. Between 1984 and 1988 the number of Saatchi employees more than quadrupled to 16,600.

[6] Martin Mayer, *Madison Avenue, USA* (London: Bodley Head, 1958). The Editors of Fortune, *The Amazing Advertising Business* (New York: Simon and Schuster, 1957).

The Saatchis took major risks, but they were also uniquely lucky in their timing. In 1978 they already employed over 600 people; they already had a 'creative' reputation in London advertising and this led to their appointment by the Conservative Party. They were widely credited with helping Mrs Thatcher to win the general elections of 1979 and 1983. In the 1980s they surfed on the crest of a seemingly unstoppable wave. Their imagery was linked with that of Mrs Thatcher and privatization; they held the British Airways account and invented the 'World's Favourite Airline' slogan.

The Saatchi brothers had to finance their multiple purchases of other agencies in ways which most other advertising people regarded as dangerously risky. So long as the boom of the middle Thatcher years lasted, the brothers performed their high-wire act. But in the late 1980s they ran into financial catastrophe, and the inflated value of their shares fell to almost nothing. They also tried to buy the Midland Bank, an attempt which the London financial world regarded as naive and frivolous. The Saatchi brothers were not mogul owner-operators; they were really only executives, although Maurice Saatchi behaved like a mogul and Charles Saatchi cultivated a (briefly) impressive reclusivity.

It also subsequently became obvious that much of the Saatchi success had depended on others, such as Tim Bell (who ran the main Saatchi agency and was the key contact with Margaret Thatcher); another key individual was Martin Sorrell, a bright young agency accountant. Martin Sorrell left the Saatchis and then started to repeat their conjuring performance—of building a massive advertising empire with almost no visible means of financial support. Martin Sorrell bought a small company called WPP which made supermarket trolleys; next he went shopping and soon purchased two of America's biggest and most respected advertising agencies—J. Walter Thompson and Ogilvy and Mather. J. Walter Thompson was the most prestigious and most traditional American agency; Ogilvy and Mather was another important New York agency which had several British strands in its background. But Martin Sorrell had repeated several of the Saatchi mistakes—he paid more than anyone in New York would pay, and then suffered from the subsequent economic downturn. WPP shares in 1992 stood at 3 per cent of their 1987 peak value. But WPP recovered and did so more quickly than did Saatchi and Saatchi.

Despite their spectacular rise-fall-rise histories both Maurice Saatchi and Martin Sorrell added something to the industrialization, the globalization, and the professionalization of world advertising. Maurice Saatchi played a part in directing advertising 'professionalism' back into a more commercially aggressive direction. He also unintentionally demonstrated the dangers of politicization in advertising; he, who rose with a party politician, Mrs Thatcher, also fell alongside her. The Saatchi brothers were in 1995 expelled from their own advertising empire, with Chicago and other US investors playing an active role.

The Big Advertising Agency Bulks Up—Specialist Media Buying and Marketing Subsidiaries

Increasingly during the 1990s the big advertising agencies followed the normal public company imperatives of trying to get both bigger and more profitable. In this they were merely following the growth, and placing the increasing advertising expenditure of, their big advertising clients. Another source of the growth imperative was the assumption that, as media companies got bigger, advertising agencies would need to bulk themselves up in order to maintain their ability to bargain for bulk discounts.

But before considering the Media Buying subsidiary, let us just consider the kind of portfolio of non-advertising subsidiaries which the bigger advertising agencies developed from the 1980s onwards. Taken together these other activities could account for nearly half of the total revenue of the advertising agency:

- Most of the large market research companies are now owned by advertising agencies. WPP's research companies (BMRB, Millward Brown, and Research International) had revenues of over $500 million in 1997.
- Similarly most of the largest public relations (including political PR) companies are advertising agency owned; WPP's PR companies include Hill and Knowlton and Carl Byoir.
- Direct marketing companies were another diversification, partly because the big agencies saw more client expenditure going into non-media or 'below-the-line' advertising such as direct mail, coupons, leaflets, and brochures. Some direct marketing subsidiaries are significant multinational companies; for instance Draft Worldwide, once a Saatchi and Saatchi subsidiary, soon after being acquired by Omnicom in 1996 was doing over $1 billion of business from thirty-six offices around the world.[7]
- 'Specialist communications' was another major area for subsidiaries. These could operate in particular markets (such as medical, real estate, or ethnic), or could specialize in shareholder relations or corporate image work. Other such subsidiaries specialize in producing in-house publications, or in economic and market forecasting.

Another much cultivated subsidiary activity in the 1990s was the subsidiary which specialized in media buying (traditionally conducted by the advertising agency's media department). The specialist media-buying agency could generate extra revenue by working not only for its parent

[7] 'Draft at 20', *Advertising Age*, 26 Jan. 1998, pp. C1–24.

agency but by media buying for other (probably smaller) agencies. This increased buying volume would add negotiating weight and should generate bigger bulk discounts for the happy advertising clients.

The basic argument for media subsidiaries was one of bulking up for the bigger bulk discount. Nevertheless the concept had a somewhat bumpy career, especially in the United States, and it was only towards the end of the 1990s that the advertising world—led by France and Britain—recognized the advantages. It was soon being predicted that, within a few years, huge proportions of all world media buying would be channelled through six or eight large buying gateways.

In the 1990s, specialist media-buying companies became an important feature on the advertising scene, first in France and Britain, and then across western Europe. If you buy television time by the hour, rather than the minute, you'll get a lower price per minute. Newspapers have always operated bulk discounts. The large media specialist company also claims to provide not only more sophisticated analysis of standard research but also its own fresh research.

Advertising clients, who have tried the service, typically stick with the media-buying company longer than they remain with the advertising agency. Thus media specialists have grown faster than agencies; the split-off media company is also typically more profitable against revenue than is the advertising agency. All of these media specialist advantages were clearly evident by 1995 when Carat (France) and two British media specialists were together placing well over $10 billion worth of advertising across Europe. Nevertheless Madison Avenue continued to see such specialist companies as more appropriate to local car dealerships or franchise food operators than to blue chip national companies. Across in France, Carat had indeed exhibited some slightly dubious tactics; as commercial radio expanded in France in the early 1970s, Carat went into the radio time brokering business, initially awarding itself massive margins such as 40 per cent. Subsequently Carat became the main target of a special law, the 'Loi Sapin', designed to tame its somewhat wild west ways. Media specialists in Britain were also (unjustly) regarded as slightly tacky; this image was not helped when the Saatchi media subsidiary Zenith was launched in the midst of the parent agencies' worst financial disasters.

Another New York belief was that what might work in one European country would not work so easily in the much bigger and more complex US media market. European media specialists argued that the scale and complexity of the US market made media specialists more—not less—relevant to the USA. However, the transition problems in the USA would be more difficult. Moreover (from a European viewpoint) the biggest American advertisers, media, and agencies tended to be huge, slow, cumbersome, and conservative.

Nevertheless, from 1994–5 onwards, the American tide started to move towards focused media-buying power. Interpublic, one of the largest US agency groups, in late 1994 bought the biggest domestic media specialist, Western International Media. WIN had begun as a small local Los Angeles operation in 1970; but its founder, Dennis Holt, then acquired some nationally important Hollywood and other west coast business.[8]

Meanwhile, New York received another media specialist invasion from Europe in the form of Zenith and Carat. Zenith arrived in New York to take over most of the media-buying activities of the Saatchi and Saatchi and Bates agencies. Zenith initially attracted considerable scepticism, but by 1997 was getting well established. 1997 was a key year for the specialist media-buying concept because Carat also arrived from France. During 1997 all of the largest advertising agency groups (including WPP and Omnicom) began to concentrate their media buying into one or more subsidiaries. The WPP specialist media subsidiary was named Mindshare, in order to emphasize that it would focus not just on bigger buying volume, but also on sophisticated research and strategic thinking.

This media-buying invasion from Los Angeles and Europe was perhaps indicative of some broader trends. Here again were British (and in this case French) ideas challenging American advertising professionalism. Within New York advertising the media specialist function had a low-status backroom reputation and attracted few graduates of the elite universities. Now the New York advertising world was being forced to learn a lesson from Europe: if agencies don't set up their own media subsidiaries, profitable business will be lost to media independents. Moreover as the eager media experts arrived in New York from Los Angeles, London, and Paris they were quick to question other traditional assumptions. One such Madison Avenue assumption was that major advertisers should spread their big TV spending across all four broadcast networks. However, the European critics claimed that it would be better to use only two or three big networks (at a lower price) and to spread more expenditure across a wider range of low-audience programming. European critics claimed to have superior computer and research back-up; they argued for example that New York media buyers were very poorly informed about detailed audience flow within a particular television commercial break.

The late 1990s swing towards media-buying subsidiaries had several implications. If media buying is regarded as a separate activity, the combined subsidiaries of the big agencies will probably account for more revenue than does the remaining 'advertising' part of the advertising agency.

The move towards buying subsidiaries has itself been driven by the assumed advantages of greater scale. This added bulk is, of course, being

---

[8] *Variety*, 16–22 Oct. 1995, pp. 33–84.

directed at the space and time sellers in the media; consequently any further knock-on consequences must be looked for within the broader media industry. The greater bulk of media buyers is likely yet further to encourage greater bargaining bulk and vertical strength within the media generally.

American Advertising: Britain as World Media Number Two, and also as Media Colony

The flow of advertising has hugely assisted the flow of American media in the world. There is an advertising sequence which runs parallel to the evolution of American entertainment genres from film to radio to TV to cable. There is a parallel sequence in the history of an advertising agency like J. Walter Thompson, which initially sold space for American religious magazines, before progressing via radio production and TV production into a world role. The US advertising agencies have everywhere campaigned for more TV channels and have thus been part of the media multiplication lobby in many countries.

What of the British contribution to Anglo advertising? We have argued here that Britain has been important—as an advertising base, as a creative force, and as a 'professional' influence on international advertising. But advertising runs counter to some British media traditions (such as the BBC), and it can be argued that the British economy and media gain little. Although Britain exerts important 'professional' influences on Madison Avenue, the main thrust of advertising development is overwhelmingly American. This can be seen in the ownership of larger London advertising agencies. Most are American owned; another substantial category consists of agencies like WPP, whose main elements are American but which are British owned.

So, although in some respects Britain is the world's advertising number two, it can also be asserted (in line with the argument of the following chapters in Part III) that Britain is in danger of sinking to colonial advertising status, with British advertising playing a totally subordinate and dependent role within Anglo-American advertising.

Are there any truly important and 100 per cent British advertising agencies still in operation in London? Not many, might be the answer, but there are a few. For example, the largest single London advertising agency (in terms of British business alone) is (the very British) Abbott, Mead, Vickers. In 1996 with all of its founders still in place, it became the largest agency in terms of solely British advertising expenditure. But was AMV really 100 per cent British? No, it was not. Since 1991 one quarter of AMV was owned by the American agency BBDO, itself part of the Omnicom group. AMV was in practice the British link in BBDO's European chain of BBDO subsidiary agencies. The partial merger of 1991 was of mutual benefit. BBDO got a slice of the most admired British 'creative' advertising agency. AMV also received benefits, financial and other. AMV—which previously had no Europe-wide connections—was after 1991 able to play a leading role, within BBDO, in the Europe-wide advertising of Pepsi-Cola, Pizza Hut, and other American advertisers.[9] The mutual agreement was that eventually BBDO/Omnicom would acquire a majority share of AMV; AMV (like many 'creative' British agencies before it) was a semi-independent territory, destined to become a fully owned-and-operated American colony. This duly happened in 1998 when Omnicom took 100 per cent control of AMV.

[9] *Abbott, Mead, Vickers PLC. Annual Reports and Accounts; Campaign,* Special Advertising Supplement, 21 Nov. 1997 (20th anniversary of 1977 launch of AMV).

Britain as Film, Television, and Press Colony

13
Hollywood and British Media Subordination

NONE of the areas in which Britain could (and can) be considered a serious world Number Two has involved a direct head-on confrontation with Hollywood. Hollywood has never been involved in news or public service broadcasting and has only been marginally involved in book publishing and advertising. Of the five areas which we have just considered in Part II, Hollywood was only significantly involved in one area, namely popular music. But in this Part III we consider segments of the British media which have had to confront Hollywood. Here Britain has long been subordinate; moreover, the stance of British video entertainment—initially in film and then also in television—has been defensive.

British film and TV entertainment has been defensive for the very good reason that Britain from 1920 was targeted by the American film industry as a key, or the key, export market. However, although the British film industry, and later both the BBC and ITV, adopted defensive tactics, there was never (and there still is not) an effective overall British defensive strategy for confronting Hollywood.

Hollywood's challenge to the British media industries was especially severe during four of the eight decades between 1920 and 2000. First in the 1920s the Hollywood assault virtually wiped out the British film industry. The second big assault lasted some two decades, 1945–65, and involved both Hollywood film and Hollywood TV. The British film industry suffered very severe blows from Hollywood in the late 1940s; especially in the years following 1955, the British public was deluged with American television series imports.

However after about 1965 the British defensive tactics seemed to be working successfully. 'Public Service Broadcasting' was effectively redefined with two BBC TV channels, a more severely regulated ITV, and a reduction in the proportion of TV programming and concepts imported from the USA.

The third massive blast of renewed Hollywood competition came in the 1990s, starting in fact in 1989–90 with the beginnings of Murdoch-Sky television in Britain. The new satellite channels relied heavily on massive imports not only of American series, but entire American channels, including movie channels stocked overwhelmingly with Hollywood products.

From 1989–90 onwards Britain ceased to be a net television exporter and became a net TV importer. By 1996 Britain's TV imports were twice as large (in money terms) as Britain's TV exports.[1] In the late 1990s Britain spent over $1 billion annually on TV imports (not including films for cinema and video).

Throughout the 1990s, then, Britain was a substantial net importer not only of cinema films, but also of television programming. However despite this 1990s increase in British subordination to Hollywood, there was no coherent industry or government strategy. British defensiveness was more a matter of ingrained tradition and experience than a considered position. Moreover Britain did not merely lack a defensive strategy, it also lacked a coherent exporting strategy. There was no attempt to consider the wider Anglo-American media connection overall.

A realistic *export* strategy for British film and TV programming in the 1990s would have needed to consider the changing European TV market, including its increasing 'Americanization' and the explosion of new commercial networks (which we consider below in Part IV). One example of these European changes was the adoption in Europe of American scheduling practices; this included a preference for big batches of episodes—such as 23 or 26 episodes per year, building to a completed successful series of 100 or 200 episodes. Australian TV producers (also facing a massive Hollywood challenge) did adopt most of the commercial practices of American television; consequently Australian producers (such as Grundy) were successful in Europe in ways that British producers were not.

British reluctance to compete head-to-head with Hollywood was indicated by British television's continuing practice of commissioning short series runs, often an annual total of just six or seven episodes. These very small production batches do not appeal to schedulers in other countries who need to fill thousands of hours of programming slots.

British reluctance to move beyond defensive instincts to a combined defensive-and-offensive strategy was evident in a range of media areas. One of these was the elite newspaper press, much of which in the 1990s was owned and controlled by non-British citizens (Chapter 14).

Britain's Defensive Posture

A defensive posture has become ingrained into most kinds of British TV and film entertainment. The defensive posture has been central to latter-day definitions of Public Service Broadcasting. For decades the British commercial television regulator required the ITV companies to limit their American imports and to engage in as much British (and thus virtuous)

---

[1] According to Office of National Statistics (ONS) trade data.

programming as possible, especially in the expensive fiction areas in which Hollywood specialized. Even when programming formats such as quiz/game shows were imported, these were to be populated with British performers; other undesirable elements—such as large prizes—were severely limited.

This defensive posture against Hollywood encouraged British television (and such British film as existed) to be inward-looking, parochial, and focused on lovable, somewhat caricatured, British idiosyncrasy and eccentricity. This idiosyncratically British material was one element in the failure of both British films and British TV fully to use the potential international advantages of the English language. Those exports which did occur mainly involved a few limited genres—such as costume drama and odd-ball comedy, and went mainly to small (and culturally close) markets (Scandinavia, the Commonwealth, and American PBS) which liked the costumes and the comedy.

Between the 1960s and the 1990s the relationship between British and American entertainment remained broadly the same. One major commercial success of the 1990s was the BSkyB satellite-to-home operation. This ensured that British video entertainment would enter the twenty-first century with four major entertainment entities: the BBC, ITV, BSkyB, and Hollywood.

From a BBC perspective two important points to note about these other three entities are that all three were growing fast in revenue terms—very much faster than the BBC; and that all three of these entities now regarded 20 per cent profit levels as normal. This, of course, was in strong contrast to the not-for-profit BBC.

This phenomenon of *high profitability* was relatively unfamiliar in the British media, although it had been commonplace in the USA, especially since commercial TV became successfully established in the 1950s. In Britain, previous to the 1990s, the media had not been an industrial area known for its high levels of profit. Commercial TV in particular had been heavily regulated and taxed and the dominant ITV network had been split into fourteen separate geographical areas. Only in the 1990s could the British mass media be seen, for the first time, as an industrial area from which big profits could be extracted over an extended period. For the first time media owners no longer needed to think in terms of the occasional 'cash cow' (such as a particular monopoly newspaper); now it became possible to think in terms of a whole herd of cash cows.

However, the mass media were not bulking up merely in profitability and company size. Another important aspect of late twentieth-century American media was the greatly increased 'entry cost' required to get established in some new media, and especially media using new technologies. In the USA this was often associated with the use of space satellites.

A British example of this scenario of high entry cost in return for high profitability was BSkyB, which made very large initial losses before moving into big profits. It is noticeable that in Britain, both Hollywood and the ITV companies are also capable of this kind of high entry investment. Hollywood companies, such as Warner and Viacom, made huge British investments in multiplex cinemas. The two main ITV companies, Granada and Carlton, both saw digital terrestrial TV as an area for high investment in return for eventual duopolistic profit.

But while BSkyB, Hollywood, and ITV were all players in these new high entry cost games, the BBC was expected to soldier on without debt, without risk, and without paying any big entry costs. So, official British government policy implied, was the British 'film industry'.

British Film Colony, Hollywood Movie Empire

British film-makers live in the twin shadows of the Hollywood big six companies and of British television. These individual British film-makers do make quite a lot of films, but their 'films' are typically low-budget productions only seen by small audiences.

The great bulk of cinema-going in Britain involves movies distributed by five Hollywood companies: Disney (Buena Vista), Columbia (Sony), Fox, Warner, and UIP (Paramount, Universal, and MGM-UA). These companies act as sales/marketing arms of their respective companies. British films have to compete in this distributor-dominated industry where there is no large British distribution company. Through the 1990s these five Hollywood distributors' films accounted for around 80 per cent of British cinema revenue. By contrast, Channel Four's Film Four Distribution accounted for around 1 per cent of cinema revenues. Most of the more financially successful British productions in the 1990s went through American distributors such as Miramax (Disney) or Fox (Murdoch) or through Polygram (Philips).

While cinemas in Britain have traditionally been British-owned, there has long been a strong 'alignment' between particular British cinema chains and the Hollywood distributors. The British cinema chains have (since the 1920s) been eager to secure an assured supply of front-line Hollywood product. Since 1980 the alignment between Hollywood suppliers and British cinema chains has become still stronger. But the colonial, dependent, aspects go well beyond the (80 per cent plus) dominance of Hollywood distributors and their films in British cinemas. In recent years a more vertically integrated Hollywood has developed a more vertically integrated export strategy; this strategy is especially well developed in Britain and involves a linked series of Hollywood practices and British responses.

- Multiplex cinema building has, since 1985, been led by Hollywood-linked companies. This was the key factor in a doubling of UK cinema attendance in the 1985–95 decade.

- Hollywood companies see the cinema as the first window key to the financially more significant subsequent windows of films-on-video and films-on-TV, where Hollywood is also dominant.
- Britain and Germany are seen as Hollywood's two key markets in Europe. Success in the British and German markets is internationally noted and facilitates successful promotion around the world. London is seen as the European distribution and publicity hub within Hollywood's worldwide operations.
- Sky movies on satellite and cable (along with France's Canal Plus) pioneered premium 'pay TV' in Europe; Hollywood intends that this British tradition will stretch into the future.
- British efforts to promote the latest British 'film renaissance' focus largely on low-budget and 'art' films. Hollywood can safely ignore most of these, but Miramax and other niche labels of Hollywood majors cherry-pick a few British films which look to have some commercial potential. When British film art turns into significant profit, the profit seldom stays in Britain.
- Meanwhile Britain still lacks a combined film/video/TV policy; in particular there is no meaningful policy for the main and expanding revenue-generating film windows of video/pay TV/cable/satellite/digital new media. 'Pay TV' film offerings in Britain are dominated by Sky, which itself is controlled by a vertical Hollywood/network company.
- The main British TV players (BBC, ITV, Channel Four) dabble in making films, but they lack a realistic multi-window distribution strategy; in terms of audience numbers reached, the initial financial investment seems not to be justified.

Between Hollywood Movies and British Television

The American industry has been dominant in Britain in every single year since 1914–15. It has always exercised this dominance in two main ways. First, British theatre revenue has gone predominantly (usually between 60 per cent and 90 per cent) to Hollywood-made movies. Second, however, the remaining British production sector has since the 1920s always been heavily Hollywood influenced, through being wholly, or partly, Hollywood financed.

The financing of British films reflects—but also tends to exaggerate—the normal boom and bust cycle in Hollywood itself. If Hollywood is booming at home, it may make more movies in Britain; if business is bad at home, Hollywood may radically reduce its British production effort. Hollywood-in-Britain finance has also always moved up and down, as changing dollar-pound exchange rates make London seem suddenly either cheaper or more expensive. Yet further causes of fluctuation include the tax policies of both governments; perceptions of whether British trade unions are currently more or less reasonable than the Hollywood unions; also significant is the Hollywood perception of whether London is currently swinging or fashionable or a comfortable place for a movie star to work for a few months.

The Hollywood switch has tended to turn the British film industry on for one decade and off for the next:

- During the 1920s there was almost no British film industry, such was the strength of Hollywood.
- The British industry (with slowly increasing domestic quota requirements) gradually grew in the 1930s, then fell back a little, and had its best decade in the 1940s; this latter success depended on wartime government support.
- The 1950s were a bad decade for British films with Hollywood itself in retreat everywhere.
- The 1960s were another good decade for the British film, as Hollywood established major offshore production locations in London and Rome. From 1958 a new wave of young British film directors and 'angry' novelists were largely funded by Hollywood. The 1960s also saw several of David Lean's biggest films (*Lawrence of Arabia, Dr Zhivago*), Tony Richardson's *Tom Jones*, and the first big batch of *Carry On* films.
- The 1970s were a weak decade for British films, not least because it was a bad decade for the domestic Hollywood industry.
- The 1980s saw what was greeted as an artistic revival. This included Channel Four, which began as a film patron in 1982, and the appearance of several ambitious new British companies (which mostly went bankrupt).
- After a steep drop in British production in 1987–9, more Hollywood money again lifted the British industry in 1994–6; then came yet another decline and revival.

The switch-on/switch-off approach of Hollywood to the British film industry reflected industrial conditions in the US market. But rapid fluctuations in finance also created uncertainty in Britain. These exaggerated market fluctuations made the establishment of a major long-term industry still less likely.

Britain largely lacked the industrial structures—of both production and distribution companies—which are required for a successful film industry. Britain also largely lacked mogul owner-operators or even baronial executives (on the Alexander Korda 1930s model). The only major owner-operator mogul in British film history was J. Arthur Rank and it was he who presided over the British film industry's best decade of the 1940s.

It was just at the beginning of the world war, 1939–40, that J. Arthur Rank began his decade as a successful movie mogul. He possessed all of the key mogul characteristics. First, he was an owner, indeed he acquired most of the British production companies and studios, a major distribution company, and two of the three main British cinema chains. In 1945 he began to buy up additional cinema chains in Canada, Australia, New Zealand, and South Africa. Second, Rank not only owned but also personally operated the Rank film interests; he was actively involved in all major financial decisions. Third, he was an entrepreneur, who became expert in buying film companies and doing deals; he was also a risk-taker, who often ignored pessimistic financial advice. Fourth, Rank had a highly individual and idiosyncratic style; he did not make decisions on specific films, scripts, and stars, but he employed most of the best producers and directors of the period to make these decisions for him. These producers and directors included Laurence Olivier (*Henry V*), Michael Balcon (Ealing Studios), David Lean, and—perhaps the most talented pair—Michael Powell and Emeric Pressburger (*A Canterbury Tale, A Matter of Life and Death, The Red Shoes*).[2] In addition to the prestige films (many of them relying on realism and semi-documentary approaches) there were also romantic, fantasy, and other mass market films.[3]

The Rank film empire ran into a mammoth crisis in 1947–8, when the British government (faced by a dollar crisis) attempted to impose a punitive tax on Hollywood imports into Britain. Hollywood responded with a film boycott on Britain. Rank tried to fill the gap by increasing production, but these new films then fared disastrously against the pent-up flood of Hollywood imports in 1948–9. This was a disaster largely created by the British government. However, the lack of understanding between the British government and the British film industry reflected the lack of a 'long tradition' of successful British film.

Subsequent to 1950, the Rank company—having been severely punished—retreated from film production risk-taking. Britain has never again had a film mogul of any magnitude. Some of the men who might possibly have become film moguls—such as Sidney Bernstein and Lew Grade—moved into the new British business of commercial television in 1955; in television they could safely earn substantial profits by presiding over a regional television advertising monopoly.

It was also television which built up what became a successful long tradition of making fiction and entertainment for television. In Britain, as elsewhere in Europe, there was no merging of TV and film into a single production industry. Moreover television in Britain did not focus solely upon large

[2] Ian Christie, *Arrows of Desire: The Films of Michael Powell and Emeric Pressburger* (London: Faber and Faber, 1994).

[3] Robert Murphy, *Realism and Tinsel: Cinema and British Society, 1939–48* (London: Routledge, 1989). Marcia Landy, *British Genres: Cinema and Society, 1930–60* (Princeton: Princeton University Press, 1991).

audiences; British television successfully developed several diverse strains of drama, from long-running super popular soaps to prestigious 'single plays', mini-series, and once-a-week series. These various TV offerings largely stole both the prestige and the audience, leaving the British film industry trying to fill any gaps which might remain.

Individual Film-Makers Looking for a British Film Industry

> But the British film industry has a long way to go before it rivals Hollywood. Almost moribund in the mid-1980s, it's regaining its health. . . . With labor costs estimated 20% to 30% lower than the US, and film talent plentiful and largely non-unionized, Britain clearly has advantages.
> The sticking point is finance. Few if any British outfits can come up with the $100m or more it takes to make a big budget movie. . . . That's why Britain largely serves as a location and postproduction site for big-budget pictures.
>
> *Business Week*, 1997.[4]

Seen from Hollywood, Britain has a substantial pool of talent which comes from four sources: first Britain's large television industry; second Britain's cottage industry of low-budget 'independent' film-making; third London has a long tradition of providing segments of big Hollywood movies— perhaps one-third or one-half of the acting and other talent, and similar fractions of filming locations, and post-production and special effects; fourth London's strength in television commercials and in music videos.

Hollywood is an industry dominated by six vertically integrated entertainment companies; Britain lacks a movie industry of sizeable companies but does have numerous individuals who make 'films'. British film people are faced with two main choices—to work either for the Hollywood movie industry or the British cottage business of self-employed film-makers. Most of those who decide to work for Hollywood move to Los Angeles for years or decades. Many of them adapt quite quickly to Hollywood genres and Californian life; some of the actors even achieve the difficult task of dropping their English accents. Some win Academy Awards, while most do not. Some return to Britain, having worked in a number of Hollywood movies.

The other main path—it is scarcely a career path—is into low-budget British film-making. It is widely agreed that when Channel Four arrived as a new British 'minority' TV channel in 1982 it became a key patron of British film-making. Certainly since 1982 an increasingly long list of auteur-directors became established in Britain. Several of them have an intense—even obsessive—personal vision and substantial bands of dedicated

---

[4] Stanley Reed and Julia Flynn, 'Moviemakers are back—but where's the big money?', *Business Week*, 7 Apr. 1997.

supporters. Peter Greenaway's films establish extraordinary connections with Renaissance art. Mike Leigh extracts anguish and melodrama from everyday suburban life in north London. But these unique directorial visions seem to lean towards the art gallery and experimental theatre. Moreover they are exceptions. Most Channel Four films have lacked both quality and audience. Channel Four used these low-budget (but 'high art') films to establish a reputation with the British and European cultural elite. But Channel Four was also successfully obtaining a lot of prestige, publicity, and newspaper 'film' reviews in return for the very modest investment of part-funding some thirteen low-budget films per year during 1982–97.[5] Typically each year one or two of these films had some cinema success and leant support to the belief that Channel Four was creating a Film Renaissance. Certainly Channel Four's output was very small compared with the BBC's output of 'single plays', drama series, and 'films'. In terms of total (cinema and TV) audience reached, Channel Four's fictional effort was a tiny fraction of the BBC's or ITV's.

Meanwhile a celebrated auteur film-maker like Ken Loach continued—even in the Channel Four era—to struggle on under cottage industry conditions. Ken Loach's *Land and Freedom* (1995) was about British volunteers in the Spanish Civil War. Despite pre-sales to a number of European TV channels and several different European film distributors, the total multi-source budget was less than £3 million ($5 million).[6] By 1995 Ken Loach was widely regarded as one of Europe's greatest film-makers and he had a thirty-year record of prize-winning accomplishment. While Ken Loach and other virtuoso film-makers have had to work hard to raise finance, trying to make projects happen probably takes up most of the working time of most of these auteur-makers of low-budget films. Thus, instead of a film industry, Britain has a chaotic swirl of individuals looking for finance, and of 'self-employed' people looking for employment.

Is there no middle way between moving to north-west Los Angeles or remaining an unemployed art film-maker in north-west London? There have been a few energetic and talented individuals who have found middle ways between the super-popular and the art ghetto as well as between Los Angeles and London. These were, however, perhaps just a few talented individuals who are the rare exceptions to the general rule. Richard Attenborough, David Puttnam, and Kenneth Branagh were three very individual individuals, who in different ways contributed to the great British actor-manager tradition. Richard Attenborough began acting bad guys in the 1940s. After a distinguished acting career, he directed *Oh! What a Lovely War* (1969) and then continued as a highly successful film-maker. He relied

[5] Stuart Kemp and Louise Tutt, 'Channel 4 at 15'. *Screen International*, 26 Sept. 1997, pp. 28–36.

[6] Ian Christie, 'Film for a Spanish Republic', *Sight and Sound* (Oct. 1995).

on Hollywood finance and specialized in bio-pics. David Puttnam, a success-ful producer with a special skill in film publicity, was briefly production head of a Hollywood major studio (Columbia); his British background led him into an unwise and ill-informed attack on Hollywood's high-budget way of life. Kenneth Branagh was a multi-talented actor-manager who achieved the ultimate mission impossible of acquiring finance to film a high-concept four-hour *Hamlet*, with more film Shakespeare to follow.

But these were high-profile individual British filmmakers, attempting to lead into battle a British movie army which wasn't there. The biggest 'British' film companies were either the London offices of Hollywood com-panies or some small-medium British distributors and (currently) success-ful production houses. The dynamic, thrusting, prizewinning independents of the mid and late 1980s—Goldcrest, Handmade, Zenith, Initial, Palace—were all dead or severely wounded only a few years later. The next 'hot London production company' was Working Title; of its thirty-five films made in fifteen years there were two big commercial successes—*Four Wed-dings and a Funeral* (1994) and *Bean* (1997). Working Title also made admired lowish-budget 'American' films such as *Dead Man Walking* (1995) and *Fargo* (1996).[7] However Polygram Filmed Entertainment which had owned Working Title since 1992 was sold in 1998 by its parent, Philips of the Netherlands, to the Hollywood major company, MCA-Universal. From hav-ing been a hot Dutch-British film-maker, Working Title became part of a Hollywood major. Also in 1998 the entire film commissioning team at Channel Four joined Miramax—which had distributed numerous British films, but was itself now owned by Disney.

The task of lobbying the British government on behalf of the 'British Film Industry' was left to the actor-managers including Attenborough, Puttnam, and Branagh. For years these energetic money-raisers and film-makers faced a near impossible lobbying task, because the Conservative governments of 1979–97 did not want a film policy.

But in 1997 the Film Lobby found itself suddenly welcomed by the Blair Labour government. Several reports were already available from the Major era.[8] These were quickly adopted by the Labour Government, which also increased the National Lottery film funding commenced under John Major in 1995.

But the British movie scene of the Blair late 1990s differed little from the Major early 1990s. There were still three categories of movie: first a largish

[7] 'Working Title at 15', *Variety*, 14–20 Dec. 1998, pp. 99–110.

[8] Geoff Mulgan and Richard Paterson (eds.), *Hollywood of Europe?* (London: British Film Institute, 1993). Monopolies and Mergers Commission, *Films: A Report on the Supply of Films for Exhibition in Cinemas in the UK* (London: HMSO, 1994, Cm. 2673). House of Commons, National Heritage Committee, *The British Film Industry*, volume i, Session 1994–5 (London: HMSO, 1995) 57-I. The Advisory Committee on Film Finance (chairman, Sir Peter Middleton), *Report to the Secretary of State For National Heritage* (London, 1996).

number of 100 per cent British very low-budget films, often part-funded by Channel Four or the BBC and perhaps best regarded as made-for-TV movies. Second there was a middling category of somewhat bigger-budget films, often depending on co-production finance; it was this category—including French-British co-productions—which the British Lottery grants hoped to encourage. Third, each year there were eight or ten 100 per cent American financed made-in-Britain productions, typically with budgets ten times as large as the first made-for-TV category. However even most of these American financed movies were still only medium budget movies by Hollywood standards.

Several things were still missing. There was no British distribution company, no British film industry—and despite some policy documents[9]—no national policy for the British film industry. There was also still a remarkable reluctance to look at the film business as one corner of a much wider audio-visual industry. Meanwhile Britain remained a film colony.

[9] The report of the Film Policy Review Group, *A Bigger Picture* (London: Department of Culture, Media and Sport, 1998).

14

Non-citizen Press Moguls: Feuds and Foreign Policy

IN March 1998 the Irish Independent newspaper company of Dublin, and its chairman Tony O'Reilly, acquired full ownership of *The Independent* (daily and Sunday). This meant that 78 per cent of the sales of non-tabloid national newspapers in Britain were owned by non-British companies, controlled by three non-British citizens—namely Rupert Murdoch (US), Conrad Black (Canadian), and Tony O'Reilly (Irish). The two sales leaders in the elite (broadsheet and up-market) national category—*The Times* and *Daily Telegraph* and their Sunday versions—were controlled by Murdoch and Black. Including the O'Reilly acquired *Independent* papers, the Murdoch-Black-O'Reilly foreign interests together controlled 76 per cent of up-market national British daily sales, and 85 per cent of Sunday sales.

How did British politicians and the British business community—proud of Britain's distinctive news and media voice around the world—allow three-quarters of the non-tabloid London newspaper press to fall into foreign hands?

An Ambiguous Long Tradition in Elite Newspapers: British Dependence on Outsiders

British media people and politicians have become accustomed to the truism that London is home to the largest national newspaper press in Europe. Nowhere else—certainly in Europe—is there such a large collection of highly competitive and aggressively tabloid papers; but London's collection of (since 1986) no less than five serious, up-market, or elite dailies is also unrivalled in Europe. However—despite some 1990s anxiety as to 'dumbing down', or tabloid, tendencies in the serious dailies—little attention has been paid to the issue of whether it is possible to have five, or even three or four, serious national dailies in a country the size of Britain.

There are several reasons for this lack of debate. Politicians do not wish to antagonize newspapers; journalists and politicians always prefer that sick newspapers—and the relevant jobs—should be rescued, with only secondary concern being focused on the rescuer's identity and the implications of new ownership.

All of this also has a long tradition which can be traced back to 1911. Ever since 1911 various rich men from the United States and Canada—and more recently from Australia and Ireland—have engaged in more than a dozen 'rescues' of British national daily and Sunday newspapers.

This has become one of a number of overlapping long traditions which together constitutes the glorious British media tradition, with its strong Anglo-American, Commonwealth, and world-girdling overtones. This particular long tradition—of elite newspapers being rescued by Anglo-American outsiders—has, like some of the other long traditions of the British media, evolved considerably over time.

As Table 14.1 indicates, the first batch of rescues, during 1911–22, involved two wealthy heirs, the Astor brothers (US) and the self-made wealthy Canadian Max Aitken, soon to be Lord Beaverbrook. But only the two Astors acquired elite newspapers; both Astor brothers were settling down (with their American millions) to become well-disciplined members of the British aristocracy. Both supported the traditional Victorian role of the Sovereign Editor. Waldorf Astor kept J. Garvin as Editor of the *Observer*. J. J. Astor similarly supported the return of Geoffrey Dawson (who had been sacked by Northcliffe) as Editor of *The Times*, a post which Dawson held during 1922–41, thus including the notorious Appeasement era. Garvin also was a leading

Table 14.1 Acquisitions of British national newspapers by 'foreigners', 1911–1998

	Up-market or elite	Mid-market	Down-market
Waldorf Astor	*Observer* (1911)		
Max Aitken/Lord Beaverbrook		*Daily Express* (1916)	
J. J. Astor	*The Times* (1922)		
Roy Thomson	*Sunday Times* (1959)		
Roy Thomson	*The Times* (1967)		
Rupert Murdoch			*News of the World* (1969)
Rupert Murdoch			*Sun* (1969)
Rupert Murdoch	*The Times* (1981)		
Rupert Murdoch	*Sunday Times* (1981)		
Rupert Murdoch		*Today* (1987)	
Conrad Black	*Daily Telegraph* (1987)		
Conrad Black	*Sunday Telegraph* (1987)		
Tony O'Reilly	*The Independent* (1998)		
Tony O'Reilly	*Independent-on-Sunday* (1998)		

appeaser, and this era of Astor ownership in retrospect seems less than glorious. But both Astors had acted like true gentlemen-owners, paying the bills, while allowing the Editor to edit.

The next wealthy newspaper acquisitor was Roy Thomson. He was a hardened advertising salesman from small-town Ontario; when he came to Britain his television background led him to bid for the ITV franchise in central Scotland. This generated huge amounts of quick wealth, and when Roy Thomson acquired the *Sunday Times* he was happy to leave the editorial side to the journalists. Subsequently the British establishment behaved with considerable condescension in allowing Thomson to buy that British treasure, *The Times*. Once again Thomson did not interfere with his new Editor, the very conventionally British, and independently Conservative, William Rees-Mogg. The Thomson takeover was widely seen as a success, a wonderfully concocted mixture of Canadian enterpreneurship and British intellectual independence. The old traditions of the elite newspaper, the rich owner, and the independent Editor were alive and well in London, a splendid example for all the world to see.

However, Thomson was the last of the gallant outside rescuers who were happy to subsidize a wonderful old piece of Britain's wonderful old press tradition. When Rupert Murdoch acquired the two *Times* papers in 1981, everyone was fully aware of his track record with the two tabloids, the *News of the World* and the *Sun*. But the previous history of the acquisition of elite newspapers by wealthy outsiders played a significant part in the 1981 transfer. The acquisition of *The Times* by an Australian, who had attended Oxford University, seemed to fit the tradition. Murdoch may have appeared to be following in the footsteps of Lord Northcliffe, whose main paper had been the mid-market *Daily Mail*, before he acquired *The Times* in 1908.

The Rupert Murdoch acquisitions, however, led to a new phase during which several elements of the wealthy-foreign-rescuer scenario were turned upside down:

- The early North American rescuers were all Conservatives; indeed J. J. Astor was a Conservative MP at the time he acquired control of *The Times*. But their politics were low key and they did not interfere with journalists and editors. Rupert Murdoch and Conrad Black, however, both went for high-profile aggressive political involvement.
- Whereas the early rescuers settled down and indeed 'went native' as British gentleman landowners, both Murdoch and Black were absentee landlords.
- Whereas the earlier newspaper buyers saw themselves as Press Lords enjoying the social flattery and privileges which are part of newspaper ownership, the new generation were professional acquisitors who continued restlessly to seek new media properties.

- Finally, a key difference. The early newspaper rescuers saw themselves as funding, and if necessary continuing to subsidize, British national institutions over an extended period. The Murdoch and Black approach was the reverse; they saw newspapers like the *Daily Telegraph* and the *Sunday Times* as cash cows, to be milked of profits which could then fund other acquisitions, especially in North America. The early tradition was of British elite papers being subsidized with US and Canadian money. The later version of this tradition found British newspapers being used to subsidize the building of new media empires in the USA and Canada.

Especially in the mid-twentieth-century years there was very little competition in the British national elite newspaper field. From 1937 there were only two elite British national dailies. *The Times* continued on its elite subsidized path with a sale below 200,000. The *Daily Telegraph* in 1937 had nearly three times this sale, and deliberately was a slightly more popular product. This comfortable duopoly continued until around 1960, when both the *Guardian* and the *Financial Times* effectively joined the national elite newspaper market. The circulation of these four by 1997 was about three times the combined *Times* and *Daily Telegraph* circulation of 1937. The elite newspaper business had become very much more competitive. This increased competition changed many other aspects of the elite newspapers, including their need for financial 'rescue' and the type of 'rescuer'.[1]

The Newspaper Cash Cows

It has often been said of Rupert Murdoch that he was prepared to risk the company—or bet the farm—on the latest high-priced acquisition. But this is hardly true. The Murdoch farm long included several reliable 'cash cows' as well as more risky-frisky new acquisitions. Among this cash cow herd, the British newspapers have loomed large ever since the *Sun* and the *News of the World* began to generate substantial profits in 1971–2.

Rupert Murdoch's first US daily newspapers (in San Antonio, Texas) were acquired in 1973; but although his US newspapers earned him a 'tabloid' reputation, none earned significant profits. In sharp contrast, the British and Australian papers were highly profitable. As late as 1986–7—when Murdoch had been in the USA for fourteen years, 'newspapers' (predominantly British and Australian) accounted for 38 per cent of News Corporation revenue, but 43 per cent of profit. In 1986–7 the UK generated 40 per cent of profits on 25 per cent of revenue. The London *Sunday Times* (acquired by Murdoch in 1981) was one of the most profitable newspapers in the world. Several years later the broad cash cow picture was still much the same. In 1992 the

[1] Tunstall, *Newspaper Power*, 35–9, 79–89, 377–90.

profit margin on News Corporation's newspaper properties was 21 per cent. The annual report showed that in 1992 News Corporation was selling 14.2 million newspapers a week in Australia and 32.7 million copies a week in Britain.

Similarly the Telegraph newspapers became the cash cows of the Black-Hollinger farm—especially in the years 1988–93. It was these profits from the Telegraph papers in London which enabled Black to acquire other properties and eventually to control (with Southam) more than half of Canada's daily newspapers.

Murdoch's British newspapers, and his Australian television properties, provided him with uniquely comprehensive experience of fierce media competition. The Australian television system from 1956 was more competitive than that in the USA. In British national newspapers, Rupert Murdoch also experienced newspaper competition much fiercer than anything then available in the USA. In Britain, Rupert Murdoch 'experimented' with nude females on the *Sun*'s page three, with tabloid journalism in general, and with aggressive television commercials about tomorrow's tabloid excitements. Murdoch was also an important minority owner of London Weekend Television. Much of this experience was redeployed subsequently on the *New York Post*, and on the Fox network and Fox TV stations.

But the key British contribution to the wider News Corporation story was financial. The British newspapers always made substantial profits from 1970 onwards; even in the financial year 1989–90, when Sky Television made a massive operating loss of £154 million,[2] the newspapers were there to nurture what quickly became another huge British cash cow. The longer-term financial significance of the British newspapers was their role as a reliable cash generator, which in turn contributed to News Corporation's reputation as an owner of 'strong assets' and hence to its ability to finance surging growth.

Pro-Thatcher, Pro-USA, Anti-Europe

Rupert Murdoch and Conrad Black were not the first owners of British newspapers to lean to the political right and to be on friendly terms with Conservative politicians-in-power. Murdoch and Black were unusual, however, in establishing a new triangular relationship between first supporting the government in power, second seeking and obtaining privileged regulatory treatment for their business acquisitions, and then third using their newspapers for belligerent advocacy of British foreign policies which just happened to match their business interests.

Conrad Black's political romance with Mrs Thatcher was the more

[2] *News International, plc, 1990 Annual Report.*

effusive. On first meeting her in April 1986 Conrad Black told Mrs Thatcher that her 'revolution' was more important than the decapitation of Charles I and the deposing of James II. She said, 'That is very good Mr Black. Do come back.'[3] He did. The Murdoch–Thatcher political relationship was also extremely friendly, but with less emphasis on lengthy Black-style speeches and more use of political nodding-and-winking. Rupert Murdoch received several Thatcher nods of high commercial value:

- In 1981 Mrs Thatcher exploited a loophole in the monopoly law and formally accepted the false claim that the two *Times* newspapers were loss-makers in danger of closure; under these (fictionally) desperate circumstances Mrs Thatcher exempted Murdoch from the normal monopoly-assessment procedure.[4] (The *Sunday Times* continued to be hugely profitable, paying very comfortably indeed for the small losses of *The Times* daily paper.)
- In 1987 the same legal loophole in the monopoly law was exploited by Mrs Thatcher on Murdoch's behalf in another equally fictional case— that of the *Today* newspaper.
- 1990 saw the nod-and-wink approval by Thatcher of the BSkyB merger in contravention of the main thrust of the Broadcasting Act, passed a few days previously.

The Murdoch/News interests also in 1986 received government support of a different (not simply regulatory bypass) kind. January 1986 saw the famous move of Murdoch's national newspapers to the new printing plant at Wapping, with the old technology and thousands of old-style print workers discarded in Fleet Street. The Thatcher Conservative government passed legislation (1980, 1982, 1984) to restrict the power of trade unions in general; the newspaper and coal-mining unions were two cases especially prominent in government thinking. When the trade unions responded to Murdoch's Wapping move, they were engaging in an illegal strike, which had severe financial consequences both for the unions themselves and for their newly unemployed members. The government also provided very large numbers of police personnel over an entire calendar year to ensure that the newspaper trucks could transport each night's production out of the Wapping plant.[5]

The Thatcher government in 1986–7 also approved the purchase of the Telegraph papers by Conrad Black. Like the Murdoch papers, the Telegraph papers next year supported Mrs Thatcher and the Conservatives in the victorious 1987 general election campaign. This Murdoch and Black two-

---

[3] Richard Siklos, *Shades of Black: Conrad Black* (London: Heinemann, 1995), 157–8.

[4] Tunstall, *Newspaper Power*, 383–8.

[5] For the 1986 events: Tunstall, *Newspaper Power*, 18–30; Suellen Littleton, *The Wapping Dispute* (Aldershot: Avebury, 1992); Linda Melvern, *The End of the Street* (London: Methuen, 1986).

fifths of national daily newspaper circulation also supported John Major and the Conservative Party in their 1992 electoral victory.

Rupert Murdoch newspapers did at times support both the Australian Labor Party and the British Labour Party, but his politics shifted decisively to the right:

- Murdoch supported Ronald Reagan in the 1980s, but thought both George Bush and Bob Dole were too moderate. In 1992 Murdoch voted for Ross Perot.[6] Broadly in US politics Murdoch was Republican, and especially hostile to Edward Kennedy and Bill Clinton.
- But in New York City, Murdoch's *Post* newspaper supported a Democrat Mayor, Ed Koch.[7]
- In Britain, Murdoch's papers supported Margaret Thatcher and the Conservatives in 1979, 1983, and 1987; they also supported John Major and the Conservatives in 1992.
- But during 1992–7 the *Sun*'s Scottish editions differed from the London editions and supported the Scottish National Party in opposition to the Conservatives in London.
- In early 1997, when Labour looked almost certain to win that year's British general election the *Sun* dumped both the Conservatives and the Scottish Nationalists[8] and supported Labour.
- In China, News Corporation in 1995 went into partnership with the *People's Daily* newspaper. By 1995 Murdoch was a supporter of the communist government and in particular did not repeat his 1993 assertion that his satellite television systems were 'an unambiguous threat to totalitarian regimes everywhere.'[9]

There were two clear themes running through Murdoch's political positions. First he moved steadily to the right. But second, the Murdoch newspapers supported politicians in power (or likely soon to be in power) in order to obtain political support and regulatory advantage for News Corporation businesses.

Both the Murdoch and Black newspapers were also deeply involved in advocating controversial foreign policies for Britain. Throughout the five years between John Major's election victory in 1992 and his defeat in 1997, *The Times, Sunday Times, Sunday Telegraph*, and (from 1994) the *Daily Telegraph* sided with the anti-Major, anti-European, faction of the Conservative party. This press campaign against the European Union (especially against political integration and monetary union) was also taken up not

[6] Andrew Neil, *Full Disclosure* (London: Macmillan, 1996).

[7] For more detail on Rupert Murdoch's political history, see William Shawcross, *Rupert Murdoch* (London: Chatto and Windus, 1992).

[8] Rob Brown, 'Tartan army left smarting as "Sun" deserts the cause', *The Independent*, 20 Mar. 1997.

[9] 'Comrade Murdoch', *The Economist*, 17 June 1995, p. 79.

only by the *Sun* but by other companies' newspapers and especially by the *Daily Mail*, the Conservative mid-market leader. John Major had the unusual experience for a British Conservative Prime Minister of being opposed by the bulk of the British national press on his most important policies.[10]

Why did Murdoch and Black and their editors oppose the official Major position and support the 'Euro-sceptical' tendency inside the Conservative Party? There was a remarkable coincidence between these anti-EU political views and the Murdoch and Black views of what was good for their businesses. Andrew Neil (editor of Murdoch's *Sunday Times*, 1983–94) noted that Murdoch: 'dislikes Europe, for example, and barely even visits it as a tourist. He despises the idea of the European Union: hence the *Sun*'s strident anti-European line.'[11] Conrad Black in a 1998 speech argued that Britain should seek to join the North American Free Trade Area (NAFTA) along with the USA, Canada, and Mexico.[12] 'In fact, what Black dislikes is anything that weakens relationships between the UK and north America.'[13]

There was clearly a rather happy coincidence in this Murdoch–Black opposition to Britain being involved in a European political and economic union and the Murdoch–Black welcome for Britain's allowing some of its major newspapers to be owned from outside Europe. The European Union was a potential business threat to continued financial nourishment from the British cash cow newspapers.

Price Cuts and Predatory Competition

The desire to preserve their profitable newspaper cash cows also lay behind another high-profile Murdoch–Black campaign of the 1990s. This was a price and circulation war against each other and in particular a contest between *The Times* (Murdoch) and the *Daily Telegraph* (Black).

Since 1931 the *Daily Telegraph* had been the up-market daily circulation leader over *The Times* by a big margin; through the years 1955–75 the *Daily Telegraph* outsold *The Times* by around five to one. Only in the early 1980s and then again in the early 1990s did *The Times* (under Murdoch ownership) make any attempt to catch up. In the first years of Black ownership (1987–92) the *Daily Telegraph* was the commercially dominant market leader in the broadsheet national daily market; under the more efficient Black management, the *Daily Telegraph* initially had well over twice the sales and

---

[10] Tunstall, *Newspaper Power*, 240–55.
[11] Neil, *Full Disclosure*, 174.
[12] Conrad Black, *Britain's Final Choice: Europe or America?* London: Centre for Policy Studies, July 1998.
[13] Raymond Snoddy, 'Telegraph chief regroups', *Financial Times*, 29 Apr. 1996.

probably about three times the revenue of *The Times*. The *Daily Telegraph* in the early 1990s was especially profitable because it was also charging a premium advertising rate. If you are the market leader, you can charge more per thousand readers, because many advertisers think they must use the paper which has the most readers in the relevant market. The *Daily Telegraph* was exploiting its strength as market leader to operate as a cash machine for the Black/Hollinger interests.

On 6 September 1993 Rupert Murdoch made a huge price cut for *The Times* (45p down to 30p daily) which was designed to attack the *Daily Telegraph*'s market leadership. Subsequently (June 1994) the *Daily Telegraph* made an even bigger cut (48p to 30p) and *The Times* immediately dropped again (30p to 20p).

These price cuts had a larger impact on the newspapers' circulation revenue than might at first appear. *The Times* at 20 pence (which it continued at for one year) was still allowing the wholesalers and retailers 15 pence.[14] Broadly *The Times* seemed to be winning the battle with its circulation 73 per cent of the *Daily Telegraph*'s in 1996, but *The Times* fell back subsequently. This circulation war moved on to other forms beyond daily price cutting. *The Times* tried selling its Monday paper for a token 10 pence; the *Daily* and *Sunday Telegraph* operated a massive cheap combined subscription which largely eliminated profits in 1996–7, and further competitive price variations continued.

The *Daily Telegraph* versus *The Times* circulation war had little impact on the *Financial Times* and *Guardian* with their separate loyal niche markets of business people and affluent Labour supporters. However the fifth up-market daily, *The Independent* (founded only in 1986), was caught in the crossfire of the sales-and-price war. In 1990 *The Independent* had about the same sales as *The Times*. But *The Independent* was a small, financially weak newcomer. *Independent* sales slipped badly and in September 1994 it made a big defensive price cut (50p to 30p); its sales now fell hugely behind *The Times* and also far behind the *Guardian*.

The *Independent* accused *The Times* and Rupert Murdoch of 'predatory pricing'. But this is an American legal concept, not a British one. Big price cuts have happened on numerous occasions in British press history. So *The Independent* was left to soldier on. There was, again, a significant international dimension. Earlier in its short life *The Independent* had been partly financed by an Italian and a Spanish newspaper group. As losses rose, however, the new main owners of *The Independent* became the Mirror Group of London and the (unrelated) Irish Independent Group of Dublin. Subsequently, in early 1998, the Mirror Group withdrew and *The*

---

[14] Author interviews in 1994 with senior advertising and circulation managers at the Telegraph Group and at News International.

Independent (daily and Sunday) became 100 per cent owned by the Irish Independent Group, and its chairman (and dominant shareholder), Tony O'Reilly.

The Independent Group was not only the leading newspaper-owning company in Ireland, but also a leading owner of newspapers in South Africa and New Zealand. As an Irishman, Tony O'Reilly was adding one fresh element to the ownership of British elite newspapers. He also had previous British ties, having played rugby for the British Lions. But despite this Irish-British connection, O'Reilly had more United States involvement since he had served as chief executive of the Heinz food company, based in Pittsburgh.

Foreign-Owned Newspapers: Why So Few Complaints or Policy Ideas?

Remarkably little serious public discussion focused on these foreign news-paper ownership issues. There were no real policy suggestions; and there was little attempt even to contemplate the possible motivation involved in the Murdoch vs. Black price-cutting saga.

Why did Murdoch continue his costly price-cutting tactics with *The Times*? Media moguls tend to study each other rather closely, not least because these professional acquisitors often buy media properties from fellow moguls. In this case Rupert Murdoch showed a remarkably sustained determination to oppose Conrad Black. Rupert Murdoch, in observing Conrad Black, may have seen in him a potential serious rival, who might try to follow in the Murdoch footsteps by using British profits to fuel growth in the United States. Well before the price cutting began in 1993, Conrad Black's Hollinger company owned over 100 very small daily newspapers in the USA; in this respect Hollinger resembled the Canadian Thomson company, which also owned small US dailies with a total sale of over one million daily copies. The Murdoch-induced British price war did greatly reduce Conrad Black's profits; when Black decided, later in the 1990s, to expand his Canadian newspaper empire, this must have been satisfactory to Rupert Murdoch, who clearly had no interest in Canada.

The lack of significant public debate in Britain was clearly connected to politicians' respect for the power if not the wisdom of newspaper owners. This is perhaps more true in Britain than in most countries, because the British national press is so competitive and aggressive. John Major, when he was a Conservative Prime Minister being attacked and vilified day after day (in 1993–7) by 'Conservative' newspapers, did not (in public) denounce *The Times* and *Daily Telegraph* or Murdoch and Black. Presumably Major feared that had he done so, the newspaper attacks might have become still more fierce. Conservative politicians who do speak out on this issue tend already to have retired (like Lord Deedes) or are about to retire (like Julian Critchley).

Only occasional complaints of 'foreign subversion' come from the other newspapers. A complaint such as *The Independent*'s against 'predatory pricing' is widely read as a sign of weakness. More importantly, most of the British press groups are playing, or trying to play, their own 'foreign' games. Already in the 1980s most sizeable British media groups had some kind of American presence. This obviously included high-profile companies such as Pearson and Reuters. But United News already had such a presence in 1986[15] and a decade later had annual United States sales of $1 billion, through UAP—'the leading publisher of free distribution advertising periodicals in the US'.[16] British owners of non-national newspapers also had such interests. The owner of the Liverpool daily papers (Trinity) obtained 32 per cent of its 1995 revenue from publishing and printing in the USA and Canada. These latter were all low-profile local publications and the investment emphasis was on advertising revenue.

However the Pearson (*Financial Times*) Group was a big owner not only

---

Two Conservative Politicians Complain About Foreign Ownership of Newspapers

'I suppose it's really the new world brought in to destroy the old. . . . I think it's a pity to get newspapers into the detergent bracket. . . . This is designed to destroy other newspapers, not to foster diversity. Murdoch is in the position to be highly destructive of other people. . . . He is a destructive individual. Rupert is not a competitor, Rupert is a monopolist.'

Lord Bill Deedes (former Conservative Cabinet Minister and former editor of the *Daily Telegraph*), June 1994

'Nowadays, the Conservative press, largely foreign owned, trumpets home and foreign policies fully suited to North American ideas and conditions, but discordant to those of Britain and Europe. . . . That the hostile press campaign against the European Union should be led by our foreign-owned newspapers is only superficially paradoxical. . . . Only large groupings such as the EU have much chance of taming them. Hence the enmity of the Murdoch and Black empire to Europe, or, to be more specific, Britain in Europe.'

Julian Critchley, (then) Conservative Member of Parliament, May 1996

---

[15] Annual Reports for 1987.
[16] United News and Media plc, *Annual Report and Accounts 1996*.

in the USA but in Europe. Pearson pursued a policy of buying financial daily newspapers initially in France and Spain; it also owned the biggest selling daily in Spain (*Marca*, a sports daily). Pearson's approach to owning foreign newspapers was a low-profile one, and this also applied to *Financial Times* coverage of newspaper foreign ownership stories.

Thus we are left with a paradox. On the one hand Britain is a world player in world news. However inside Britain the bulk of the serious press is foreign owned. These foreign owners have been quite willing to use supposedly elite papers for savage political vendettas, and crudely to support transparent commercial self-interest. In doing so these press owners—while claiming to support British independence—themselves personified the contrary image of Britain as colony of North America.

15
British Broadcasting Containment and Competition

By the end of the 1990s Britain had three separate types of well-funded and competitive television. There was the old BBC system still funded by a substantial licence fee; there were also three commercial channels (ITV, Channels 4 and 5), funded by substantial advertising revenue. Third, there was a formidable satellite and cable sector with a large portfolio of popular entertainment channels and a substantial, mainly subscription, revenue.

Although not unique, Britain was internationally unusual in having such competitive strength in all three categories. But this competitive strength largely took the form of internal competition between British national networks. It was an inward-looking kind of competition, not a competitive urge strongly directed towards exporting into other national markets.

The traditional British pattern, of just one new broadcast TV network every decade or two, was continued in the 1980s and 1990s. Channel Four appeared in 1982 and Channel Five finally was launched, fifteen years later, in 1997. Such very slow gradualism was not the whole story, but it was part of a broader picture of a British television revolution which made haste fairly slowly. Other key factors included these:

- The most (for Britain) revolutionary changes were the mainly Sky, satellite offerings, and the linked roll-out of cable. But these 'revolutionary' changes took place outside the traditional broadcast sector and grew fairly slowly. Up to an additional 3 per cent of households received the satellite-cable channels each year; but the satellite-and-cable share of British audience time grew more slowly, by between 1 per cent and 1.5 per cent per year through most of the 1990s.
- What could loosely be called the Public Broadcasting Sector—BBC1, BBC2, and Channel Four—held on to a 50 per cent share of the UK audience until 1999.
- ITV, which through most of the years 1955–85 had a 50 per cent audience share, fell below 33 per cent for the first time in 1998. Nevertheless ITV remained one of the strongest TV networks in Europe.
- At the end of the 1990s the four 'old' networks BBC1 and 2, ITV, Channel Four—all of which already existed in 1982—still had four-fifths of the British TV audience.

Nevertheless there was more change to come. A decade after she left office in 1990, Mrs Thatcher's 'poison pills' still had not yet had their full effect; like other aspects of the national television scene, these poison pills observed the British tradition of gradualism.

Public Service Broadcasting as an Un-American Activity

Those who are most critical of the BBC are those who have most loved it. To work for the BBC is to be told (especially by TV and radio people in other countries) that you are working for the most respected and most professionally distinguished broadcasting organization in the world. As a senior TV producer in the BBC, you have a remarkable amount of autonomy; within quite broad guidelines you are free to decide what you will put out on the air.[1] It is like being a doctor who works for the most admired hospital in the world (although, as with many British hospitals, the building may be in obvious need of repair).

But all good things come to an end. You cannot go on for ever being executive producer of this BBC show or deputy head of that department; it is a fast-moving, young man's and young woman's business. One day you find yourself in a less desirable and more bureaucratic job, or you resign in disgust at some new management madness. At this point, spurned and rejected by the much-loved BBC, you vent your anger. You denounce the BBC to those friendly press journalists upon whom you previously relied to obtain advance publicity for your next series.

' "End of BBC as we knew it" says senior BBC producer' has been a frequent newspaper headline, at least since 1945; this was the year in which many hundreds of BBC European Service personnel—having just won the 'word war' against Germany in Europe—were unceremoniously dumped out of their Bush House offices onto the badly bombed Aldwych street outside. It is always the end of the BBC as previously known; it is also always true—as senior BBC managers reply to the criticism—that 'We face a period of unprecedented change'.

The 1970s were the BBC's last Golden Decade. The ITV network, with its early American 'excesses' now cut back, had about 50 per cent of the audience; the BBC by 1970 had got its two-channel strategy running smoothly—the 'majority' BBC1 and the 'minority' BBC2 together taking about 50 per cent of the audience. The switch to colour, which began in 1967, led with its higher licence fee to a very comfortable BBC financial background. Also the political picture was positive—Prime Ministers Edward Heath, Harold Wilson, and James Callaghan were all strong believers in the BBC's unique virtues.

[1] Tunstall, *Television Producers*.

But two periods were especially painful for the BBC. In both the 1950s and during 1985–90 the British consensus behind the BBC broke down; and in both of these periods the door was opened to massive importing from the United States. In the 1950s the introduction of competition from commercial television was the BBC's worst nightmare come true. In 1955–7, in households which could receive both channels, the ITV channel took the bulk of the audience, leaving the BBC with as little as one-quarter. The BBC's fundamental television mistake during 1946–55 had been to regard television as radio-with-pictures or as radio-with-tabloid overtones, and therefore to be kept in an inferior place (with low budgets).

Especially during 1955–7 it seemed, from within the BBC, that this was an American bulldozer which was crushing BBC television. The ITV companies—able initially only to reach a small fraction of even the people with TV sets—were starved of early advertising revenue, and desperate for appealing programming. By 1956 the bulk of programming on ITV was either an imported American cowboy, crime, or comedy show or an American quiz-game or other format hurriedly recast with British faces and voices. In some cases British performers were required to use the original American scripts with only the most minimal of re-editing. And then there was the television advertising, which, also, was heavily influenced by American models and American-owned advertising agencies.

Some thirty years later, Mrs Thatcher became increasingly determined to punish both the ITV and the BBC versions of public broadcasting. Her chosen punishment had a distinctly American accent. There would be more commercialism, more advertising, more American programming and channels; there would be a Sky satellite system far more dependent on American programming than anything seen or heard in Britain, since the American Forces Network of 1942–5.

The Last Years of the 'Comfortable Duopoly' and Mrs Thatcher's 1990 Poison Pills

During her years as Prime Minister (1979–90) Mrs Thatcher expressed acute dissatisfaction with British television's performances. At various times she wanted to shake up British television with competition from cable and satellite; she wanted to cut back trade union overmanning; and she wanted to make the BBC carry advertising. In fact none of these things happened during her eleven years in office; the main innovation during Mrs Thatcher's long spell as Conservative Prime Minister was a fourth TV channel, which not only pursued BBC-style public service goals, but which even leaned to the political left.

However, Mrs Thatcher ultimately had her revenge. Shortly before leaving office in 1990 she left behind not one poison pill, but two poison pills. Her

1990 Broadcasting Act and her nod-and-wink acceptance of Rupert Murdoch's satellite commercial monopoly ensured that British broadcasting would experience turbulence in the 1990s and that more British money would be spent on importing more Hollywood programming.

In 1980 (Mrs Thatcher's first full year in office) the 'comfortable duopoly' was still in place. The BBC (with two channels) and ITV (with its one channel) were each quite happy to have about half the audience; ITV had a monopoly of British TV advertising, while the BBC had a monopoly of the licence fee, paid by all households with a TV set. Even when Channel Four launched in 1982, the three pre-existing channels initially only had a very modest drop in audience share.

After 1990 some audience shares dropped more steeply; this was caused mainly by the steady growth of satellite and cable through the 1990s. But cable and satellite (and Channel Five from 1997) took audience share mostly from the two big channels—ITV and BBC1. The two established 'minority' channels, BBC2 and Channel Four, were each able to hang onto about the same 10 per cent audience share as in 1990. With 'minority' being very vaguely defined, it was not difficult to make either BBC2's or Channel Four's programming mix just a shade more popular.

ITV and BBC1 had less flexibility, because both were already largely entertainment channels; moreover continuing regulatory requirements—especially for news and other factual programming—meant that neither channel could transform itself towards much more popular programming. Although after 1990 both BBC1 and ITV did move a bit further in the entertainment direction, both still suffered audience losses.

Senior BBC managers looked back on the late 1980s as a time of acute anxiety as to whether Mrs Thatcher would be successful in breaking up the BBC. In the 1980s the four-sided consensus, which John Reith had first cultivated in the 1920s, seemed to be cracking even more dangerously than it had in the 1950s. First the governmental machine and the civil servants supported the now established duopolistic version of Public Service. The official regulators at the IBA/ITC (Independent Broadcasting Authority, later Independent Television Commission) badly wanted to maintain 'public service' in ITV and Channel Four; these regulators fought hard in the negotiations leading up to the 1990 Act to minimize the impact of what they saw as Thatcherite excesses—for instance Mrs Thatcher's insistence that ITV franchises should be reallocated in a blind auction to the highest bidder. Second, the educational, religious, and cultural establishment continued to support the BBC—thus probably confirming Mrs Thatcher's perception of professional conspiracies.

A third traditional coalition element—the political parties—were more divided. The Labour Party and Liberal Democrats (in several versions) stood solidly with the BBC. Mrs Thatcher's own Conservative Party was divided; some young, radical, Conservatives wanted to punish the BBC. But in the case of the BBC, the Conservative politicians' cultural conservatism proved stronger than their ideological free market conservatism. This cultural conservatism also prevailed in the BBC Board of Governors and the Peacock Committee (of 1985–6). The latter committee, under a free market economics professor, was invited by Mrs Thatcher to investigate the introduction of advertising to the BBC. Predominantly packed with Conservative supporters—of upper-middle age and income—both the BBC Governors and the Peacock Committee wanted, at least for a while, to preserve the BBC more or less as they knew it.

The fourth side of the old consensual square, which now took a predominantly anti-BBC stance, was the Newspaper press. This was especially true of the Murdoch-owned papers—*The Times, Sunday Times, Sun,* and *News of the World*—which together sold about one-third of all British national newspapers. But some other papers—especially the *Daily Mail* and *Daily Express*—joined the anti-BBC campaign, thus giving it over 60 per cent of national daily newspaper sales. At various points in the mid and late 1980s senior people in the BBC and also in the IBA/ITC regarded themselves as on the receiving end of a 'press vendetta'. In the late 1980s they saw this vendetta as being transparently driven by the commercial ambitions of three press groups to get into television and new media channels.

'Comfortable duopoly' was a term which the Peacock Committee coined to describe the whole British television system.[2] Mrs Thatcher—while accepting Peacock's advice against BBC advertising—seized on this phrase and directed a somewhat reluctant Home Office (the then broadcasting department) to shake up the ITV side of the duopoly.

ITV had been invented in 1954–5 (and reinvented in the 1960s) as a commercial network which included some public service goals. But while the television world had moved on since the 1960s, the ITV system, as even its top regulators believed, had become 'ossified'. Independent Television or ITV in the 1980s was a single channel, but was split up into fourteen British regions, with fifteen regional companies, a news company (ITN), and a breakfast company. Thus, no less than seventeen separate companies ran this single 'public' TV network through a complex arrangement of trade association committees. Another C-word was crucial here; ITV was a cartel of seventeen companies each with its particular fiefdom. An inner ring of five bigger companies supplied the bulk of the networked programming.

ITV was controlled, and maintained in its unchanging and inflexible state, by three interlocked forces—the cartel of seventeen companies, a group of civil servants and regulators who typically favoured BBC-style 'public service', and third the broadcasting trade unions. Consequently

[2] Alan Peacock (chairman), *Report of the Committee on Financing the BBC* (London: HMSO, 1986), 38–42.

when the Thatcher spotlight was switched onto ITV after 1986, what the spotlight revealed was a particularly rabid example of the disease of 'corporatism'. ITV, in the Thatcher spotlight perspective, was a classic corporatist conspiracy of commerce, government, and trade unions living off the fat of a commercial (advertising) monopoly.

Nor had ITV been greatly altered during the 1980s by the new Channel Four. The new fourth channel was a child of the pre-Thatcher Labour–Conservative broadcasting consensus. But Mrs Thatcher allowed Channel Four to go ahead, in order to reward the political loyalty of William Whitelaw (deputy Prime Minister, 1979–83). Although Channel Four was to carry advertising, it was also designed to shelter under the maternal wings of ITV, rather than to compete head-on for advertising. During the 1980s even Channel Four's American programming was acquired for it by ITV— meaning that Hollywood still dealt with a restrictive purchasing duopoly (ITV and BBC) in Britain. Moreover Channel Four was to be a 'minority' channel, like BBC2 but more so. Channel Four was only aiming for a 10 per cent audience share and it started with a much smaller share.

From a Thatcher viewpoint Channel Four's performance must have looked like one commercial step forwards, but two or three public service steps backwards. Certainly Channel Four was not the answer to the Thatcher problem.

Channel Four's Achievements in its Early Years, 1982–1990

Channel Four's main pro-competition and anti-corporatist achievements

- Pioneered in Britain the concept of the TV channel which buys all of its programming from outside suppliers.
- Pioneered in Britain the commissioning of much of its new programming from 'independent producers'.
- First British television channel in which trade unions had little power over either policy or programming.

Channel Four's main public service achievements

- Extended the range of British TV programming, especially in factual areas, and outside the boundaries of established genres.
- Maintained the autonomy of the television producer, once commissioned, to make programming.
- Extended the powers of senior departmental producers ('commissioning editors') inside Channel Four.
- Pioneered in Britain the one-hour 7–8 p.m. TV news.

Channel Four was, thus, yet another reason why the two 'poison pills' of 1990 were still, from a Thatcher viewpoint, vitally necessary. The first poison pill was the 1990 Broadcasting Act. This Act (although somewhat watered down from Mrs Thatcher's initial preferences) did ensure that in future the duopoly would be a lot less comfortable. The Act compelled ITV companies to bid in a blind auction to retain their franchises; ITV was also required in the future to compete head on with Channel Four (and a new Channel Five) for advertising. Equally important, both trade union power and job security would be radically reduced by legal requirements for substantial levels of 'independent production'. This meant that the Channel Four system of self-employed (and weakly unionized) independent producers would now spread across the entire system and would shatter the old 'comfortable' heavily unionized internal TV production factories of both BBC and ITV. This was the first poison pill, which duly had the desired results during the early and mid-1990s.

The second poison pill involved Rupert Murdoch and Sky television and is discussed in the next chapter.

The 1990s: Channel Multiplication Begins, Containment Weakens

Pre-digital channel multiplication continued steadily in Britain during the 1990s. But at the mid-1997 launch of Channel Five all of the new satellite and cable output together only accounted for a 12 per cent share of total TV viewing. Nevertheless by then the existing multiplication already included some fifty nationally available extra networks plus some other local cable services.

But along with fragmentation, there also went important elements of concentration. The most dynamic entity in 1990s British broadcasting was Sky, which offered a steadily expanding number of services, but which was also itself highly centralized and focused into the 'Sky Multi-Channel package'.

Both fragmentation and concentration were also evident in the old ITV companies. The 1990 and 1996 Broadcasting Acts allowed the fifteen companies to merge into just three major companies. But this did not have the intended result of strengthening ITV. The three dominant ITV companies— Carlton, Granada, and United—all could see the limitations of ITV. From a commercial viewpoint ITV was a single network trying to compete against the multiple networks of both the BBC and Sky. ITV still had some 'public service' regulatory requirements; in particular the requirement for big amounts of national news and fourteen separate regional news shows between 5.30 p.m. and 10.30 p.m. took away valuable resources and valuable schedule time from more profitable entertainment. The ITV companies were required to pay several different kinds of licensing payment and taxation; they also paid generous dividends to shareholders. Altogether these requirements meant that ITV was devoting less than 40 per cent of gross revenue to producing (and buying) nationally networked programming. This meant, in practice, that ITV did only the minimal regulatory requirement in most programming genres, while focusing heavily on fiction—soap series, mid-evening drama series, and films. The dominant fictional focus did (happily for ITV) appeal to women viewers and hence to advertisers. But ITV's fiction focus was vulnerable to potential competition, not least from a future expanded British fiction effort on Sky One and other satellite channels.

The ITV big three companies could see this as an additional incentive towards their broader strategies. By 1998 each of the big three was seeking to use its foothold within ITV to expand into other areas of television.

- Granada (owner also of London Weekend TV) had its main interest in hotels and catering; but Granada also owned 50 per cent of On Digital, the terrestrial digital operator.
- Carlton (owner also of Central) was traditionally a film and television hardware and services company; Carlton also owned 50 per cent of On Digital.
- United News and Media controlled three of the middling ITV companies (Anglia, Harlech, and Meridian). In addition to being a big press company, United also owned 29 per cent of Channel Five.
- Pearson, while not an ITV company owner, was the other main player in British (conventional) commercial TV. Pearson's main activities were books and the *Financial Times*, but it was also a big owner of independent production houses which by 1997–8 included Thames TV, Grundy (of Australia), and All-American Fremantle.[3] Pearson also owned 24 per cent of Channel Five.

The ITC (the commercial TV regulator) was acknowledging ITV's other business activities when it allowed ITV to move its main news away from 10–10.30 p.m. in 1999. But the move of ITV's main news to 6.30 p.m. also reflected the traditional *News at Ten*'s declining audience, and the increasingly fierce competition faced by ITV as a network.

Channel Five would clearly be an important element in this more vertical world. Channel Five, already linked to two of the big commercial TV companies, was structured and launched in a more aggressively commercial manner than any previous British terrestrial channel. Channel Five was now a third channel aiming for (at least) a 10 per cent audience share; this inevitably meant increased competitive pressure on the existing 10 per cent channels (BBC2, Channel Four) and on ITV.

[3] Michael Katz, 'Pearson buys All American for $513m', *Broadcasting and Cable*, 6 Oct. 1997, p. 12.

British Broadcasting Containment Taking Priority Over Exports

This British system was overwhelmingly concerned with domestic national competition. In 1997, as in 1987, the bulk of the highest rated programming was drama, situation comedy, and game shows.[4] But most of these entertainment genres were still commissioned in the small numbers which were well known to be unsuitable for export. Apart from its three soap dramas, ITV ran only five dramas in the year 1997–8 which had as many as ten episodes.[5]

Television drama was expensive, of course, and a typical batch of say six drama hours would cost perhaps £3 million or $5 million. There was extreme reluctance to order a (more exportable) batch of say twenty hours, costing £10m or $15m.

Commercial caution—in the gradually evolving British system—still also combined with traditional respect for artistic autonomy. British television—even in increasingly commercial times—still found it important (or some might say commercially less risky) to respect the artistic integrity of the writer, the director, and the working producer. In situation comedy, the traditional British practice of employing a single writer or at most a 'team' of two writers, remained in place. Indeed as late as 1998 the BBC commissioned a new sitcom *Dinnerladies* whose comedienne star, Victoria Wood, was also the writer. The British TV view continued to be that the large comedy writing team of Hollywood TV tradition was not suitable (or was too expensive) for Britain.

British television did have some high-volume productions. These included the super-popular three or four times a week soaps, like *Coronation Street* (ITV) and *EastEnders* (BBC). There were also in the later 1990s many new forms of leisure-based game shows such as Bazal (Peter Bazalgette) Productions' *Ready, Steady, Cook* and *Changing Rooms*. But all of the high-volume programming formats were also seen as low-budget—or cheap per hour—productions; and, although not unexportable, these formats were not suitable for significant export earnings on the pattern of the high-volume/high-budget Hollywood sitcom and melodrama series.

One final reason why Britain lacked major television exports was that none of the major British television organizations had the necessary commitment, ambition, or interest. The main British commercial players—Granada and Carlton—were too involved in trying to protect ITV and to launch On Digital. Both Channels Four and Five were focused much more on imports than exports. The BBC had long favoured the safe practice of co-production especially with American upmarket networks in drama, natural

---

[4] William Phillips, 'Anatomy of a hit', *Broadcast*, 31 July 1998.
[5] William Phillips, 'A dramatic irony', *Broadcast*, 26 June 1998.

history, and documentary. Nor were the new independent production companies able to be serious exporters; under British conditions these independents found themselves engaged in unequal deals with the British national networks. The independents were too beholden to these British networks and were kept to such modest contracts and series runs that they were unable to compete seriously against big American, and other, exporters. In this perspective Reuters TV was probably unique in British television in that most of its business was exporting; but of course Reuters as a company was predominantly involved in sales outside its home country and was thus heavily committed to export actively.

16

Mrs Thatcher's Farewell Waive, Sky's Satellite and Cable Monopoly

> News International and BSkyB between them have a monopoly of satellite distribution in the UK, dominate the provision of programmes to cable homes, and have a near-monopoly of those programming 'battering rams', sport and movies. And, on top of all that, they own the proprietary technology that will control digital access, subscription management, and programme navigation systems.
>
> Sir Christopher Bland, Chairman BBC Governors, 19 November 1996

> The reason Murdoch owns 50 per cent [of Nickelodeon, UK] is that we couldn't have got a distributor in England in any other way.... He really has got a stranglehold on the market....
>
> Sumner Redstone, Chairman Viacom, 6 Dec. 1995

BSkyB in the early 1990s completely transformed Britain's audio-visual landscape, because it became, in effect, a second system of national broadcasting parallel to, and, in many respects opposite to, the existing system. The existing system was heavily British, heavily regulated, competitive, funded by advertising and licence fee, and paying substantial sums into the national finances.[1]

The new parallel Sky system was heavily American, subject to minimal regulations, highly monopolistic, funded by subscription, and contributing (in its first years) almost nothing to the national finances. Sky had strong overtones of the offshore tax haven; Sky was only possible because it used the Luxembourg licensed (but unregulated) Astra satellite system.

The parents of Sky were Rupert Murdoch and Margaret Thatcher. The story has operatic elements. It is late 1990 and Thatcher is on her political deathbed. Michael Heseltine is about to persuade the Conservative Party to dismiss Mrs Thatcher. Now, enter right: Rupert Murdoch. He has a small problem, he tells his political friend, Margaret. Current losses require him to merge the official British Satellite Broadcasting into his own unofficial Sky television to create a single satellite-to-home operator. Can the Prime Minister accept this? Thatcher nods; here is perhaps her last chance to wound not

---

[1] 'Newscorp Investments is Rupert Murdoch's main British holding company. Although the group's profits over the past eleven years add up to £1.4 billion ($2.1 billion), it has paid no net British corporation tax.' *The Economist*, 20 Mar. 1999, p. 83.

only the BBC, ITV, and Channel Four, but also the cultural conservatives of the Tory left. Thatcher nods again and waves graciously. Murdoch grunts and departs. The merger is announced. Within a month Thatcher is gone.

The BSkyB story is not short of paradox and oddity. This avalanche of Hollywood output was widely seen in Britain and across Europe as quintessentially American; yet this BSkyB system was far too monopolistic, far too dominant, and far too vertical (even by US 1996 standards) to have gained regulatory approval inside the United States. Fellow Hollywood moguls (like Sumner Redstone of Viacom) were genuinely startled to discover the extent of Murdoch's monopolistic domination in Britain.

How was such a combination allowed in Britain, with its proud tradition of making media policy slowly and carefully? The original merger of BSB and Sky illustrated some gross weaknesses in the British system:

- The tradition of several weak regulators made Murdoch's regulatory bypass possible. The main watchdog regulator, the Independent Television Commission (ITC), played the role of poodle and failed to generate a whimper of dissent, let alone an angry howl of protest.
- The British Parliament was also made to look ineffectual and irrelevant. The BSkyB merger transgressed the Broadcasting Act of 1990 which had just completed its lengthy legislative passage.
- Leading politicians, not only Mrs Thatcher—but also John Major and Michael Heseltine—showed an extraordinary willingness to waive laws, regulations, and self-respect in order to please Rupert Murdoch.

Rupert Murdoch himself demonstrated a virtuoso ability to intimidate politicians and to exploit their political insecurity and electoral anxieties. He also showed that he had a unique combined understanding of both newspaper and TV politics and of competition across three English-speaking countries.

Finally Murdoch showed that the desired end result of competition and political support was market domination; that the most desirable kind of such domination was vertical monopoly; and that newspaper power is an extremely effective (because politically focused) route to the vertical destination.

Murdoch and BSkyB were playing with the rather significant advantage of a government-conferred—but unregulated—commercial monopoly. Other 1990s Murdoch attempts in the satellite-to-home TV business—in Hong Kong, Japan, and the United States—did not enjoy this unregulated, government-conferred, monopoly advantage. In all three of these latter cases Murdoch was dramatically less successful than under the dream conditions of the British operation.

Solving the TV Comfortable Duopoly Dilemma with Comfortable Monopoly Satellite and Cable

Both satellite-to-home and cable TV experienced substantial growth in 1990s Britain. Both used predominantly American programming packaged directly, or indirectly, by BSkyB. Throughout the decade after its early 1989 launch, Sky's programming hours were always predominantly composed of American material. As late as 1996 when Sky One (Sky's most popular channel) had been running for seven years, only 6 per cent of its programming budget was being spent on British production.[2] Of the suppliers of programming indicated in Table 16.1 only 'Sky Premium' had a large British component; even within these Premium ('Pay') offerings, the film channels (heavily Hollywood) took up a little more audience time than the sports channels (heavily British).

Table 16.1 Share of all British satellite and cable audience hours, January–December 1996 (%)

Sky Premium	27
Sky Basic	22
Flextech Basic	21
Viacom Basic	10
Turner Basic	10
Others	10
Total	100

Sources: BARB/Sky/Flextech/Broadcast

This preponderance of American programming was something which Mrs Thatcher's relevant ministers (1979–90) had always said they wanted to avoid. The Thatcher government from 1981 tried to encourage highly British versions of both satellite and cable television. But both satellite and cable policy in 1980s Britain constituted a comedy of errors. The key policy error was to ignore the simple lesson that the then successful cable services in Belgium, Netherlands, Canada, and the USA all involved delivering attractive fresh programming at attractively modest prices.

Britain's satellite and cable policy in the 1980s was not unique in its errors. Most countries which attempted policy-making in these 'new media' fields were plagued with a host of unanticipated consequences. The distinctive feature of Britain's comedy of errors was its complete U-turn in 1989–90 from an extreme regulated approach to an extreme unregulated regime for just one privileged monopoly player.

The British Thatcher government in the 1980s saw both satellite and cable

[2] Steve Clarke, 'BSkyB hails rise in original output'. *Broadcast*, 25 Sept. 1998.

in terms of industrial policy; government support was seen as necessary to encourage satellite and cable to become leading elements of the national information technology industry. A 1981 document called *Direct Broadcasting by Satellite*[3] led to a Thatcher government policy in which GEC-Marconi and British Aerospace were to launch a high-power and high-technology satellite system; the channels of new programming were to be generated by the BBC and the whole satellite TV project was to be a triumph of all things British. This consortium—and some subsequent ones—soon fell apart. The cost of the operation just seemed likely to be too great and the demand too small.

Eventually—five years after the original document—British Satellite Broadcasting was given the go-ahead in late 1986 to pursue a revised version. But, when, after a forty-month delay, BSB's satellite-to-home offering was launched, it was a disastrous failure. BSB was too high technology, too high quality in terms of expensive programming, and too expensively advertised, while not enough households signed on in the early months. BSB collapsed in late 1990.

Cable in 1980s Britain followed a similarly disastrous course. The Thatcher government's 1982 policy document[4] (and the 1984 Cable Act) also called for everything to be high. British broadband cable franchises were awarded to companies promising to take a high (expensive) technology route. In most cases the local cable company initiated a trial operation, by cabling a small area, and then found almost no demand. British consumers did not understand what all the fuss was about—a cable company building an expensive under-the-streets system to deliver some rather unappealing programming; the cable company—finding little demand—stopped digging and waited for some new encouraging sign. None came in the 1980s.

But in 1989–90 the satellite scene was transformed. In late 1990—with Mrs Thatcher's approval—the official and high-concept BSB satellite operator was merged into the unofficial and low-concept Murdoch Sky satellite-to-home operation. Rupert Murdoch, although starting later, beat BSB into the field and in fact established a winning lead before the BSB debut in early summer 1990. Everywhere that BSB was high, the Sky offering was low; Sky was lowly—hardly at all—regulated, because it was using the new SES/Astra satellite and was thus legally located in Luxembourg. The technology was inferior—Astra was a 'medium power' satellite. The Murdoch/Sky programming was also lowish concept—initially its one expensive ingredient was its (Hollywood) film channel; much of the rest was super-cheap US and Australian material.

[3] Report of a Home Office study, *Direct Broadcasting by Satellite* (London: HMSO, 1981).
[4] Lord Hunt (chairman), *Report of the Inquiry into Cable Expansion and Broadcasting Policy* (London: HMSO, 1982).

A crucial difference was in marketing. BSB's marketing involved large amounts of expensive high-concept advertising about the high-tech square antenna ('Squariel') which—like much fresh high technology—did not operate smoothly. The Murdoch Sky operation also made its own disastrous mistakes; but the need was quite quickly seen to sell both the Sky services and the receiving equipment direct to households. The News International newspapers (with a third of UK national sale) were ruthlessly pushed into the promotional battle with huge amounts of advertising, big 'news' feature coverage, and very extensive listings of the very thin programming provision. News International journalists were given the Sky service at a nominal cost. Satellite television during 1990 was forced onto the national news and comedy agendas. Moreover anyone looking around their locality could see that the Murdoch round dishes were quite numerous, while the BSB dishes were as rare as they were square.

After Murdoch and Thatcher nodded-and-winked in late 1990, BSB was rapidly merged into Sky in early 1991 and Sky continued on its low-concept, hard-sell path. BSkyB's successful chief executive of the 1990s, Sam Chisholm, had extensive experience in Australia not only of managing a big television network but, previously, of direct selling and of TV advertising sales.

Cable in Britain went through a very unsuccessful time for a full decade, following the 1982 policy document. But eventually in 1991 cable companies were allowed to offer customers telephone service combined with cable TV. Then, at last, British cable started to grow; or, rather, American phone and cable companies came to Britain to practise offering a combination which was not yet allowed by the domestic American system of separately regulated boxes. British cable expanded from 1992; it was low regulated. Very little was offered by way of high-technology interactive services. Most of the sophisticated two-way services so enthusiastically discussed in the 1982 policy document had still not appeared fifteen years later. The programming on cable was—with few exceptions—the same as on BSkyB. But there now at least was a real demand for the cable offer of either Cable TV or Cable Phone or both.

Enter Murdoch Winking, Exit Thatcher Waiving

The unequal merger between BSB and Sky was announced on Friday, 2 November 1990. Rupert Murdoch warned Margaret Thatcher of the imminent merger four days earlier, on Monday 29 October. This was just twenty-four days before Margaret Thatcher announced that she would resign as Prime Minister.

Thatcher and Murdoch were old political allies and their nod-and-wink routine was already well practised. On two previous occasions Thatcher had waived the law, for the Murdoch acquisitions of Times Newspapers (1981) and the *Today* newspaper (1987). On this Sky occasion Thatcher nodded and winked again and—by not objecting to the Sky-BSB merger—in effect waived the law. This case differed from the two newspaper cases, however, in that here the law being waived was the 1990 Broadcasting Act (the result of five years of reports and debates) which had only just been signed into law by the Queen; the Thatcher–Murdoch agreement broke both the spirit and letter of the 1990 law. In contrast to the newspaper merger case, the Broadcasting Law did not include an optional waiver clause. Thatcher and Murdoch were actually breaking the law. The Home Secretary—David Waddington—as the broadcasting minister, subsequently acknowledged this 'technical' illegality.

The nodding-winking-waiving exercise took place in an unusual transitional time warp. This was a time of transition from one official British square dish to an unofficial (illegal-but-legal) round dish. It was a time of transition between two broadcasting laws and also a time of transition between two Prime Ministers. Once again, Rupert Murdoch was astonishingly lucky (and politically adept) because he found Mrs Thatcher on that Monday at an unusual point in her sinking career:

Sunday 28 October 1990 marked the end of a European Union heads of government 'summit' in Rome, hosted by the Italians. At the end of the meeting Mrs Thatcher gave radio interviews in which she denounced the summit's discussion of a single European currency.

Monday 29 October. Back in London, Mrs Thatcher received Rupert Murdoch; he reported the discussion as having dealt mainly with 'international affairs'. However, Murdoch briefly reported the 'inevitability' of a Sky-BSB merger and Mrs Thatcher made no objection. According to one report, she made a note, but said nothing.[5]

Tuesday, 30 October. At Prime Minister's Questions in the Commons, Mrs Thatcher gave her famous 'No ... No ... No' reply to a question on the future European currency.

Thursday 1 November. Sir Geoffrey Howe, deputy Prime Minister, resigned in protest at the Thatcher Europe comments.

Friday 2 November. The Sky-BSB merger was announced.

13 November. Geoffrey Howe made a Commons personal statement, highly critical of Mrs Thatcher's leadership.

20 November. Conservative leadership election. Mrs Thatcher failed to beat Michael Heseltine by the required margin.

22 November. Mrs Thatcher announced her impending resignation.

27 November. John Major, elected as Conservative leader, became Prime Minister.

---

[5] Peter Chippindale and Suzanne Franks, 'How the Sky fell on BSB', *Guardian*, 11 Nov. 1991.

Rupert Murdoch's usual combination of luck and political adroitness did not consist solely of obtaining Mrs Thatcher's Prime Ministerial nod at a time when her thoughts were focused on Europe and on personal political survival. His political adroitness stretched across another unusual time-span. The Murdoch waiver just happened to be granted during a short legal hiatus between the powers of the IBA and the satellite powers of the successor regulatory body (the ITC) under the new 1990 Broadcasting Act. Sir George Russell was chairman of both the old IBA and the new ITC but he has confirmed that neither body possessed the relevant powers on the relevant days.[6]

The Satellite Monopoly Established and Extended to Cable

At the time of the late 1990 Sky-BSB merger the total losses of the two companies were about £14 million a week, or at the rate of over $1 bn per year. But almost all of BSB's 600 employees were fired; the five BSB and four Sky networks were merged; and the Hollywood contracts—negotiated in competitive panic at inflated prices—were renegotiated downwards. It was during the years 1991–4 that the merged BSkyB company developed its monopolistic dominance. This had several key components:

1. BSkyB achieved monopolistic control of pay movie channels and of leading sporting competitions including English Premier League Football and a dozen other key sports. Movies and sport were (apart from pornography) the only types of premium programming for which Britons would pay substantial sums each month.

2. Sky also bundled up its own basic channels with other basics, mainly from American companies like TCI/Flextech, Viacom, and Turner (Time Warner). Sky was thus able to offer—apart from its movie and sports premium channels—a big basic tier which it launched as the 'Sky Multichannel' package in autumn 1993; initially there were 11, and by 1996 there were 31 channels in this basic multi-channel offer. Not only was the big basic tier a broad and attractive offer, but it made effective competition impossible. BSkyB even acquired 50 per cent of the British versions of Nickelodeon, the History Channel, and National Geographic, as well as smaller shares of QVC, Paramount, and Playboy.

3. Sky became the dominant British customer of the Luxembourg-licensed Astra satellite family; or, in US parlance, it controlled Britain's hot bird. Sky also persuaded the British government effectively to shut out the official European, Eutelsat, satellite system; Sky had successfully lobbied the

---

[6] Mathew Horsman, *Sky High* (London: Orion Business Books, 1997), 72–5. Shawcross, *Murdoch*, 508–12. Hugo Young, *One of Us* (London: Pan, 1993), 575–91.

Department of the Environment in London to allow unrestricted use of 70-centimetre (Sky) dish antennas, while the DOE insisted on special official planning permission for 90-centimetre (including Eutelsat) dishes.

4. From 1991 cable companies began to grow, because the British government allowed them to offer both telephone and cable services. But these, mainly American, companies quickly became dependent on Sky for nearly all of their popular basic, as well as their premium, programming.

5. Sky steadily developed a monopoly of relevant technology. An American trade paper commented: 'Rupert Murdoch's News Corp has built itself a number of key technology companies. The reasoning behind this strategy: Control the technology and it becomes far easier to exploit your own content. Plus, other content providers have to pay you to compete with you.'[7] There were two key News technology subsidiaries, both with special British connections—News Datacom (based in London) and DigiMedia Vision (formerly part of the IBA/ITC Engineering Division). The News Corporation technology used by BSkyB included a TV set-top box to decrypt the signal and the smart cards (which unlock the services for which a specific subscriber is paying). Another key technology was the computerized management system for handling subscriptions and payment. There was also special Navigation System technology—which provides information to the subscriber both about scheduled programming and about interactive services. News Corp/BSkyB's own technology did indeed constitute a monopoly gateway which other channel providers could not duplicate. In addition these specialized technology companies were supplying other News Corp companies (in the USA, Asia, and Latin America) as well as other telecoms and data companies and other pay TV operators. Consequently BSkyB was also entering the digital multiplication era equipped with unique commercial insights into its competitors' technology investments.

Monopoly pricing is a classic ingredient of effective monopoly. BSkyB's customers through the 1990s found that its prices rose much faster than inflation. The cable companies found that Sky charged them such amounts as 60–70 per cent of the retail satellite tariff. Sky's subscribing households experienced large, above-inflation increases each year. Sky's public justification was that it operated a 'benign circle'—a steadily bigger multi-channel offer, and more and more movies and sports justified steeply rising prices. A more honest assessment—that this was charging people extra for extra channels they mostly didn't want—was made by Frank Barlow (BSkyB chairman in its early years).

The BSkyB management had the unique advantage of having been given the Thatcher monopoly dispensation back in 1990. Linked to this was the

---

[7] Toby Scott, 'News Digital Systems: Murdoch's Delivery Doorway', *Broadcasting and Cable International* (Oct. 1996), 22.

strength of the News International newspapers. Moreover the key executives (Murdoch and Chisholm) had experience of running dominant operations in commercial markets; their Australian and New Zealand backgrounds gave them a much better instinctive understanding of the British market and British television than was exhibited by executives in charge of most other foreign companies.

The BSkyB management conducted several series of divide-and-rule negotiations with the US cable network suppliers and with the builders of local cable systems. Often the divide-and-rule approach involved doing a special deal with a TCI company; TCI's chief executive back in the USA was a Rupert Murdoch business ally (John Malone). BSkyB offered the TCI-Flextech network bundle a place inside the Sky multi-channel package, which was accepted—thus making the emergence of a rival bundle virtually impossible.

The American builders of British cable systems were equally deftly handled by similar divide-and-rule tactics. The key company here was Telewest (TCI and US West) and when it agreed to take the BSkyB movies, sport, and multi-channels, the prospects faded of a serious competitive cable combination offer of attractive programming. The American builders of local British systems were all from the cable and telephone industries. The US telephone companies were excited by the prospect of offering house-holds both phone and cable service. The American senior executives of the British cable operations mostly had engineering backgrounds. Even on their home ground these American executives were probably not the best and the brightest. Both they and their American bosses seemed to assume that 1990s British cable would be like US cable in the 1970s, with the local operators holding all the cards and not needing to worry much about content, pro-gramming, or marketing to customers. But they had misunderstood the US experience. US cable in the 1970s was indeed dominated by monopol-istic local multiple system operators (MSOs). But in Britain the vertical trend was even stronger than in 1990s USA; in Britain the satellite mon-opolist delivered straight into households and had tied up the key pro-gramming in advance of the cable companies. Consequently in the early and mid-1990s, while Sky built itself a hugely profitable satellite-to-home business, the cable operators signed few customers, despite digging up many streets and building up a mammoth debt. Saddled with this debt, the cable companies had no spare capital with which to develop unique programming.

1994 Onwards: Strong Profits, Weak Policy and Press

The American cable and phone companies (being themselves local mon-opolists at home) mutely accepted BSkyB's rapid rise to dominance over both satellite and cable in Britain. Equally accepting and equally mute were the British government and the entire British media industry.

The British government under John Major accepted Margaret Thatcher's 1990 nod-and-wink deal with Rupert Murdoch. British media policy continued on a twin-track basis—an unregulated regime for Sky and a still heavily regulated (and taxed) regime for everyone else. Government fear of the Murdoch/News International national newspapers was the key to this twin-track strategy. Having decided to accept much Murdoch press punishment, rather than to fight back, the John Major government found itself proposing fresh broadcasting legislation which broadly accepted (or pretended not to notice) the established BSkyB monopoly; this, then, was the position adopted in the Broadcasting Act, finally completed in summer 1996. For broadly similar reasons, the Labour Party in opposition, and after 1997 in government, also did not mount a frontal assault on BSkyB.

The main broadcasting players also declined to attack BSkyB. They too were hoping for friendly treatment in the legislation finally passed in 1996. The BBC was on its very best neutral political behaviour and keen to demonstrate to the Conservative government its new-found lean and mean efficiency; the 1996 legislation duly renewed the BBC's mandate to continue as Britain's champion public service broadcaster. Similarly, the larger ITV companies were looking forward to some relaxation of the ownership rules (which they obtained in 1996), so they also were not ready to engage in a bruising battle with Murdoch and his newspapers. The ITV companies, indeed, followed the BBC lead in doing deals with BSkyB.

The only significant media players with both the necessary political firepower and lack of regulatory constraint were the non-Murdoch national newspapers. But these newspapers, also, were reluctant to attack the BSkyB monopoly. All of these newspapers collectively had certain attitudes in common; most of their senior people, in the early 1990s, still had some residual admiration for Rupert Murdoch's 1986 confrontation at Wapping with the newspaper trade unions. Nor would any of these newspapers have wanted to adopt an overtly 'anti-American' line of criticism. Four ownerships—the Pearson, Telegraph, Mail, and Guardian groups—formed themselves into the British Media Industry Group (BMIG), whose common purpose was to loosen the cross-ownership rules so as to allow newspapers to acquire significant television holdings. Pearson already had major TV interests, but it also owned a significant slice of BSkyB; consequently Pearson's *Financial Times* felt compelled to give the issue strictly neutral and low-key coverage. The Telegraph group was itself controlled by a Canadian (Conrad Black) and thus would also have felt uncomfortable in attacking BSkyB as an American monopoly.

It was the *Daily Mail* group which provided, in the person of Sir David

English, the main leadership for BMIG. But David English was especially focused on cross-ownership and had pushed the Mail group into developing a cable channel. Called Channel One Television, this offered news and features initially in London, with subsequent local editions in other cities such as Liverpool and Bristol. Channel One was certain to be high on initial cost and low on revenue for some years. The Mirror group (not in BMIG) launched a somewhat similar (but entertainment) channel designed for local cable systems, and it also found its predictions of high initial losses to be fully justified. Lumbered with these loss-making channels, and locked into a small cable market, both the Mail and Mirror group managements may have felt that direct criticism of BSkyB would have looked too like sour grapes. (The Mail's Channel One was eventually closed in 1998, shortly after the sudden death of David English.)

Several very senior print and broadcast journalists during 1990–4 described BSkyB to this author as an 'unregulated monopoly'. Some journalists pointed to the contrast between Rupert Murdoch's free market rhetoric ('choice' for consumers, let the competitive market decide) and his actual behaviour and informal comments ('cash cows', 'we have the pipeline', and the compulsory bundling of Sky channels). But journalists (including editors) had their own reasons for staying silent; in conditions of insecure employment, they naturally did not wish to antagonize the biggest single employer of national newspaper journalists in Britain.

The Murdoch/BSkyB team in 1996 again showed that they had enough lobbying skill and clout to guard and to protect their existing monopoly. A provision in what was to become the 1996 Act would have prevented a foreign company from owning a controlling share of a domestic British satellite service; but Michael Heseltine (deputy Prime Minister) had lunch with Rupert Murdoch and a few days later (March 1996) a government amendment duly altered the position so as to ensure that BSkyB (despite being 40 per cent owned and effectively operated by Murdoch) would qualify as a British-controlled company.[8] This lobbying intervention itself neatly illustrated that BSkyB was indeed controlled by Rupert Murdoch, a US citizen. Incidentally Murdoch's dominant control had also been illustrated a couple of months earlier when he appointed his 27-year-old daughter, Elisabeth, to the job of 'general manager, broadcasting' at BSkyB.[9]

In late 1998 BSkyB launched its digital satellite service with (initially) 140 channels; and the On Digital terrestrial digital service also began.[10] This was

---

[8] Mathew Horsman, 'Sky favour for Murdoch followed Heseltine lunch', *The Independent*, 11 Apr. 1996.

[9] Horsman, *Sky High*, 187–90.

[10] 'Sky Tenth Anniversary Issue', *Broadcast*, 5 Feb. 1999, pp. 1–20. 'BSkyB 10th Anni', *Variety*, 1–7 Feb. 1999, pp. 35–50.

the beginning in Britain of a new digital era (see next chapter). Eight years earlier a very British Prime Minister (Mrs Thatcher) had opened the door to American domination of both satellite-to-cable and direct satellite television in Britain.

17
Will a British BBC Survive until 2022?

THE BBC is a great survivor and will surely survive to its hundredth anniversary in 2022. The BBC's internal reforms of the late 1990s prepared it well for the new digital age. However the years up to 2012 are still certain to see a substantial reduction in the BBC's share of audience viewing time; these years will also see an increased American element within the BBC's productions and co-productions. Moreover the most severe difficulties will face the BBC during its tenth decade, in the years 2012–22.

A key difficulty is that successive British governments have wanted the BBC both to serve the British domestic audience with truly British programming, and at the same time to attract audiences around the world. In the meanwhile the BBC clings to the tradition of the licence fee, knowing that, ultimately, it will have to rely on other sources of finance. Reliance on a static licence fee, adjusted only for inflation, as the dominant revenue source must mean that the BBC will fall financially ever further behind commercial broadcasters who will depend on more buoyant advertising, subscription, pay-per-view, and interactive revenue streams.

The 1990s were one of the BBC's best decades—led by one of its best-equipped leaders, John Birt. In the 1990s the BBC held onto its audience better than did ITV (from which BSkyB took much of its audience share). The BBC got itself into better and slimmer fighting shape; it embraced channel multiplication and launched new services. But John Birt's success at apparently enabling the BBC in the 1990s to do more (and better, and cheaper) distracted attention from the longer-term problem. After the levelling out—or audience plateau—of the 1990s, the audience share would fall steeply both up to 2012 and during 2012–22. A tangled web of linked dilemmas included these:

1. At the 1998–9 dawn of digital television in Britain, total television revenue was spread roughly equally between ITV, Sky-and-cable, and the BBC's two TV channels. But in the next decade the BBC's income would grow only just ahead of inflation; meanwhile ITV income (from advertising and new 'pay' and digital services) would probably double, while satellite-cable revenue might treble. The BBC faced a huge drop from about one-third to perhaps only a fifth of total British TV expenditure by 2010 or 2012.

2. Behind the financial dilemma lay the old BBC dilemma of the licence fee. Declining expenditure and audience share were not politically compatible with a significantly increased licence fee. Therefore, the BBC must innovate new services and sell its wares. However the licence fee-payers cannot fund risky investments. Consequently risks must be taken only with extreme caution; translated into business reality, this meant that services might expand quickly but revenue from these services would not.

3. In an age of fast-moving consumer goods and fast-moving consumer television, large blocks of audience time and cash can only be earned by large blocks of popular programming; this requires both lengthy popular series and whole networks dedicated to streams of attractive material. In the 1990s the BBC experienced difficulty in generating large blocks of popular material even for its home audience, let alone for export audiences.

4. 'Prestige' and 'quality' have always been the BBC's strongest cards, and especially so in terms of programming exports. But big prestige and high quality are rewarded more with praise and prizes than with big finance or big profit. Moreover much of the 'prestige' reputation comes from English-speaking audiences in north America, northern Europe, and Australia. The key conferer of these prestige and quality accolades is the United States.

5. The BBC entered the expanding bouquet business with some trepidation and also with some enthusiasm. But the BBC was damned if it did multiply and also damned if it did not. By deciding to go for the BBC as Big Bouquet Corporation, the BBC went into business with assorted American bouquet bundles. The twin risks were that it was spreading itself too thin as well as too American.

6. The BBC, like other big broadcast players, uses programming at all price levels from expensive (a million dollars or pounds per hour) to cheap (only 1 per cent or 2 per cent of the expensive rate). In the 1990s the BBC found new ways to make both cheap and middling-price programming. If you had (like BBC1) £2 million per day to spend on 20 hours of programming, £1 million-per-hour programming was hard to finance. Increasingly much top-of-the-line programming requires some kind of foreign (American and other) support and co-finance.

7. The BBC's new digital channels could be provided on a separate subscription basis; or digital television households could be charged a higher licence fee (as occurred with colour TV when first introduced). However, either measure would discourage digital TV and would contravene the universal principle of a common licence fee for all.

The Government believes that the BBC . . .

1.1　The Government believes that the BBC should continue to be the United Kingdom's main public service broadcaster. Its primary role should be making and broadcasting programmes for audiences throughout the country.

1.2　However, the next 10 or 15 years will bring rapid and exciting changes in broadcasting. New technologies are emerging and the boundaries between broadcasting, telecommunications and other media are becoming blurred. New services are being created, which combine aspects of different media, and which have become known as multi-media services. There will be new opportunities for United Kingdom businesses in providing such multi-media services in an expanding global market.

1.3　The Government believes the BBC should be able to evolve into an international multi-media enterprise, building on its present commercial services for audiences in this country and overseas. These ventures should be separate from its public services, which are funded from the licence fee and the Foreign and Commonwealth Office Grant-in-Aid.

Source: Department of National Heritage, *The Future of the BBC* (London: HMSO, July 1994), 1.

Britain's Three-Way Digital TV Launch, 1998–1999

Britain was not unusual in launching digital TV; indeed it was well behind the USA, France, and several other countries in launching digital satellite TV. But Britain did claim to be the first country in the world to launch terrestrial digital TV (receivable through an old rooftop antenna).

Britain was certainly unique in launching all three main digital TV technologies within a single year in 1998–9. Table 17.1 indicates some of those launch details. First came *satellite-to-home digital* (launched by BSkyB); within six weeks came *terrestrial digital* (launched by the two main ITV companies, Granada and Carlton). Then in 1999 came *digital cable* launched by the dominant cable companies.

The main 'old' BBC1 and BBC2 channels were on all of the systems, as were the BBC's newly launched and more niche-themed new digital channels.

The launch of all three technologies (plus a big range of pay-per-view film services) at roughly the same time led to intense competition, massive

Table 17.1 The UK's three-way launch of digital television, 1998–1999

System	Channels initially offered	And also
Satellite-to-home Sky Digital Launched 1 Oct. 1998 (BSkyB)	*75 TV channels* 7 Free (5 BBC) 68 Pay (6 BBC) Also 48 pay-per-view channels	44 audio channels some interactive services
Terrestrial On Digital Launched 15 Nov. 1998 (Granada and Carlton)	*30 TV channels* 9 Free (5 BBC) 10 Pay (3 BBC) 11 Premium	
Cable Launch: 1999		Numerous Audio channels Numerous fast Interactive services including fast Internet

launch advertising, and widespread anxiety as to the ultimate winner. One of the safest predictions was that not all of the very different forecasts would be correct.

Some possible indications as to which channels would be most popular were the existing preferences within the one-third of homes that in 1999 already received multiple channels from either satellite or cable. These audience data suggested a steep hierarchy of channel popularity along the following lines:

- Two big channels with 20 per cent plus audience shares: ITV and BBC1.
- Three big little channels with perhaps a 6 or 7 per cent audience share: BBC2, Channel four, Channel five.
- Five channels with a 2 to 4 per cent audience share: Three Sky channels (Sky One, one movie, and one sports), UK Gold, and the Cartoon Network.
- Another twenty or so channels with an audience share between 0.4 per cent and 1.9 per cent. This group would include several more Sky channels and perhaps as many as ten American channels (including Nickelodeon, MTV, Discovery, and the Disney Channel).

Of course, because of the launches of many new channels (and the mergers and closures of both old and new channels) this would not be the actual list of channel leaders in 2010 or 2012. However, from the perspective of 1999 these were the current front runners, the ones new entrants must try to beat.

The early stages (at least) of the digital era seemed to favour the satellite operator. Sky in the 1990s was a pioneer in delivering a large, centrally coordinated bunch or bouquet of channels from a single 'platform' (or group of satellite transponders). Sky demonstrated the benefits of cross-promotion and integrated scheduling. Sky also had sufficiently big profits to be able to pay ever higher fees in order to stock its sports channels. In its first decade it relied overwhelmingly on subscription revenue; but strong entertainment offerings (such as Sky One)—as they reached more households and bigger audience numbers—generated larger amounts of advertising revenue.

Almost all known successful networks eventually turn towards more domestic programming. After 1992–3 Sky had the financial resources to produce its own British soap operas, expensive drama, and so on. Sky chose not to do so but to spend its programming budget mainly on British sport and Hollywood movies. However, Sky One, programmed with more fresh British material (in addition to some of the most popular American TV series), will pose a strong challenge especially, perhaps, to ITV.

In the history of both BBC and ITV decline, the launch of Channel Five on 30 March 1997 is likely to feature as a key event. Channel Five got off to an unimpressive start and the newspaper 'disaster' treatment traditionally accorded to new TV channels in Britain. Channel Five needed to try harder, because as the final conventional TV channel it could not reach 100 per cent of households; it also entered a much more competitive market than had Channel Four at its launch back in 1982. But Channel Five—unlike Four, not sheltered from advertising competition—was much more commercially scheduled and much more aggressively marketed. Without any established popular programming, Channel Five initially leaned heavily on what Hollywood movies it could get. The top twenty audiences for Channel Five's first month included no less than sixteen enticing Hollywood movies (such as *My Stepmother is an Alien* and *Memoirs of an Invisible Man*). Channel Five also had its British daily early evening soap (*Family Affairs*). The chief executive of Channel Five, David Elstein, came direct from Sky. Initially Channel Five had 2 per cent and 3 per cent audience shares. But with increasing audiences and revenue and with more expensive (both British and American) programming, Channel Five was a different kind of 'minority' channel from BBC2 and Channel Four, both of which have tried to balance middling and smallish audience programming. Channel Five, in the more competitive late 1990s, was given fewer 'public service' obligations than any other conventional British channel, including ITV. It was therefore certain—despite predictable lamentations from the ITC regulator—to draw ITV into a more aggressive defence of its leading audience share and also to draw Channel Four into a more aggressive defence of its 10 plus per cent audience share.

The BBC Enters the Digital Era and the Bouquet Business

Major reorganizations of the entire BBC have tended to occur at three- or four-year intervals. A key focus especially of the 1996-7 reorganization was to split the BBC up into semi-autonomous business units; for example 'BBC Resources' went into business to make its office, studio, editing, and post-production services available to commercial broadcasters and others. Another effort was to try to supplement licence fee income by launching new digital channels funded by subscription. More cash would be generated by more effective exports through 'BBC Worldwide'. However the BBC remained entrepreneurially inhibited. Not allowed to go into significant debt, the BBC had to be 'relatively risk averse'; it had, in practice, to find business partners to take the commercial risk. But the (somewhat) more commercially minded middle and senior managers recruited by the BBC in the 1990s mostly came from 'old ITV', and their management thinking derived mostly from the old monopolistic era of Thames, London Weekend, and Central back in the 1980s. The BBC recruited few of its top managers from newer ITV, Channel Four, satellite, or cable. This would be another BBC disadvantage in the years ahead.

BBC, 1997 Onwards

From 1997 the BBC had these six directorates:

- *BBC Broadcast:* commissions and schedules programming for all TV and radio channels
- *BBC Production:* produces all internally made TV and radio programming (except news)
- *BBC News:* makes all TV and radio output in news and current affairs
- *BBC Resources:* provides resources such as studios, editing facilities, and technicians
- *BBC Worldwide:* the BBC's commercial arm, handling both export and domestic sale of programming, audio, video, books, magazines, other products, and the associated rights
- *Corporate Centre:* finance, personnel, planning, and other central services

---

As the BBC's management looked forward to 2012 and 2022 there were (in addition to the household licence fee) four other present, or possible, sources of revenue, profit, and loss:

1. The payment for BBC World Service radio from the Foreign and Commonwealth Office; this amounted to some 8 per cent of BBC revenue.

2. Sales and services combined under the title 'BBC Worldwide', which in fact involved UK domestic sales as well as foreign export trading. The optimistic way of describing the activities was to quote the gross sales revenue figures. But these activities—such as selling TV programming and videos, books, magazines, and educational materials—generated fresh costs amounting to about two-thirds of revenue. The most successful revenue generators in 'Worldwide' were the (programming-linked) magazines for the domestic British market, such as *BBC Good Food* and *BBC Gardeners' World*. This entire 'BBC Worldwide' operation was greatly expanded in the mid-1990s and its revenue did grow; however, its net benefit was much smaller, reaching 4 per cent of BBC net income in 1998–9.

3. Channel subscriptions promised to be a significant source of revenue as the BBC developed its digital channels. However, new channels inevitably faced significant start-up costs and initially low numbers of subscribers. The launch of the new digital channels in 1997–9 was assisted by some windfall finance from the sale of the BBC's national transmitter system. But BBC planning for the first five digital years (1997–2002) allowed 9 per cent of licence fee income per year, or about £1 billion over the whole period. In this early period the digital channels would generate losses rather than profits.

4. Advertising revenue was still forbidden on domestic services (to justify the licence fee) but was introduced to fund BBC World, the new competitor to CNNI. The sums initially generated were very small.

The central BBC management recognized that the reputation of the BBC was highly fragmented between the BBC's different services and publics. There was also the problem that the places where BBC world service radio had its biggest regular (listening) audience (such as West Africa and North India) were not necessarily the places which could, or would, generate the most future sales revenue.

In view of such inconsistencies (and the generally weak export performance in financial terms) it was decided that the BBC should try to consolidate its reputation as a single 'brand'. At BBC Worldwide's offices (just north of BBC Television Centre in west London) there was much talk of the 'brand'. The strategy was to phase out the contradictions and fragmented imagery of the past. The BBC branding mark was to be attached to all existing products and services, including books, video, CD-Roms, radio and television programming. Then new services (such as new TV channels) would be launched 'off the back of the brand'.

In its 'rebranding' and other marketing exercises the BBC was trying to emulate its commercial competitors, who were also attempting to sharpen their 'brand identities' as the arrival of hundreds of new offerings bewildered the public. But talk (and action) along rebranding lines was cheaper than paying big sums of money each month and each year for big projects, big stars, and big executives. In terms of big projects Sky had seriously raised the price threshold by its huge bids for Hollywood movies and sports rights. An obvious BBC anxiety was that, just as it was priced out of live football, it would increasingly be priced out of other programming.

The cost of star talent was a related anxiety. More competition and more revenue leads to bigger demands by the agents of the top-rated stars. Star salaries in British television and radio escalated in the 1990s. An instructive case was that of Chris Evans, whose million pound salary deal for presenting the BBC Radio One breakfast show was not sufficiently attractive. (His specific 1997 request was to do the show four, rather than five, mornings per week).[1] Chris Evans soon departed to acquire (with associates) ownership control of Virgin Radio. An era which saw a young radio star become chief owner of one of the largest radio companies in Europe was a worrying one for the BBC. The BBC now faces the prospect of building up star performers (often from radio into TV) only to see them disappear—like football players—to become absurdly highly paid competitors. As in football there was inflation also in the salaries of lesser stars. A performer who could help to generate a 2 or 3 million audience on BBC2 or Channel Four could also demand a huge salary increase.

The same applied to managerial and senior producer talent. John Birt's salary as BBC Director-General was a very high one by previous BBC standards. But Sam Chisholm's 1996–7 salary (with bonuses) in his last year as Sky chief executive was £6.8 million (or $11m).[2] More importantly, the BBC will find that its executive producer and senior management salary structure is increasingly uncompetitive.

The Future BBC: Further Down the Anglo-American Path

In 1997 the BBC moved decisively in a more American direction by concluding several agreements with the Denver-based cable giant, Telecommunications Inc (TCI), with its chief executive John Malone, with other associated companies, such as Flextech, Liberty Media, and the Discovery Channel, and with the part-TCI-owned Telewest cable company in Britain. All of this took place before, in 1998, TCI agreed to be acquired by the telephone giant, AT&T.

The BBC needed a commercial partner with which to pursue the more commercial strategy it had agreed with the British government. The BBC did not seriously consider a major European partnership; all of the European public broadcasters were perceived to have difficulties similar to, or worse than, those of the BBC. Thus the BBC looked towards the USA and saw several positive aspects in TCI. The big American cable company might

---

[1] Simon Garfield, *The Nation's Favourite: The True Adventures of Radio 1* (London: Faber and Faber, 1998), 100–29.

[2] *British Sky Broadcasting: The Annual Report, 1997*, 46.

be able to offer the BBC better access to the US market than the BBC's scattered previous pattern of sales to PBS and to small cable channels; TCI might help the BBC to launch not just a few mini-series but a niche network or two into the USA. TCI was also a known existing force in Britain through its 51 per cent ownership of Flextech; this latter company owned and/or operated about one-quarter of all 'basic' satellite-and-cable channels in Britain with about 10 per cent of the total satellite-and-cable audience. Flextech was also a minority owner of Scottish TV and it had British senior management.

TCI was thus already part of the British scene and its people and channels were well known to BBC executives. In 1997 three main agreements were announced.

- Flextech and the BBC would jointly (50/50) own and launch a batch of new British subscription channels, primarily for digital transmission. These would include UK Horizons (science), UK Arena (arts), UK Style (lifestyle), and UK Play (pop music and comedy). The first three were launched on Telewest (part TCI-owned) cable systems in late 1997.
- Flextech assumed full control of UK Gold, which was already one of the most successful channels on British satellite and cable, and which mainly showed BBC and Thames 'classic' comedies and other popular rerun programming. The intention was to develop other output from UK Gold.
- The BBC also agreed another joint venture with the US Discovery channel (49 per cent owned by Liberty Media and controlled by John Malone). Discovery already existed as a British (and European) channel with an additional Home and Leisure channel in Britain. The BBC would increase its existing programming contributions to the various Discovery channels, including US Discovery and Animal Planet.

These BBC–TCI accords acknowledged in practice that only in news could the BBC convincingly go it alone on a global scale. BBC World, the BBC all-news channel, was steadily building up its household total especially in Europe and South Asia; some news and news-feature programming was produced for showing on BBC World as well as on the BBC's domestic News 24. BBC World also recycled other factual material from BBC1 and BBC2.

But the BBC was admitting that it was losing the bulk of live domestic sport. It was finding it increasingly difficult to compete with ITV in popular fiction series. The BBC was anxious to generate more TV drama between the twin extremes of costume drama and its social problems/working-class *EastEnders* soap.

In terms of television programming for the world outside news, the BBC recognized that its main strength lay in the areas targeted for the first pay digital channels—especially science, arts, lifestyle, education. In particular the BBC was especially strong in general documentary and natural history/environmental (and some would say, gardening) programming. The BBC also remained strong in domestically oriented comedy (some 200 fresh half-hours each year).

The TCI–BBC agreements had obvious advantages for the BBC; not least was the fact that TCI took all of the financial risk (and would take half of the profit). But these agreements also represented a recognition by the BBC that its most significant potential market was the USA and that the BBC could only be a significant world player in the digital era if it was allied with at least one big American company.

One inevitable criticism of all of this American-assisted bouquet building was that the BBC—still overwhelmingly dependent on a licence fee, spent primarily on its two domestic TV networks—was spreading itself across too big a bouquet. Indeed even before Britain's first 1998 digital transmission, it was already quite difficult to add up the BBC's total number of networks. The information in Table 17.2 lends itself to more than one way of counting, depending on the definition of network. But the total was around 20 radio and TV networks and due to rise soon to about 25.

Table 17.2 The BBC bouquets, 1999

Domestic TV	Domestic, Digital, Cable, and Satellite TV	International TV
BBC1	BBC News 24	*BBC Worldwide*
BBC2	BBC Choice	BBC World
	BBC Parliament	BBC America
	BBC Knowledge	UK TV (Australia)
	BBC Text	
	UK TV (with Flextech)	*With Discovery*
	UK Gold	Animal Planet
	UK Arena	People and Arts
	UK Horizons	(Latin Am.)
	UK Style	
	UK Play	

Domestic Radio	Interactive	World Service Radio
BBC Radio One	BBC Online	English service
Radio Two	BBC news online	40 other language
Radio Three		services
Radio Four		
Radio 5 Live		
Local Radio		

Even more obvious criticisms were that these developments were too American and also too involved with one US company, TCI, the creation of the highly idiosyncratic cable (and capital gains) mogul, John Malone. The BBC, in fact, did expect to continue its PBS relationship, not least with WGBH (Boston). There might be other US partners.

For the early years of the new century the BBC was firmly committed not only to the licence fee but to an American alliance. It still greatly preferred both of these to the obvious alternative of transformation into a more 'commercial' organization, partly, or entirely, dependent on subscription and advertising.

The reorganizations of the 1990s gave the BBC quite strong prospects for much of the next decade. For some or most of the years up to 2010–12 the BBC still had several advantages:

- The BBC would continue to be the biggest and most vertical broadcaster in Britain—still doing much of its own production and delivering it down BBC network-pipelines into all UK homes.
- In the new world of big bouquets of channels and networks, the BBC—with its substantial bundle or bouquet of radio networks, old broadcast, and new digital TV channels—was in a unique position within Britain.
- BBC Radio (especially the five national channels, four of them on FM) would still be in a strong position and still occupying huge amounts of audience time.
- The BBC would continue to have unique strength in cross-promotion between its numerous networks. In particular its big traditional TV and radio networks would be able to provide invaluable promotion for the new digital niche channels.
- The BBC even had good 'Interactive' prospects. BBC Online was generously funded and perfectly placed to recycle information across the huge range of BBC programming. For language teaching and other interactive learning the BBC had obvious strengths. BBC Online also added significant firepower to the overall cross-promotional onslaught.

However all of these advantages would tend to weaken—alongside declining audience share—as 2010 and 2012 approached. By that time BBC resources would be weaker in comparison with those of its main commercial competitors.

Moreover by 2012 the date for the switch-off of analogue television may either have happened or (more probably) will have been agreed. Even in the late 1990s the BBC's senior management were, of course, aware of government (UK and most others) plans to switch 'broadcasting' entirely onto digital.

Unfortunately for the BBC this will be only one of a whole batch of linked severe new difficulties. Indeed most of the advantages of the years immediately after 2000 will, not many years later, be transformed into disadvantages.

- The analogue switch-off will remove the BBC's own broadcast networks. In a more vertical era, the BBC itself will be less vertical. Its main distribution home will be inside On Digital, an enterprise owned and operated by its competitors, the ITV (company or companies). BBC channels will also appear on satellite and cable systems, but the owners of these systems will obviously protect their own channels.
- The BBC bouquet of new digital channels may be looking a lot less broad. All of the BBC's 'new' channels were—to a greater or lesser extent—based on recycling existing BBC productions. Subsequent possibilities of this kind must be quite limited.
- BBC Radio, by 2010–12, will probably be much weaker. Digital satellite and cable technology facilitates a huge increase in the possible number of audio channels; by 2012 BBC radio's audience share is likely to have been radically diminished.
- As both the TV and Radio bouquets shrivel by comparison with the commercial competition, the cross-promotion possibilities must also be severely reduced.
- In Online/Interactive terms the BBC is also likely to have fallen behind. Few of the possible big money-spinners of the future (such as interactive shopping, banking, gambling, pornography, game shows, dating/mating, pay movies, pay sport) are likely to seem suitable for the BBC brand.

If the BBC does approach 2010–12 in this sort of weakened state, it is likely to be even more dependent upon a continuing American alliance strategy.

PART IV

Europe Adds Deregulation to Media Nationalism

18
France and Germany Copy Italian Accident: Britain Follows Later

In the 1980s and 1990s Britain was quite often accused of being a Trojan Horse for American media within Europe; Britain was said to have used its membership of the European Community/Union to help the American media to conquer the European media. There is some, but not much, truth in such an assertion.

The real Trojan Horse was Italy—which in the late 1970s did not merely deregulate its media; Italian politicians deliberately allowed totally unregulated broadcasting anarchy of a kind which had not been tolerated in the United States since 1927. The main beneficiaries were the charismatic advertising salesman, Silvio Berlusconi, and the Hollywood exporters. Also in at the beginning was little Luxembourg—an eager Trojan pony— supposedly one of the homes of the new Europe but also a traditional European base for Hollywood.

In the media Trojan Horse business the next eager runners were France and Germany. Both France and Germany in the mid-1980s embraced policies of deregulation without much concern for the likely anti-European and pro-Hollywood consequences. It was only after these four countries—Italy, Luxembourg, France, and Germany—had done their Trojan Horse acts, that Britain finally (in 1990) joined the Trojan Horse sequence with Mrs Thatcher's regulatory exemption for Rupert Murdoch and the BSkyB monopoly.

The late 1970s Italian lurch into broadcasting anarchy occurred before Brussels, and the then Economic Community, had yet entered the media policy field. A politically delicate policy field even at national level, media policy was inevitably going to be extremely politically delicate at the European level. Population differences between large and small countries made for radically different amounts of finance available for film or TV production. Most media activity across Europe was either national and semi-national or global and semi-global; there was no neat collection of distinctly 'European' media activity, comparable to, say, the European coal, steel, or agriculture industries (with which Brussels had previously grappled). Amongst such Europe-wide media activity as did exist in 1975–80, Hollywood occupied a prominent place. Brussels had thus to face the dilemma that the most European-wide media were often the most American.

Another key difficulty was that in 1980 most of Europe's national media industries were either nationally controlled 'Public' TV and radio broadcasters (funded typically by both advertising and licence fee) or newspaper publishing companies, deeply entrenched into the national political system. Even two decades later, several of the largest media organizations in Europe were traditional press companies, which had diversified into television. Bertelsmann in Germany, Havas/Canal Plus in France, and Pearson in Britain were all historically derived from news and print companies.

There were several waves across Europe of what might politely be called 'injudicious' deregulation, but which, more bluntly, was Mickey Mouse policy-making whose main beneficiaries were Disney and the other Hollywood companies.

- The initial wave of injudicious deregulators (or Trojan Horses) were Italy, Luxembourg, France, and Germany; all four of these had committed themselves to massive deregulation by 1986.
- Britain was in a second wave (around 1988–92) which also included some heavily cabled nations such as the Netherlands and Belgium.
- Next came most of the smaller nations of Scandinavia and the Mediterranean including Sweden, Greece, Portugal, and—most important of all—Spain. This wave occurred mainly in the early 1990s.
- The final wave involved a number of newly independent and newly ex-communist nations in eastern and east-central Europe.

By 1995–6 some thirty-five separate countries—from the Atlantic to the Ural Mountains and the Caspian Sea—had been through a major TV channel multiplication exercise; these exercises invariably involved thousands of extra hours of Hollywood TV imports.

Europe's era of injudicious deregulation and channel multiplication lasted some two decades, 1975–95. But around the mid-1990s another media policy era began. Instead of half-hearted quota and other attempts to limit TV imports from the USA, after 1995 the new era focused on telecommunications deregulation and upon anti-monopoly policies, increasingly pursued in cooperation between Brussels and Washington.

Media Nationalism, and Italian Media Anarchy

Europeans are media nationalists who prefer their own national media in their own national language. All across Europe people are happy to drive German cars, use Italian refrigerators, and to consume French wine and cheese. But few foreigners want to read French newspapers, watch Italian TV programming, or listen to German pop music. There are only two main exceptions to this rule. First, people will accept media from a same language neighbour with a bigger population. French speaking (South) Belgians devote about 30 per cent of their TV viewing to TV channels coming from France; similarly citizens of the Irish Republic devote about 30 per cent of their TV viewing to TV channels coming from the UK (Northern Ireland). But apart from these (same-language) exceptions there is very little interest in a neighbouring country's media. In Germany, for example, ten TV channels each have an audience share of 2 per cent or over; all ten of these are German-language channels.

The second exception to the national preference rule concerns American media. Across Europe 20–30 per cent of all viewing involves Hollywood or American programming. The proportion is highest out of evening prime time and in the smaller population countries.

Media nationalism originated with the national and sub-national character of newspapers, which historically had close ties with *national* political parties. Almost all European countries also until the 1970s had a predominantly public service type of both radio and TV, which also mainly reflected national political and cultural concerns. All of these national (and regional) media systems in Europe have been—and still are—inward looking in terms of content. In each country, debates which take place about media policy are predominantly national.

Language is crucial and western Europe is generously endowed with a large number of different languages. Their national language is of high significance to the citizens of each country; they naturally wish to preserve their national language and the national media which help to sustain the language. But its national language is also sustained by each country's schools, homes, work places, and politics.

Against this traditional background of national language, western European countries—when they adopted media deregulation—did so on the basis of national impulse, national mythology, and national political advantage; such few concessions to 'European' thinking as did occur, were minimal and semi-ritualistic.

Injudicious media deregulation had a number of common, or parallel, characteristics between countries and especially between the core Brussels member states of the first two waves:

- The decision to engage in radical deregulation—and channel multiplication—was more of a sudden lurch, rather than a carefully planned (and extensively debated) policy.
- Party political advantage played a prominent, or dominant, role in the key decisions. Parties of both the left and the right made these decisions; often the key intention was to wrong-foot, to pre-empt, or to do the opposite of, the main political opponents.
- Major newspapers (and their owners) typically gave public support, in the expectation of obtaining regulatory favours in general and ownership of new channels in particular.

- The media-political deals and alliances often involved a leading politician—such as Craxi (Italy), Kohl (Germany), Mitterrand (France), and Thatcher (UK)—in alliance with one or more media moguls.
- Individual media moguls were often prime beneficiaries of these deregulatory lurches. Indeed in some cases an individual mogul's company was able quickly to establish a monopolistic or dominant position within the new channel multiplication pattern on the audio-visual landscape. Silvio Berlusconi quite quickly established monopolistic control of television advertising in Italy. In France the TFI consortium, led by the construction mogul, Francis Bouygues, achieved dominance in TV advertising. In Britain Murdoch achieved monopoly control in both satellite TV and in cable programming. In Germany the main business beneficiaries were the two media 'families' of Kirch and Bertelsmann.
- All examples of sudden channel multiplication led to severe shortages of cheap-and-cheerful programming; in all cases this was met by direct imports from Hollywood and also by format importing and format copying, mainly of cheap American programming.
- But the larger European countries also made some modest gains, especially in terms of media exports to smaller neighbouring countries which spoke the same language. Thus media nationalism made one modest break-out from the nation state; media nationalism was partly redefined around language nations.

But in most of this Britain was not the leader, instigator, or Number One Trojan Horse. Italy was the initiator and provided an extreme—and tragicomical—example of deregulation lurching quickly into chaos, illegality, political corruption, cheap glitz, and hard-core pornography. Perhaps Deregulation Italian Style at first appeared so ludicrous that the lessons were ignored.

Trojan Horse Number Two was France, because France was, and is, the leader in European media policy. In terms of media regulation, what France does today Europe tends to do the next day. Unfortunately for Europe, France has been inept at media policy-making. Unfortunately for the reputation of the Socialist President of the Republic, François Mitterrand,[1] he was the jockey of a Media Trojan Horse. Britain and Mrs Thatcher were well behind Italy and France in this deregulatory exercise.

Italy was the country which introduced comprehensive channel multiplication to Europe. Italy came upon channel multiplication accidentally. As the result of a 1975 Constitutional Court decision, broadcasting was opened

---

[1] Michael Palmer and Jeremy Tunstall, *Liberating Communications: Policy-Making in France and Britain* (Oxford: Blackwell, 1990), 199–211.

to all comers and Italy by the mid-1980s had added eleven national commercial networks (and part-networks) to the existing three RAI, public service, channels.

These chaotic Italian happenings were the beginning of policy changes which had Europe-wide consequences. Let us just consider France, Germany, Italy, and Spain. In 1980 these 'large' countries each on average had 2.75 TV channels, all of them public. A decade later in 1990, each country had 8.25 channels—a trebling of TV channels in one decade. By 1990 half of the TV channels were public and half were commercial.[2]

These changes obviously involved a big decline in the audience share of the public channels. By the mid-1980s Italian television stabilized in an approximate balance between the three RAI public channels and the three leading commercial channels controlled by Silvio Berlusconi. RAI had already been financed by a mix of advertising and licence fee; it managed to hold onto 40 per cent plus of the audience only by moving in a more entertainment direction.

The Italian version of 'public service' involved a strong party political element. In the 1950s and 1960s RAI basically followed the Christian Democrat Party and their allies, the Roman Catholic Church. Later only RAI One was Christian Democratic, while RAI Two was Socialist and RAI Three Communist. The Berlusconi private television revolution around 1980 did not sweep away all political influence. The Berlusconi commercial channels became still more politicized in the 1990s when Silvio Berlusconi established a new centre-right political party, briefly became Prime Minister (1994), and meanwhile used his television channels and huge advertising resources brazenly to support his political party and political career. There were some Latin American elements in the Berlusconi phenomenon—not least the use of the national football slogan, 'Italia Forza', as the name of his political party.

An immediate consequence in Italy after 1976 was a ravenous demand for batches of Hollywood movies and prime-time TV series. But American prime-time network output actually generated quite limited numbers of hours and there was, as yet, little fresh production for American cable. The Italian networks quickly gulped down the US prime-time programming and looked round for more; they then imported older movies and big slabs of daytime soap operas, games, and talk shows. After this they turned to Brazilian and other Latin-American soap operas. Then, gradually during the 1980s the Berlusconi and the RAI channels made more of their own soaps and glitzy Italian versions of American game shows.

Despite such Italian innovations, the dependence of Italian television on American television in the early and mid-1980s went to extraordinary

---

[2] Karen Siune and Wolfgang Truetzschler, *Dynamics of Media Politics* (London: Sage, 1992), 103.

lengths. CBS and NBC worked with the Italian commercial channels while NBC worked with the RAI channels.[3] By the 1980s the commercial channels were making more of their own programming; the leading Berlusconi channel (Canale-5) was showing every weekday Italian versions of *Family Feud*, *The Dating Game, Blockbusters, The Price is Right, The Newlywed Game*, and *Hollywood Squares*. But even by 1987 (after a decade of Berlusconi) such 'Italian made' programming accounted for only 38 per cent of Canale-5's output. 49 per cent was 'acquired' (mainly American) programming, while 13 per cent was advertising (also, of course, heavily American influenced). However, Italian advertising had never accepted all of the Anglo-American 'professional' advertising rules. The key element in Berlusconi's extraordinary empire was his advertising company, Publitalia; the real cash engine of the whole Berlusconi enterprise, Publitalia effectively operated a monopoly of television advertising in Italy.

Another Italian TV innovation of the Berlusconi era was the TV sex show, or 'TV a luci rosse'. Like other TV genres, this one had quite a complex history—deriving both from the commercial disasters of the Italian feature film industry and also from the late night programming put out by local operators in the early days of Italian TV chaos. Like other genres, this one was made up of several sub-genres, including the strip-quiz, the porn show, the sex chat-phone show, the quiz-sale show, and an 'Erotica' soap opera.[4]

France Takes a Commercial Leap

While the Italian political system lurched into unregulated commercial television by mistake, France deliberately moved into commercial channel multiplication in the mid-1980s. In the French media there is a characteristic tension between the elite and the popular. There is one elite, intellectual, highbrow pole of the French media celebrated in a newspaper like *Le Monde*. This tradition is Paris-based; the tradition has in the past favoured a substantial state involvement in television, subsidies for newspapers, tax-breaks for journalists, and subsidies also for the cinema film, seen as an art in which France excels. This tradition, while favouring the cosmopolitan and international, is unhappy about large quantities of American media entering France; however, small numbers of carefully selected American 'classics' are greatly admired and Hollywood production resources are envied. There is a quite opposite tradition in France which is popular and provincial; it is found in the chains of popular French radio stations playing much Anglo-American music and in the large quantities of American programming, and French versions of US genres, to be found on French television.

---

[3] 'Not so innocents abroad: US webs in Italy', *Variety*, 18 Apr. 1984.
[4] Neil Blain and Rinella Cere, 'Dangerous Television: The TV a luci rosse phenomenon', *Media Culture and Society*, 17 July 1995, pp. 483–98.

There is another characteristic French tension between the media seen as avenues for artistic expression, intellectual elegance, and domestic and democratic debate and, on the other hand, the media as instruments of the state and of politicians in power. During the decade up to May 1968 De Gaulle 'governed by television'. Radio and television were state dominated and political opponents were kept off the news; De Gaulle himself had excelled as a radio performer (initially from London) and he now adapted his style to become a master of the televised address and the grand televised press conference. He also appointed his political supporters to all of the top management and news positions in French TV and radio. Television was held back in terms of hours and finance; advertising as an additional form of TV finance was not introduced in France until 1968 (against 1955 in Britain).

After De Gaulle's 1969 departure, the system changed; the state became less dominant, but the politicians-in-power continued to exert their influence, in somewhat more indirect and subtle ways. The regulatory arrangements went through a series of reinventions. In 1984–5 President Mitterrand, accurately anticipating the Socialists' loss in the 1986 parliamentary elections, made the key decisions about two new commercial channels, which came into existence in 1986, the same year in which Jacques Chirac (again) became Prime Minister.

The Mitterrand Grand Design was very much a political design and it stretched over the years 1984–6. Of the three pre-existing channels, only two (FR 2 and 3) would remain as public channels. There would be two completely new commercial channels; and Channel One was privatized, indeed TF-1 became one of the most dominant single large TV channels in Europe with (initially) over 45 per cent of the audience.

Also in 1984 Canal Plus was launched and after a shaky start it quite soon became a big success. Canal Plus was a pay (subscription) network. TF-1 and Canal Plus became the two most financially successful channels in France. Both channels are idiosyncratically French, but both channels also rely quite heavily on American imports and influence. TF-1 is 100 per cent focused on delivering popular programming and commercial profits. Bouygues—a leading French construction company—has been the dominant ownership/ management force. TF-1 is developing its own group of digital channels; it owns the all-news LCI (La Chaine Info). TF-1, especially in its early commercial years, used much American programming. TF-1 is now much like a French version of an American commercial TV network. But it is Canal Plus which incorporates an even more intriguing collection of different influences:

- Canal Plus is close to the French state. At its birth Canal Plus received the priceless advantage of a conventional TV channel; the state also temporarily shut out imports of Japanese video machines, a potentially

competitive way of viewing films at home. Havas, close to the French
state for well over a century, was the leader of the ownership
consortium.

- Canal Plus followed a classic 'pay TV' path in rounding up exclusive
sports and film rights.
- Canal Plus was also conceived as the saviour of the French film industry. It has been a part financer of most French feature films since the
mid-1980s.

After 1990 Canal Plus moved on to additional triumphs outside the
borders of France. As other countries began to copy its success, Canal Plus
became involved in Canal Plus Espagne, Canal Plus TVCF in Belgium, and
in Première. Then in 1996 Canal Plus acquired the pioneering Nethold
(Filmnet) channels which were thinly spread around Italy, Scandinavia, the
Netherlands, and Belgium (with an additional presence in Eastern
Europe). With a total 8.5 million subscribers at the merger in 1996, Canal
Plus was unambiguously number one in pay TV in Europe. Already in
1996 Canal Plus saw itself as poised to take the European lead in digital
television.

Germany as 1990s Channel Multiplication Leader in Europe

Germany became during the early 1990s the first of the larger European
countries to get a satellite and/or cable package of about thirty TV channels
into the majority of its domestic households. East and West Germany also
became reunited with western Europe's largest (80 million) population; and
in the mid-1990s, having become the satellite-and-cable leader in Europe,
Germany also came to see itself as the probable European leader for the
'digital era'.

It took very few years for Germany to switch from a public system of three
TV channels to an 'American' system of thirty channels. In 1986 just two
big public service channels (ARD, ZDF) still had 84 per cent of the German
TV audience; seven years later (1993) these two public channels had only 34
per cent of the TV audience.

The German public system, created by the American and British
occupying forces in 1945–8, stayed more or less in place for forty years. The
forced-to-be-free German media system of the late 1940s was a deliberately
provincial system; the British actually favoured a centralized system (with
Hamburg playing the role of London) but, when the British zone was combined with the American and French zones, the result was a Germany with
several major media locations. The Americans took the lead, but paradoxically, they favoured a version of British public, rather than American
commercial, broadcasting. Crucially both Americans and British insisted on

the location of broadcasting authority at the regional (*Land*) level. The press also was licensed on a city-by-city basis and this produced a strong collection of city-region newspapers, with the main national press initially modelled after American magazines.

This German provincial media system was challenged on several occasions by politicians-in-power but was defended by Federal Constitutional Court decisions in 1961, 1971, and 1981. For a country which came to possess Europe's leading capitalist economy, the Germany media system incorporated remarkable restrictions on market forces. Two national channels, plus regional public offerings, all continued to be mainly licence-fee financed. As late as 1988 only 10 per cent of German advertising expenditure went into television. It was a highly politicized system with key factual programming usually reflecting the political majority of the *Land* where it was produced. This was also a highly regulated and legalized system; there was an in-built tension between the regions and the federal level, as well as within some of the key regions.

Big German companies and advertising agencies wanted more television advertising time; both the newspapers and the federal telephone operator wanted to get into the electronic media. But it was the federal election win of the Christian Democrats (CDU) in 1982 and a Constitutional Court decision of 1986 which led to the big change. The public broadcasting monopoly was rejected as a socialist policy previously preserved by such SPD politicians as Helmut Schmidt.

A decade later the German media scene had been transformed into Europe's nearest approximation to the United States media system (the three leading networks now had only 46 per cent of TV viewing). But the German media were still politicized; indeed two of the major media companies became the two dominant and politically opposed media 'families'. Bertelsmann operated a media family which was distantly friendly with the Social Democrats (SPD). Bertelsmann is historically a print and publishing company; in 1993 it still drew only 9 per cent of its revenue from radio and television. Most of its revenue came from magazines (Gruner and Jahr), printing, music, newspapers, book publishing, and book clubs. However from the mid-1980s Bertelsmann moved vigorously into television, in particular a German language RTL channel, jointly owned with CLT (of Luxembourg). In a very few years this commercial channel became the German ratings leader—available by cable, by direct satellite, and also increasingly on conventional (terrestrial) television. In 1996 Bertelsmann bought out its partner to acquire majority control of the various RTL TV channels.

The other leading German media 'family' was created by Leo Kirch. After the death of his fellow conservative, the newspaper owner Axel Springer, Kirch became the leading German example of the media mogul—an owner-operator-acquisitor with right-wing political views. Kirch was a movie mogul of a special kind; he became the main go-between for Hollywood films onto the ARD and ZDF national TV networks. He acquired the German language TV rights to most of Hollywood's film output, and much Hollywood TV series output. Kirch and the Axel Springer interests together controlled SAT-1, the second major new satellite channel in the late 1980s and the 1990s. In 1996 (and aged 70) Leo Kirch launched a collection of digital channels.

Bertelsmann's control of all of the RTL channels from 1996 confirmed it as the leading European media company within Europe. RTL had important TV channels in Belgium and the Netherlands. Bertelsmann was a big owner of magazines across Europe, and not least in France. Bertelsmann also owned one of the worldwide music companies, BMG (formerly RCA/Arista), and became the 'world's largest book publishing company'. Bertelsmann and other German magazine publishers also had a significant magazine presence in the USA. German companies were very active in former communist central and eastern Europe.

But the German situation was broadly comparable to the British one, although with very different detail. On the one hand the German media had an impressive 'export' performance; however, the German media scene also exhibited a huge level of importing from the USA. This was evident across most national media fields within Germany, but was especially evident in the big commercial television sector. It involved both the importing of programming and the part-ownership of TV channels.

In the late 1990s German television had six big channels (each with at least 9 per cent of the audience). Three of these six were public service and three were the largest commercial channels. These six channels had about 80 per cent of the total audience, but the picture was made additionally competitive by the presence of a second batch of another five channels each averaging at least a 2–3 per cent market share. This large number of largish channels left German television still very dependent on the USA for imports of more expensive programming, especially drama series and movies. During one week in 1997 the five biggest German channels showed 110 American drama series episodes, 58 Hollywood feature films, and 16 British/Canadian/Irish/Australian/New Zealand feature films. Two-thirds of the films shown were English language.[5]

National Media Rivalry: France, Germany, Britain

From a European media policy viewpoint, the 'British problem' was not that Britain differed greatly from France or Germany. Rather the problem

[5] *TV Movie*, 29 Mar.–4 Apr. 1997 for ARD, ZDF, RTL, SAT1, Pro Sieben.

was one of similarity. All three countries—France, Germany, and Britain—had strong national media traditions. Despite agreeing in the 1980s to commence a European media policy, France, Germany, and Britain—their governments and media industries—all wanted to be the media industry leader of Europe. As would-be leaders each saw the others as rivals.

Despite the close France-German alliance in the political and economic spheres, there was no close Franco-German media alliance. True there was a joint-owned TV channel, Arte; while this was a government-subsidized effort, it had a distinctly lopsided existence, because Arte was on a French terrestrial channel but only on a cable channel in Germany. France and Germany in general took very little interest in each others' television series or films. The broad media relationship between Germany and France was not face-to-face, but rather back-to-back.

Meanwhile all three of these would-be European media leaders operated with quite similar international media goals and trading activities.

- All three countries' policies prefer domestically produced to imported programming.
- However, all three are willing to look up the popular culture pecking order and to import large quantities of entertainment from Hollywood.
- German, French, and British companies also own significant media companies in the United States—mainly in lowish-profile areas.
- All three countries own some media properties in other European countries.
- All three countries export TV programming and films mainly to their smaller neighbouring countries, especially ones which speak the same language (e.g. French Belgium, Switzerland, Austria, Ireland).
- All three countries see their media as having a wider international appeal. Germany focuses on its small neighbours and on eastern Europe. France looks towards its former empire, to Quebec and to Latin America. Britain, of course, looks towards its former empire and its smaller northern European neighbours from Belgium to Finland.

19

Television without Frontiers: Brussels Misreads US Satellites and British Privatization

THE ill-judged mid-1980s channel multiplication exercises undertaken by both France and Germany were encouraged by the emerging 1980s Brussels policy of 'Television without Frontiers'. Paris, Bonn, and Brussels were all pursuing similarly unwise policies at the same time, and thus learnt nothing from each others' mistakes.

Through the 1980s decade Brussels developed—under its banner of 'Television without Frontiers'—what was supposedly a television policy for Europe. Behind this policy lay the basic anxiety that, in the new 'satellite age', television signals would soon cross frontiers on a large scale. But the Television without Frontiers 'policy' had several crippling weaknesses, including the following:

- The central policy objective was to reduce the level of Hollywood imports into Europe. Because international trade treaties did not allow policies targeted against a specific country in this way, the real objective was never openly stated. There were no realistically informed debates and no clearly articulated goals. The result of the policy was to increase—not to decrease—imports from Hollywood.
- The policy was heavily influenced by internal bureaucratic struggle and by commercial lobbies in Brussels.
- The policy failed to digest the obvious lesson of the Italian channel explosion after 1975. The Italian experience indicated that it was conventional broadcast TV channels which could most rapidly transform the TV landscape. Conventional channels could be (and had been in Italy) rapidly increased in number and spread across the country, whereas new satellite and cable channels—both US and European experience showed—could only build up their number of subscribers much more slowly and hesitantly.
- Nevertheless the Brussels policy focused especially on satellite television and argued that satellites would make 'Television without Frontiers' available across Europe. The policy ignored the lessons of already heavily cabled countries such as Belgium and Canada; consumers only

really welcomed channels from other countries, if they understood the language used by the channel.

- The Brussels policy not only greatly exaggerated the likely competitive threat of US satellite channels in Europe, but also misunderstood the role of Britain. Frequently quoted in the relevant Brussels documents was the lone 'Sky' channel which Murdoch's News International transmitted by satellite and which was picked up by many local cable systems around Europe. This lone Sky channel—packed with old US and British programming—was an interesting novelty especially for local cable systems in areas of widespread English-language ability; these areas were mainly in the smaller countries such as Belgium, the Netherlands, and Scandinavia. What the policy-makers, however, did not understand was that this Sky service was highly unprofitable and non-viable; it carried little advertising and increasingly attracted the opposition of local cable regulators in the Netherlands and else-where. The continuing losses eventually led Rupert Murdoch to close down this particular (Euro) Sky and to launch a quite separate multi-channel Sky aimed at Britain.

- The Brussels policy-makers also misunderstood 1980s British policy in another way. They misunderstood telecommunications 'privati-zation'—leading to British Telecom (BT) as a commercial telephone company; this privatization enabled Murdoch to get his lone Sky onto a Eutelsat transponder with the support of BT. The policy of privatizing telecoms, but moving very cautiously on television expansion, was the official British policy through the 1980s and into the 1990 Broadcasting Act. This official British policy prevailed, until it was effectively abol-ished by Mrs Thatcher just before her late 1990 loss of office. But right through the 1980s and until 1990, Brussels policy ignored the fact that Britain—despite allowing American networks free entry, and despite the common language—had only a tiny fraction of its households actually paying to receive extra American channels.

Despite some attempts to blame London for Europe's media problems, a much more real threat to European media was Europe's second head-quarters city and state of Luxembourg, which had a long history as the leading media 'pirate' of Europe. From 1933 advertising-funded radio broadcasts were directed from Luxembourg into France, Germany, Britain, Italy, and the Netherlands. Such radio operations were also important after 1945 and the Luxembourg government subsequently allowed a television development along similar lines. By the mid-1990s there were major Luxem-bourg (RTL) television channels in French, German, and Dutch which were having a big impact on the internal television scene in Belgium, Germany, and the Netherlands. The German RTL channel became the ratings leader in

Germany; as the leading channel in the largest European media market, this Luxembourg-originated channel advertised itself as 'Number One in Europe'. This German RTL channel, when it first appeared, transmitted a service of mainly American programming.

Luxembourg was also significant from 1989 for an English-language service, namely the Murdoch/News Sky channels. It took two governments to allow Rupert Murdoch to establish his BSkyB satellite TV monopoly in Britain—not only the British Thatcher government but also the Luxembourg government—because the Sky channels used Astra/SES satellites regulated by, and controlled from, Luxembourg. Subsequent Astra/SES satellites in the early and mid-1990s became the key engine of satellite-and-cable channel multiplication across western Europe.

These Luxembourg activities were more than merely symbolic of Brussels media policy weakness. Luxembourg, one of the six founding members of the original European Economic Community, was the location of several European institutions and agencies. After coal and steel, Luxembourg had two 'modern' industries—'offshore' banking and 'offshore' media. Or to put this more brutally: the Luxembourg economy relied upon legalized media piracy. The massive Luxembourg cross-border American-leaning media exercise made any kind of successful European media policy effort look unlikely.

Another key Brussels weakness in the early 1980s was its inexperience in non-economic policy in general, and in media policy in particular. 'Television without Frontiers' was not only a (supposedly) comprehensive policy for European television. The TVWF policy was also a pioneering claim that the Commission was competent in the media area; there was no previous track record of Brussels activity or legal competence in this area. Due to a perceived need to establish the Commission as competent, there was also a political decision to take the line of least resistance; this meant not confronting either the press of member states or the public service broadcasters. In practice Brussels looked towards new networks funded by advertising; Brussels also effectively recruited the most powerful of the old media—the press—and used the support of the newspapers to encourage the launch of new commercial TV offerings.

'Television without Frontiers' Equals National Commercial TV plus Hollywood

Prospects for a single coherent European media policy were not helped by the fact that no less than four of the Commission Director-Generalships had significant media responsibilities:

- DG3: Internal Market and Industrial Affairs

- DG4: Competition
- DG10: Audio-Visual, Information, Communication, Culture
- DG13: Telecommunications, Information Technology, Innovation

DG3 and 4 both favoured free market approaches with an industrial emphasis and during the crucial 1984–8 period both were presided over by British Commissioners. DG10 and 13, in contrast, both favoured French-style interventionist, or state leadership, policies.[1]

The main Brussels media policy of the 1980s was Television without Frontiers. Altogether it took nine years to go from the first proposals (1982), through the first main documents (1983–4) to the Directive (1989) and its ultimate coming into effect (1991). The final wording of the Directive was meek and half-hearted. The Directive's major requirement was that at least half of the content of any TV channel should be 'European', but there were some exceptions and even the requirement for half European content was qualified by the phrase 'if practicable'. The Directive also incorporated the notion of free reception and the regulation of a channel by its own domestic authorities. Also present was encouragement for Independent Production, and a number of detailed advertising rules—concerning children, tobacco, and the length and frequency of commercial breaks.

The surrounding debate was probably more important than the ultimate Directive. Against the position which obtained in European television in 1982, this was a massive switch towards a more free market, deregulated, and commercial television system. The early documents focused heavily on making the (not previously accepted) case that the Brussels Economic Community was competent to develop policy in the media. DG3 argued that television was an economic and industrial activity; having made this *economic* argument, DG3 then asserted that new television channels should be *commercial* channels, financed by advertising. The DG3 people knew that there would have been major obstacles to their calling for more *public* channels. First, public channels were not commercial (and thus outside the then solely Economic competence of the Community) and second to stray in the public television direction would have meant confrontation with the (in 1982 still) dominant public broadcasters across Europe.

The key strategic flaw of the Television without Frontiers approach was to swallow the bait of the then common American argument that satellite-and-cable developments made 'inevitable' a huge expansion of new television channels; this, it was claimed (and naively believed in Europe), would make national media frontiers no longer viable. Brussels completely failed to recognize this as American public relations hype, rather than American reality.

[1] Richard Collins, *Broadcasting and Audio-Visual Policy in the European Single Market* (London: John Libbey, 1994), 17, 145.

American and Hollywood rhetoric claimed that a profusion of international channels was 'inevitable'; the reality of the US experience, however, was completely different, because every single significant new US channel was not international, but domestic.

The Brussels policy-makers were also misled by European 'high-tech' enthusiasm for satellite-to-home television; the French and Germans in 1979 and the British in 1981 had all proclaimed their intention to pursue these satellite technologies. But Washington's own more cautious and better-informed assumption around 1980 was that satellite-to-home television was still some years away in the future.[2] The DG3 authors in Brussels convinced themselves of the Television without Frontiers arguments not least because the 'inevitability' of channel multiplication helped to justify DG3's territorial claim that television fell within its (Internal Market and Industrial Affairs) bureaucratic competence.

Certainly, it was correct in 1982–4 to argue that some increase in the number of European TV channels was inevitable. But what was also probable (given the slow pace at which the public adopt major new gadgets) was quite slow growth in cable and satellite household numbers. The then current predictions of a rapid growth in channels, a rapid growth in multi-channel homes, and a big growth in channels crossing frontiers by satellite were greatly exaggerated by the familiar combination of commercial hype and self-interest. These exaggerated predictions were proclaimed by a Brussels DG3 (wanting to expand its area of competence), by management consultants and forecasters (hoping for extra business), as well as by eager American marketing and public relations people.

This satellite pie-in-the-sky thinking about the inevitability of huge amounts of cross-border international television, which became accepted as the Brussels orthodoxy in the mid-1980s, had a number of consequences. It encouraged several European governments to believe that—since (Brussels said) numerous extra satellite channels were inevitable—it might be adroit politics to make a sharp increase in the number of conventional ('terrestrial') channels. Moreover since this was something your political opponents would probably want to do, you could pre-empt them by allocating the new channels yourself.

DG3, by defining extra TV channels as being mainly commercial channels, was supporting a type of television for which the United States was the leading model. DG3 was also accepting the arguments of the Brussels press lobby, which wanted newspaper-owned new channels, and the advertising lobby, which wanted more TV advertising in a Europe where TV advertising was still quite restricted. In fact the Television without Frontiers green paper of 1984 was heavily dependent on statistical appendices and other support-

---

[2] Tunstall, *Communications Deregulation*, 68–77.

ing documentation supplied by the Brussels advertising lobby (in which Anglo-American advertising agencies were prominent).[3]

DG3 found itself in opposition to the more interventionist DG10 and 13. But one continuing (or compromise) theme which united them was a focus on satellite-to-home television. This enthusiasm was also to be found in a later policy (coming from DG13) for an agreed European standard for High Definition Television (HDTV). The Commission tried to force an agreed HDTV digital standard—initially to be a satellite-to-home standard—on all European countries. Britain objected strongly although, paradoxically, Britain had been the initiator of the first version of this D-MAC technology. The Commission entrusted the innovation to two large and (by now) none too innovation minded electronics companies—the French Thomson and the Dutch Philips. Like much top-down technological innovation (outside the military field) this exercise was not successful. Moreover, while Brussels and the European governments were arguing about imposing an HDTV high-tech standard, Rupert Murdoch (assisted by Mrs Thatcher and the Luxembourg authorities) pushed forward with his PAL low-technology, medium-power system which had the twin virtues of being workable and also acceptable to the public. The official British system (British Satellite Broadcasting) which Murdoch/Thatcher/Luxembourg defeated used the Euro-MAC technology.

What did Television without Frontiers achieve? Not very much positively. But it did legitimize an all-comers-welcome official European approach to satellite channels, and this led to Britain as the European launch pad, in the 1990s, for American channels. The policy also helped to eliminate television frontiers between neighbouring countries which used the same language. This led to countries such as Austria and (French-speaking) Belgium partly merging their television markets into the national markets of their larger same-language neighbours. Thus in television terms Germany 'acquired' not only East Germany but a total market of some 90 million German speakers in Germany, Austria, and Switzerland. Similarly France acquired a total French-speaking TV market of over 70 million people in France, Belgium, Switzerland, and Quebec, plus more in Africa. Moreover the Netherlands plus the Dutch-speaking (Fleming) Belgians became easily the biggest of western Europe's 'small languages' with a total TV market of about 20 million. So Germany, France, and the Netherlands were assisted to some modest TV export successes.

But along with these modest successes for the Germans, French, and Dutch, Hollywood was provided with a much expanded European market. The 50 per cent European content rule was still only required 'if practicable'. Moreover since news, sports events, games, advertising, and teletext

---

[3] 'European Media Lobbying', in Jeremy Tunstall and Michael Palmer, *Media Moguls* (London, Routledge, 1991), 93–101.

were all exempt, a channel might carry well under 50 per cent and still meet the requirements of the (voluntary) regulation. Even so, in 1997 (fifteen years after the TV without Frontiers policy was first proposed) of 214 European channels studied by the EU, 37 per cent fell below the required European quota. One of the worst offending countries was Belgium (the EU's home). Moreover two French-controlled FilmNet channels had only 25 per cent European content.

The Press-Led European Alliance for Commercial Television

What Brussels proclaimed as a pioneering policy voyage into the all-singing, all-dancing, all-satellite-and-cable future, was also seen by Europe's public broadcasters as a conspiracy against public, and in support of commercial, television. But 'conspiracy' was too strong a term, not least because much of Europe's public broadcasting was by 1980 quite accurately seen as politicized and unpopular broadcasting.

Nevertheless, in addition to the efforts of such politicians as Craxi, Mitterrand, and Kohl, there was a loose alliance of media interests (both in Brussels and in the capitals of member states) which lobbied for more television and especially for more commercial television. The most politically potent members of this loose alliance were large press organizations; also important was the advertising industry. Not insignificant were other television industry interests such as 'independent producers'.

Newspaper owners are still the media aristocracy—or the oligarchy families—of the German, French, and Italian media. In all of these countries the press was relaunched (officially cleansed of any taint of fascism or Nazism) in 1943–7. Since then the ownership, in many cases, has only moved on by one or two generations. This is especially clear in Germany. Much of the history of the German media since 1945 is the history of six families: Kirch, Mohn (Bertelsmann), Springer, Holtzbrinck, Bauer, and Burda.

In any country the people who own and operate the major publications help to set the tone of the entire national society. It would be difficult to exaggerate the importance of the *New York Times*, *Washington Post*, and *Los Angeles Times*—all family-controlled publications—in setting the tone of the United States. These leading newspapers, of course, not only strongly influence the entire press, but also the entire mass media. However, these great American papers—like the leading British papers—are also more commercially transparent than are many French or German companies.

Each of these European countries' newspapers have developed in different ways. Most of the big Italian papers have become the flagship possessions of major companies such as Fiat. France has a mixed picture of monopoly provincial newspapers, a declining Parisian daily press, and a more vibrant magazine sector. Germany has one massive 'tabloid' but most of the press consists of commercially strong and highly partisan papers in the larger and smaller cities. All of these national newspaper presses have enormous political influence. Politicians come and go, but newspaper families tend to stay in power for several generations. These powers involve:

- Personal alliances of owners and editors with top politicians. Many of these alliances are based on common political beliefs. But the Conservative Silvio Berlusconi had a political alliance with the Italian Socialist leader, Bettino Craxi. Even the Socialist President of France, François Mitterrand, had at one time been a parliamentary party colleague of the right-wing press mogul, Robert Hersant.
- Newspaper owners used their political power and connections to diversify into television and radio, and they did this in advance of declines in newspaper advertising revenue of the 1990s. Various Italian press owners went into commercial TV, before profitably selling out to Berlusconi. Robert Hersant used his ownership of *Le Figaro* to become one of the owners of the French fifth TV channel (which later collapsed). In Germany, Bertelsmann, Axel Springer, and other press owners were the major forces behind the leading new satellite commercial TV channels (RTL and SAT-1), which transformed German television.
- Newspapers also had a massive influence on national press policy, or lack of press policy. In France various attempts—including an 'Hersant Law' of 1984—were made to punish the press mogul for his collaborationist past and his anti-Semitic utterings; but Hersant initially ignored the law, and then successfully got the law changed (1986).

Nor is it only at national level that the press law remains weak, while newspapers are less regulated than almost any other industry of national significance. The same lack of press regulation also prevails in Brussels. European communications policy focused in the 1980s on television and in the 1990s moved on to telecommunications; but it decided to ignore the press. Why? Because the EU Commissioners are politicians who require at least tacit support from their own national domestic newspapers in order to function effectively in Brussels.

While the press played a strategic political role in the move towards commercial television, cable TV had by 1980 already altered perceptions of TV across Europe. Moreover Brussels, Europe's new capital, happened to be located in one of the most heavily cabled corners of the world. Ten small population countries of (mainly) northern Europe (Austria, Belgium, Denmark, Finland, Ireland, Luxembourg, Netherlands, Norway, Sweden, and Switzerland) are now the most heavily cabled group of nations in the world.

But despite its long history of cable television—dating back to 1960—

northern Europe (and especially its policy-makers and public broadcasters) had not anticipated the key role which cable would play in the rapid TV policy revolution around 1990. For nearly three decades the public broadcasting system of the Netherlands, for instance, managed to coexist quite amicably with the steady growth of cable. In 1985 just two Dutch public NOS channels had 80 per cent of the evening audience; the widely available cable channels already accounted for 20 per cent but they did not seem especially threatening. This 20 per cent share for the cable-imported channels included two very unthreatening Dutch-language channels from the north Belgium public broadcaster (BRTN); after these in audience popularity came German language channels (such as the public ARD).

Only in 1985–6 did it begin to be apparent that transborder television in Europe might become something quite different from Belgian channels hopping across the border into the Netherlands. In 1985–6 there was a rapid expansion in the number of satellite-carried channels now available to European cable systems.

Table 19.1 records the rapid growth of the larger channels during just seven months of the year 1986. The larger channels belonged to several quite different categories:

- Sky Channel was the (Murdoch-owned) pioneer which transmitted mainly American reruns; it was accepted by cable systems in several countries but lost money. Music Box was another British-based channel, just converting into 'Super Channel' which would offer British (ITV) reruns.
- There were several public subsidized channels. TV5 was a combined

Table 19.1 Satellite channel home connections across Europe, 1986

Channel	Language	Homes connected (millions)	
		Apr. 1986	Nov. 1986
Sky Channel	English	5.6	7.3
Music Box/Super Channel	English	3.8	5.2
TV5	French	3.5	4.3
RAI	Italian	1.4	2.9
Europa	Various	1.3	2.8
3-SAT	German	1.4	2.2
RTL-Plus	German	1.4	2.0
Worldnet	English	0.5	1.6
SAT-1	German	1.2	1.5
Children's Channel	English	0.1	0.2
Screensport	English	0.1	0.2

Source: Young and Rubicam Media (Jan. 1987).

effort of French language channels (Belgium, France, Switzerland, Canada); 3-Sat was a similar, German language offering. RAI was the Italian public service broadcaster. Worldnet was from the US Information Agency.

- Europa was a somewhat half-hearted offering subsidized by Brussels and the Netherlands government and featuring programming from public service broadcasters in Germany, Netherlands, Italy, Portugal, and Ireland. A muddled effort, without a clear goal or funding, it closed down before the end of 1996.[4]

Of these efforts the English language channels were quite significant—they were the forerunners of a subsequently small group of successful English language European channels, such as MTV and CNN. But it was two German-language channels (RTL Plus and Sat-1), transmitting into Germany, which were to establish what subsequently became the predominant satellite television pattern in Europe. 'Television without Frontiers'—or across frontiers—came to mean in particular the Home-Channel-from-across-the-frontier such as the German-language channel transmitting from Luxembourg into Germany; it also came to include, for example, the Swedish-language channel transmitting from London into Sweden. This home-channel-from-abroad transformed domestic television in a number of key countries, including Germany, Belgium, Netherlands, and across Scandinavia.

Linked to these new channels was one further important ingredient of the European swing to commercial TV. Advocacy of the 'independent production company' was common amongst European television people who accused the public broadcasters of being too bureaucratic and traditional. The Brussels policy-makers incorporated a substantial role for independent production into their plans. But the growth of 'independent production' in the 1980s did not merely encourage TV auteur-entrepreneurs; it also encouraged what became a big independent producer like Endemol, which specialized in cheap assembly line production of game shows, copied from American daytime television. The Dutch NOS, like other public service broadcasters, played its part in training up independents, who subsequently took their popular entertainment across the street to become the driving force behind new channels which were not only commercially financed but which entertained the public with their fellow citizens playing games in their own language.

One of the Endemol founders, Joop van den Ende, in 1989 switched all of his successful programming from the Dutch NOS to RTL's (Luxembourg-based) Dutch language, RTL4. Subsequently many of these shows were adapted for the German-language audience of the Luxembourg-German

[4] Richard Collins, *From Satellite to Single Market* (London: Routledge, 1998), 116–55.

channel, RTL Plus. Endemol, as a sizeable independent production company showed how a major new German channel (RTL Plus) could hold down programming production costs in two ways. First, RTL could give big programming contracts to a foreign (non-German) company. Second, Endemol could generate economies—for example in studio and sets—by making both Dutch and German versions of the same game show.

Another somewhat similar company was the Australian-owned Grundy, which developed ways of producing different local versions of the same show in a number of different countries. The (British) Pearson company subsequently acquired Grundy; with other acquisitions, including Thames Television and All American Fremantle, Pearson claimed by 1997 to be the world's largest game show company.

'Independent Production' in the late 1980s became a key ingredient in the alliance to deregulate television and to expand advertising finance from a minor to a major role in European TV. Independent Producers could see that more channels would bring them more work and less trade unions. 'Independent Producers' also generated lively stories for the newspapers, helping to create the impression across Europe that commercially oriented independents like Endemol were the wave of the future. Newspaper stories about plucky independent companies like Endemol and Grundy also conveniently obscured the more strategic point that the main winners of the 'Television without Frontiers' era were the old media, especially the newspapers and commercial television.

Spain Tries and Fails to be a Good European Media Player

The weakness of European media policy—and of TV without Frontiers—was especially evident in the case of Spain. When Spain entered the European Economic Community in 1986, it was the last of the larger population nations to join. Spain was certain to be an especially important test case for the emergence of an effective European media policy for some obvious reasons.

- Spain was a larger (almost 40 million) population country which joined the Community in 1986, at the height of enthusiasm both for TV without Frontiers and also of European enthusiasm for media deregulation in general and new TV channels in particular.
- General Franco did not die until 1975, ending four decades of military dictatorship in Spain. Against this recent background, Spain was keen to be seen to be Democratic, to be a good European nation and to have a correctly democratic mass media system.
- But Spain was also important for the future evolution of European media; Spain was the motherland of one of the world's most widely used languages. If European media were to be significant on the world scene, Spain would surely need to play a leading role.

- Finally, dictatorship had had in Spain the familiar impact of depressing and restricting all of the media. The Spanish media were shrivelled and backward by European standards; these media would surely be able to benefit from suitable assistance supplied by Spain's new European partners.

But in Spain a big European opportunity was largely wasted in the 1986–96 decade. Despite its initial wish to be a good media European, Spain behaved much like the other larger European countries; it somewhat reluctantly adopted, and somewhat spasmodically obeyed, Brussels's half-hearted collection of media regulations. Spain did enter into some European relationships—especially with the French media—but there was a strong element of European media companies seeing Spain as a market to be exploited, rather than as an equal partner.

It was, however with Hollywood and other US interests that Spain's more strategic media (and telecommunications) relationships were developed. Spain became an ever bigger importer from Hollywood of TV programming, movies, and also senior personnel. Spain was an enthusiastic supporter of pay-TV, which depended heavily on Hollywood movies. Moreover Spain's existing news agency (EFE) and telephone (Telefónica) markets in Latin America increasingly led Spain into strategic alliances with United States and Latin American companies. Thus Spain developed a media strategy which paralleled that of Britain (by looking towards Spanish speakers in North and South America). The Spanish strategy, of course, also paralleled those of France, Germany, and Italy in being nationalist first, American-leaning second, and European only third.

The Spanish media continue to be broadly spread and thinly financed. Emerging from dictatorial darkness into the democratic light, the Spanish media have followed a common European model by becoming intensely party politicized. Spain has a low level of daily newspaper circulation per population. Spanish women are especially unlikely to read a daily and Spanish newspapers are overloaded with politics and/or sport. Such is the daily barrage of partisan politics that most Spanish people find the press impenetrable. Even journalists themselves comment that they write stories with the relevant politicians, rather than any public readership, in mind. The state finally ceased to own newspapers in 1984, after a period in which many newspapers required subsidies in order to survive.

During 1975–89 Spain tried to follow the European public broadcasting path, but reached 1989 with its two public TV channels still (unusually for Europe) lacking licence fee finance. This meant that, as new channels were created, there was a destructive fight for advertising revenue. First came one (advertising and regional government supported) regional channel in six of the seventeen Spanish regions (two in the Basque Country). Next came the launch of two major commercial channels, Telecinco and Antena-3, in 1989.

This transformed the market and saw the public broadcaster (RTVE) sink into massive debt which from 1996 onwards increased by $1 billion per year. Obviously this increased RTVE's dependence on the government of the day.

Television competition radically reduced the price of advertising spots, and led to television being overloaded with commercials. The European Directive's maximum, of twelve advertising minutes per hour, was completely ignored and both Antena-3 and Telecinco were frequently fined by the European Commission. The shortage of television finance led to a heavy reliance on imported programming, mainly from the USA, but some also from Latin America. There was a high degree of concentration between the major press and TV companies. Each of the three main commercial TV companies—Antena-3, Telecinco, and Canal Plus España—had ownership links with a major newspaper group.

Spain followed the French-European lead when it allowed individual foreign companies to own 25 per cent of a Spanish commercial TV channel. But in return Italian, German, British, and French media companies all saw Spain as an investment opportunity. In their Spanish media activities several of these companies seemed to engage in self-caricature. Berlusconi's Italians were brash and flamboyant; the Germans did their 'panzer publishing' routine of introducing new publications with huge blasts of launch publicity and inducements; the British assumed a gentlemanly low profile, while acquiring two leading national newspapers. Hollywood got on with its standard routines of selling TV programming, dominating the movie business, and building multiplex cinemas in suitable suburbs.

The main Italian involvement was that of Silvio Berlusconi's Fininvest as 25 per cent owner, and management operator, of Telecinco, initially the more successful of the two big new commercial channels. But audiences tired of its quizzes, erotic programmes, and American imports and started to switch to Antena-3, which had poached most of Telecinco's best talent. Berlusconi brought with him to Spain not only his Italian advertising and programming practices but some of his famously mysterious finances. Spanish law restricted foreign ownership to 25 per cent of a channel, but Italian prosecutors at one time asserted that Berlusconi controlled 83 per cent of Telecinco.

The French connection was substantial. Hachette-Filipacchi became the number one magazine publisher in Spain. But it was the French connection with the Prisa company which was most significant. El País, Spain's leading elite (small format) newspaper was loosely modelled on Le Monde, France's leading elite (small format) newspaper. Like Le Monde, El País was an elite newspaper which leaned to the political left and was close to the left-of-centre governments which dominated Spanish politics in the immediate post-Franco years.

When Canal Plus came to Spain it did so in partnership with Prisa. Canal Plus was able to avoid some of the problems which hit the other channels. Only 10 per cent of its income came from advertising and this kept it out of the rate war that bled other networks. After 1993 Canal Plus España started to make substantial profits by offering the popular pay TV (subscription) channel mix of mainly sport and movies. As with Canal Plus in France, Canal Plus in Spain became not only a patron of its national film industry, but the major force in Spanish films.

In the mid-1990s Prisa was expanding further and further into the audio-visual media through Sogecable, Sogecine, Sogepaq, Sogetel, and other subsidiaries. This meant that Prisa was now a leading force in four media fields: first it owned *El País*, the leading Spanish newspaper; second it owned a major chain of radio stations; third it was the operator of the successful Canal Plus pay TV channel; fourth Prisa had become the leading player in the Spanish film industry, deeply involved in both film production and film distribution.

Then Prisa from 1995 began moving into yet another field—digital television. Like Canal Plus in France, Canal Plus España had strong digital television ambitions; this brought Prisa into head-on conflict with the Aznar Conservative government (elected March 1996). Spain was following the fashionable European idea of having two or more digital players. But the launch of the platforms was steeped in politics. The Conservative Aznar government attracted the attentions of Brussels as it somewhat crudely tried to hamper the progress of the Canal Plus digital service (Canal Satelite Digital), controlled by Grupo Prisa and friends. The government was reluctant to allow its old enemies to dominate in digital TV. They already had to endure continual criticism through the country's most prestigious newspaper, *El País*.

The Aznar government's conflict with Prisa and Canal Satelite also spread to Brussels, as Prisa protested about several Spanish media laws and government decisions. One government decision was a legal veto on Canal Satelite's use of a Canal Plus decoder already in use in France. A new element of tragi-comedy was a linked confrontation about televised football. Football games typically account for about half of the twenty largest TV audiences in Spain each year. The Aznar government—seeing the increasing control of TV football rights by the Prisa/Canal Satelite/Antena 3 forces—struck back with a 'Football Law'. Free-to-air channels were to be given more or less guaranteed control over football by having priority choice of weekly matches. This did not go down well with Canal Satelite or with the Spanish football league. Pay TV companies throughout Europe rallied together to lobby the European Commission.

This 'football war' was one aspect of a much wider conflict between two feuding 'media families'. In many ways this conflict was reminiscent of the two leading media families in Germany and other, somewhat similar, rivalries in Italy, France, and Britain.

But Spain was perhaps an extreme example of such conflicts in that so many communications issues were involved in one big confrontation. This happened partly because the Aznar government—arriving rather late on the scene in 1996—decided to oppose the Prisa 'family' on all available fronts, including an alliance with the state telephone operator, Telefónica, which, paradoxically, was already approaching total privatization. The conflict after 1996 encompassed not only the digital, and especially digital satellite future; also involved was cable TV, with half of all local franchises destined to belong to Telefónica. The Aznar government also had international media ambitions and became a strong supporter of a consortium which included Telefónica, the public broadcaster (RTVE), Televisa (the Mexican TV giant), and a number of newspaper, radio, and TV interests.

Like other new governments, the Aznar government could claim that they did not cause this extreme politicization into two communications families, one Socialist and one Conservative. Aznar could argue that Prisa and the Socialists were the first sinners. The Aznar government could also claim that clear Brussels policy on such issues was largely lacking. Indeed when the two founding digital TV operations decided to merge in 1998, Spain (like several other countries) found these merger arrangements being challenged on monopoly grounds by the Competition Directorate (DG4) in Brussels.

Once again, Europe seemed not to be learning the lessons of its previous media policy failures. Once again a significant European media power became somewhat disillusioned with Europe, and instead increasingly looked westward across the Atlantic. Europe, the home continent of two of the leading world languages (Spanish and English), had no plans or policies for—or thoughts about—either of these precious media assets.

20

A Policy for Film Auteurs, but None for Hollywood

EUROPE's numerous national 'film' industries have long had difficulty in competing with the Hollywood 'movie' industry. A crucial problem is the difference in scale. Just take the example of Italy, traditionally one of the world's great film-making nations. In the 1990s the Hollywood industry outspent the Italian industry, in terms of film production, by margins of around 25 or 30 to 1; in 1997 Hollywood outspent the Italian film industry by 33 to 1.[1] For publicity and production expenditure the imbalance is even greater. Other key inadequacies and difficulties for Europe include the following:

1. Europeans usually fail to assess the entirety of the Hollywood industry, with its numerous market windows across several kinds of television, cable, and video, besides theatre/cinema. Europe also tends to have a dated view of Hollywood and its contemporary commercial challenge. The 'bulking up' around 1995 of Hollywood into movie/TV network/cable network companies of greater vertical reach and strength seemed to be largely ignored in Europe.

2. Scale in general, and vertical scale in particular, has always been crucial to Hollywood's commercial strength. Europe has long been at a disadvantage because the Hollywood playing field is about as level as the Santa Monica Mountains. Two scale-related conundrums, which have long perplexed and immobilized European film people, are whether Europe should make its own big-budget 'Event' movies, and whether Europe needs its own Hollywood style worldwide distribution company. But these questions cannot be logically answered in the absence of a broader overall policy or strategy.

3. Meanwhile Europe has 101 separate industries—each with its own separate policy—across Europe's more than thirty countries. Each country effectively has three separate industries—a TV industry, second a small feature film industry (dependent on direct state subsidy and indirect state subsidy via television), and third a cinema exhibition industry which shows, and gets its profits predominantly from, Hollywood films. Against this

---

[1] *Screen Digest* (June 1998), 136.

comprehensively fragmented background, such European policy as exists is itself fragmented and contradictory.

4. Brussels has, in particular, pursued highly contradictory policies for television and film. The Brussels *TV without Frontiers* policy encouraged deregulation, channel multiplication, and commercial television. But the Brussels film policy accepted French assumptions about film art, film auteurs, and a complex collection of mini-subsidies. One of the few common characteristics of the film and TV policies was that both (unintentionally) assisted Hollywood exports into Europe.

5. Opposition between French and British policies was significant in film as also in television. Only in the late 1990s—with France and Britain accounting for three-fifths of EU film production expenditure—were these two countries beginning to recognize the errors of their previous opposition. Britain through most of the 1980s and 1990s acted as a laissez-faire, very junior, partner of Movie Hollywood. France persuaded Europe to adopt a slimmed down form of French film ideology, film subsidy, and lack of commercial dynamism.

6. Film is an extreme example of the general tendency of Media Europe to add up to less than the sum of its parts. Film Europe does not make adequate use of the available physical, cultural and financial resources. Not only Italy and France—but other European countries—have wonderful unique visual material. While TV Europe achieves huge sports audiences, Film Europe ignores such subjects. Even the end of the cold war—with its many dramatic and melodramatic (and criminal) elements has not received major film attention. Europe is natural road movie territory, but it makes few road movies. European film-makers and film policy-makers have focused obsessively on small fragments of subsidy money, while ignoring the involvement of truly large companies in the American industry.

Film Europe: From 1960s Co-Production into Continuing Decline

The film industries of Europe were at their most European in the decade 1958–68; but this successful European co-production era depended heavily on American finance. The years around 1960 were glory years for the European film industry. This was the era especially of Italian-French co-productions—which were distributed and part financed by Hollywood companies; Fellini's three-hour *La Dolce Vita* (1960) was one of numerous European films which were box office successes in the USA. The European industry had about 5 per cent of the US market (against 0.5 per cent three decades later).

The co-production era was part of Hollywood's solution to the problems of television; but, for the European film industry, the co-production era represented a high point before the main audience decline. The US movie (theatre) audience was roughly the same in 1960 as in 1995; but in 1995 the European movie audience was less than one-quarter of its 1960 level.

Why was the co-production era part of the solution for Hollywood but a key part of the problem for Europe? This happened partly because by 1960, the main impact of television had already been absorbed in the USA; moreover, Hollywood, having lost much of its cinema audience was now busy making TV programming. Hollywood was also cutting back on its annual production of feature films. By contrast, Europeans had been much slower to buy TV sets and in 1960 cinema attendance numbers were still high.

Also relevant was the post-1945 reluctance of European governments to allow the Hollywood distributors to repatriate their foreign-earned profits back to the USA. 'Blocked earnings' were, however, only one of several reasons for Hollywood's investment during the 1950s in making movies in Europe; production costs were significantly lower in Europe and there were fewer trade union problems than in Hollywood. Some European films offered an attractive mixture of sexual and intellectual titillation of a kind not found in American films in this conformist period; Hollywood's notoriously conservative and puritanical 'Production Code' was not dropped until 1966, meaning that previous to 1966 European films seemed more adult. The sheer size of the 1960 European market was enticing; moreover the production facilities especially in London and Rome (thanks to Mussolini), but also in France, compared favourably with Los Angeles. The European governments were quite Hollywood-friendly; much bending of the subsidy regulations was allowed, so long as the Hollywood companies provided plenty of cash for plenty of local employment.

This 1950s phase of European production by Hollywood shaded off into the next phase of 'co-production'. By 1955 the pattern was established. When co-production peaked in 1965 it had become the predominant film production pattern in Europe; three-quarters of all French and Italian films (and half of all German and Spanish films) in 1965 were co-productions.[2] Many co-productions involved two or three European countries plus a Hollywood distributor. Such a film might be able to pick up separate subsidies from two, or even three, countries. An Italian-French-Hollywood production, with perhaps some scenes filmed in Germany or Britain, could appeal to audiences in all four countries.

Increasingly, however, these Italian-French, and then other, co-productions did not work smoothly. As more Europeans purchased TV sets, European cinema audiences fell by nearly half in the 1960s decade. Moreover, as more normal international trade conditions returned, Hollywood's 'blocked earnings' problem declined in importance. The Hollywood

[2] Thomas Guback, *The International Film Industry* (Bloomington: Indiana University Press, 1969), 164–97.

companies began to pack their bags and return home to California. In 1966 the Production Code disappeared and Hollywood began to make movies which were more adult, both sexually and politically.

But, while the ending of the co-production era in the late 1960s was a fairly gentle transition for Hollywood, it was a much more uncomfortable experience for Film Europe. European film companies faced several linked difficulties; the Hollywood distributors were no longer providing production finance and access to world markets; the European cinema audience continued its relentless decline. Meanwhile Hollywood was a more aggressive competitor, and an 'independent' film industry was added to the Hollywood majors' mainstream; these insurgent independents made lower-budget movies, and became the junior league—and training arena—for big league Hollywood. With their more innovative, sexy, and nonconformist approaches these 'independents' invaded the segment of the US market which the Europeans had held.

Different European countries had different problems. Britain was the earliest to experience steep decline in box office revenue (in the 1950s). Germany had a massive drop in the 1960s. The Italian box office held up well until 1975 and then plunged down very steeply in the Berlusconi era of many TV channels.

France had a different experience from all of the other larger countries (including Spain). Compared with other bigger countries, the French box office experienced a much gentler decline. France was unusually short of cinemas in the 1950s and better supplied with cinemas than the rest of Europe in the 1980s and 1990s. Some of this was due to subsidy. But the French film industry never suffered crisis and disaster on the same scale as did other film industries across Europe. The French industry has remained more confident (or self-satisfied) and more financially successful (or subsidized) than have the other industries. In 1997 the official government film office (CNC) gave various subsidies to the French film industry which equalled about two-thirds of the entire production cost of all films made in France that year.

Cultural Subsidy, National Auteurs, Canal Plus

In the 1980s France backed its national film policy with added infusions of subsidy money and regulatory detail. In the same period, French films—once admired across Europe—largely lost their remaining European audience and reputation. Nevertheless Brussels began to establish its own Europe-wide film policy, closely modelled on France's unpopular and unsuccessful measures. The French state in the late 1980s and through the 1990s had three main film policy planks. Canal Plus, a 1980s innovation, was added to the French doctrines of the *auteur* and the *subsidy*.

What became the officially French state-approved doctrine of the film auteur had print-on-paper origins; the notion of the authored film was propagated by a group of French film critics, which included such subsequently celebrated film directors as Claude Chabrol, Jean-Luc Godard, and François Truffaut. From its Marxist literary intellectual origins, Auterism venerated the film director as artist-author; auteur doctrine was explicitly opposed to the Hollywood industry, although a few Hollywood directors were seen as heroic exceptions to the commercial norms of the American dream machine. Auteurism then developed from a cultural doctrine into an official French state doctrine, supported by ministers and indeed by President Mitterrand; it involved a somewhat sentimental remembrance of things past, of the heroic 1960s, and of the lost time of Great French Film Art.

By the 1990s auterist doctrine was deeply embedded in the French film industry. Auteurism, of course, was used to justify extensive subsidies; these filmic authors were to be celebrated for something other than their popularity with the great French cinema public. In practice the doctrine of the Director/Author atrophied the key film skill of scriptwriting; many French films either had an inadequate script or a scriptwriter (having won the subsidy prize) now performing inadequately as the director.

By focusing fame and subsidy on a single auteur, the doctrine ignored the fact that many good films have depended on the combined performance of four roles (writer, producer, director, and lead actors) by three, four, or more people. The auteur doctrine taught the film-maker that neither box office popularity nor subsequent television rating was crucial. What mattered most was 'artistic merit' as defined by highly politicized committees of cultural bureaucrats in Paris and by committees of auteurs, press critics, and cultural bureaucrats at film festivals.

Canal Plus was the key French film policy innovation of the 1980s. Canal Plus was awarded the crucial combined advantages of being both a conventional terrestrial TV channel, and also being a pay channel funded by subscriptions. Moreover in order to give Canal Plus a successful launch, the entire new medium of video (itself destined soon to become a huge market window) was deliberately delayed, taxed, and handicapped by the French state. After a shaky start (like many new channels), Canal Plus became successful and increasingly profitable. In film terms, however, it was an ambiguous innovation. In addition to being a showcase for new French films, Canal Plus also served up a continuous menu of fresh Hollywood films; it also carried sporting events and documentaries. Moreover, Canal Plus was aided by yet another special policy dispensation, giving it a monopoly French legal franchise to show pornographic films on a mainstream channel. Flagged as 'érotique' and 'pour adultes seulement' the month's porn film was shown after midnight, with repeats. As an example, Canal Plus was showing during October 1996 *Devil in Miss Jones 5* which included such characters as Rip Hymen (*Le diable*) and Barbara Doll (*une créature blonde*); the auteur-director of this film was Gregory Dark, whose previous films included *New Wave Hookers 2*.[3]

Canal Plus itself played a key role in French film subsidy policy. Canal Plus was required by law to show French films and this meant in practice that nearly 100 new French films were shown on Canal Plus each year. For a typical lowish-budget French film, the fee paid by Canal Plus would cover about 40 per cent of the film's production cost; the main ASR (*avance sur recettes*) film subsidy would pay for 20 per cent or more. The ASR subsidy process, heavily slanted towards 'artistic merit', was crucial in greenlighting a film project. Canal Plus in practice had little choice and would normally accept almost any film project with an ASR subsidy. Thus the Canal Plus money was itself subsidy-triggered, and the initial ASR committee decision typically generated directly and indirectly about two-thirds of the film's total production cost. Nor did the dominating influence of state policy stop even here. All French TV channels were also legally required to show French films; consequently the typical French film could expect (some months after its Canal Plus showing) to appear for a substantial fee on one of the 'free' TV channels.[4]

A representative French film, before it appeared in any cinemas, might have secured around 80 per cent of its production cost. Given the crucial importance of the initial subsidy decision, based on artistic merit, French film-makers inevitably were less than totally committed to commercial success at the cinema box office. Indeed through the 1990s the average French citizen saw just one French film per year in a cinema.

French television channels were forbidden to show films at certain hours on certain days of the week; the intention here was to encourage French citizens into cinema visits. Another regulation prohibited the advertising of films on television; this measure was intended to outlaw the heavy TV marketing of American blockbuster movies, although the TV promotion of films-on-video was still allowed.

These cultural and film policies were associated especially with Culture Minister Jack Lang in the 1980s. In 1981 French films still had 50 per cent of their home market; in 1991—after a decade of higher subsidies—the share was down to 30 per cent. But official supporters of Auteurism, Canal Plus, Subsidy, and Regulation could point to the relative 'success' of the French film industry compared with all other countries in western Europe. Through the 1990s decade French films held about 32 per cent of the French cinema

[3] *Canal + Le Magazine des Abonnes* (Oct. 1996).
[4] Martin Dale, *The Movie Game* (London: Cassell, 1997), 135–8, 187–8.

market, with the American share kept down to the low (by European standards) share of about 57 per cent.

Such domestic French film 'success' as was achieved had led to negative consequences abroad, as well as at home. During the period of increased film subsidy, the French film industry had largely lost its previously strong export markets in Italy and Germany. French films also lost in terms of 'artistic merit', as judged at prestigious international film festivals.

Most Brussels film initiatives of the 1990s were based on these French policies, which gave little weight to the preferences of either the cinema audience or the television audience. Film has traditionally depended largely on the preferences of young adults; to give middle-aged (and socially elite) judges of 'artistic merit' such a big influence ran against the traditions of French film. The weight of state support for auteurism in this extremely politicized country, led to the politicization of French film both in terms of political partisanship and in terms of the centrality of lobbying to acquire subsidy support.

French audio-visual policy of the 1990s was still heavily shaped by the decisions of the 1980s, especially the Mitterrand decisions in TV commercialization. These decisions in effect generated three separate French audio-visual products: first super-commercial and highly Americanized TV (as represented by TF1); second the two remaining public channels, still retaining some public service element; and third the elite 'artistic' ghetto of the French film (as opposed to the vulgar American movie).

The French film policies were merely the most high-profile example of film subsidy policies operated around Europe. In the later 1990s the fifteen EU countries were producing over 600 films each year; a typical subsidy level was $1 million per film. This subsidy might be paying most of the costs of a Norwegian film, or perhaps 20–25 per cent of the production cost of a German film. Individual countries often had several different bodies engaged in film subsidy. In Germany a regional subsidy system developed, which helped to create a regionally fragmented German film industry; this film industry—of Europe's leading commercial power—was in the 1990s quite happy if it could achieve a 15 per cent share in its home market.

Brussels adopted the French approach of a battery of several small film subsidies. But Brussels failed to adopt either France's matching provision of a few big subsidies or the French policy of giving extra subsidies and support to the already highly privileged. This European film policy was little more than a token 1990s correction to Brussels' enthusiastic advocacy (and competition policy support) for commercial television in the 1980s. The 1980s swing to commercial television inevitably penalized the public television channels. Subsequently national governments decided—and Brussels approved—to penalize their public channels further. The remaining public channels were required to pay highish prices for fairly unpopular films; this was in effect a public TV subsidy for film.

The public TV 'subsidy' of film not only pleased the film industries across Europe but was also highly acceptable to major press groupings as well as to their political and business friends in commercial television. Several press/commercial TV companies (such as Prisa in Spain and Bertelsmann/UFA in Germany) entered the film business.

Because prestige and political connections were so important, press comment and press support played a central part within each national film industry. Moreover, because so many European films were distributed by small companies, free news coverage and friendly reviews were more important for national films than for Hollywood blockbusters.

The Brussels launch of a European film policy took shape mainly in the form of MEDIA I (1990–5) and MEDIA II (1996–2000). These two MEDIA efforts were the work of the Brussels DG10. MEDIA I spent $250 million on a bewildering array of small projects; it had no less than nineteen separate support schemes dealing with archives, business (film) education, cartoons, documentaries, and so on. MEDIA I's European Script Fund supported 800 scripts of which, one critic says, only twenty were linked to films which achieved a modicum of either commercial or critical success.[5]

MEDIA I was widely criticized for its 'watering can' approach of sprinkling small drops of subsidy in all directions. MEDIA II concentrated primarily on film distribution. But here again the 'think small' approach was in evidence; the distribution subsidy was spread around on many low-budget film projects. These included 1,700 distribution campaigns in theatres covering 280 films; 2,000 works published in video by 200 companies; 250 television programmes, 100 catalogues, and 100 'promotion initiatives'—over 4,000 items, many of which were receiving grants of $30,000 or less. Behind this there lay the European assumption that small independent companies were good, while small independent companies from Europe's smaller countries were even better. This was a policy likely to cause more laughter than sleepless nights in Beverly Hills.

Britain and a European Film Revival?

Film has seen the familiar European pattern of national markets dominated by a combination of Hollywood and national product, with the output of other European countries only receiving a very small market share. Although a large minority of all European films are 'co-productions', many of these involve such same-language combinations as France–Belgium and Germany–Austria. During the 1990s German-French co-productions became rare, almost to the point of non-existence.

[5] Dale, *The Movie Game*, 216.

During the 1990s increasing attention focused on the advantages of Euro-British film projects of various kinds. Polygram built up Europe's largest film enterprise in the 1990s; although controlled by Philips of the Netherlands, Polygram Filmed Entertainment developed a collection of film 'labels' in which British subsidiaries (such as Working Title), and British personnel, were prominent; the management focused on London and Los Angeles. The biggest commercial success of PFE was the stereotypically British *Four Weddings and a Funeral.*

Lower-cost, and perhaps lower-risk, strategies were pursued for a variety of Franco-British projects. Such activities included French productions filmed in English; traditional French-British co-productions; British Lottery funding supporting an Anglo-French company; British art films being financed by Canal Plus and even achieving larger audiences in France than in Britain.

Most 'film revivals' have had a short time span. Even against the background of a gradual move towards a single Euro-American media industry, the cinema film (especially the bigger budget film) may be an exception and may remain exclusively American. British participation may not be enough; but without prominent British participation a continuing European film revival seems unrealistic.

Still no Hollywood Strategy

Hollywood does not need to operate a specific policy of divide-and-rule, because in audio-visual terms Europe is already so deeply divided into separate national markets, each of which has a well-developed taste for what Hollywood offers. Each country has its own 'film industry'; even Iceland (population 260,000) makes about two feature films a year. Most smaller population countries make ten or more a year; invariably there is a national film subsidy and a 'film policy' presided over by a mix of several departments and ministers. Typically the national film subsidies go to films of artistic ambition and national historical or cultural significance.[6]

It is domestic (own-language) comedies which often attract the biggest national cinema audiences; many successful comedies acquire their popularity by using the leading national television comedy talents. Such 'commercial' and TV-linked genres as comedy are not favoured by the film subsidy process; and most such national comedies are unappealing, while the comedians are unknown to the publics of other European countries.

A key European dilemma is the remarkable recent weakness of the film industries of some larger countries, especially Germany, Spain, and Italy. Despite Germany's sizeable population, only seven German films in 1997

---

[6] Tytti Soila, Astrid Söderbergh Widding, and Gunnar Iverson, *Nordic National Cinemas* (London: Routledge, 1998), 233–42.

attracted a German cinema audience of even one million (while thirty-nine US films and two UK films achieved this). The commercial and artistic successes of Italian films belong to the past; in the era of Berlusconi the Italian film industry became a prominent casualty. In Spain, also, the performance of the film industry has been very modest. In Spain, as in Germany and Italy, even the weak film industry which does exist would be completely dead without television finance.

The European film industries, meanwhile, effectively provide several kinds of financial support for Hollywood. The European industries buy the local rights to large amounts of Hollywood product. In some cases European distributors are willing to take on some of the risk of funding a Hollywood movie; in order to obtain the local national rights to a particular Hollywood movie, a European distributor may contract for advance, or pre-sale, payment. European retailers each year sell over 250 million video-cassettes, most of which are Hollywood products.

European companies have also rather generously outbid the field in order to purchase failing Hollywood companies; one example was the wasteful Canal Plus investment in Carolco. However, easily the most disastrous Hollywood adventures were those of the huge French bank, Crédit Lyonnais. In the early 1990s it funded Hollywood companies to the tune of $2.5 billion. The bulk of these unwise loans involved MGM and the Italian 'financier', Giancarlo Parretti.[7]

The early 1990s were among the worst ever years for several national film industries around Europe. But optimists noted in the later 1990s several signs of improved life chances; box office returns were up; there was a boom in new pay film channels; European co-productions were hugely increased in number and general significance.

However, the European film business needs to advance quite quickly even to stay in the same (bad) position relative to a relentlessly expanding Hollywood industry. As it bulked up in the mid and late 1990s Hollywood was anticipating further sizeable growth at home (especially in new channels and via the various video windows). But Hollywood was anticipating faster film business growth abroad and in Europe particularly.

Distribution remains the key to the international movie business. For any would-be major player the serious money is in distribution; in order to ensure a steady flow of attractive product you must also be in production— both directly making your own movies, and also picking up productions from independents. You need to be in both film and television; and you need to be a serious player inside the US market. The ultimate business goals are to make an annual profit and also to build a valuable library of product available for reshowing around the world. To succeed in this you require big

---

[7] 'The bank, the studio, the mogul and the lawyers', *The Economist*, 23 Jan. 1993, pp. 79–80.

capital resources, some luck, and a lot of company commitment over an extended period of years. Those people who argue that Europe's film industry could seriously rival Hollywood are implying that Europe would need to own and operate not just one, but more than one, international distribution major. This appears unrealistic. Europe might do better to leave the big budget 'event' films to Hollywood.

Still no TV-Video-Film European Strategy to Confront Hollywood

Europe—at both the national and Brussels levels—seems to suffer from too many separate policies. In particular there is a lack of fit between film and TV policy. Television policy is politically and commercially driven; film policy is politically and culturally driven. In contrast there is little or no interest in having policies for video or audio; meanwhile the newspaper press lurks in the background, exerting crucial pressures—and conferring prestige and artistic kudos—across the entire media range.

Despite the huge fragmentation of policy, a sole Hollywood bulked-up vertical entertainment industry is the biggest single entity within European media. Hollywood films account for about two-thirds of all European cinema visits. Television audiences—even in the five largest countries—have become used to the bulk of fictional programming (drama series, situation comedies, and feature films) coming from Hollywood.[8] In video rental and purchase across Europe Hollywood feature films account for about half of all expenditure; other Hollywood material (including television series and mini-series) takes the total well above half of all European video expenditure.[9]

Europe is inward looking, not only in films, but also in television. Over 90 per cent of European television fiction is set and located within its home country of production. The lack of concern with TV exporting is exemplified by the very small number of episodes in a typical European TV production run; France, Germany, Britain, and Italy were averaging runs of seven episodes per year in their 1996 television fiction output. In contrast, a less confident and more humbled Spanish TV industry was following American (North and South) patterns with a typical annual production run of twenty-six episodes. France, as late as 1996 was still making TV fiction lasting either 25 minutes or 90 minutes and ignoring the one-hour length almost entirely.[10] Only in the late 1990s did French television producers start to

[8] Milly Buonanno (ed.), *Imaginary Dreamscapes: Television Fiction in Europe.* (Luton: University of Luton Press, 1998.)

[9] 'European Video Software', *Screen Digest* (Aug. 1998), 177–84.

[10] Buonanno, *Imaginary Dreamscapes*, 8–11.

make TV fictions to match the international standard length of one hour (or 50 minutes).

In retrospect it was widely agreed that in the 1980s or early 1990s most west European countries had increased their numbers of television channels ahead of their capacity to fill them with domestically made programming. Nevertheless, a decade or more later, much more programming was being produced. Germany, for example, despite having seven or eight largish audience channels was now producing much more, especially of its prime-time programming. But these seven or eight German channels were still showing some 100 films a week (mostly from Hollywood). They were also importing large quantities of Hollywood television series.

A big contrast had developed by the late 1990s between the largest audience slots in the schedule and all of the rest of the twenty-four hours. Across Europe by the late 1990s most of the prime-time slots, especially on the larger audience channels, were occupied by domestically made dramas, soap operas, comedies, game shows, and sports. But this was just during the three or four prime-time hours.

However, across Europe there was still a huge amount of Hollywood material in the 'fringe' hours just before (such as 4–7 p.m.), and in the hours immediately after, prime time (such as 11 p.m.–1 a.m.). Huge amounts of Hollywood material were also scheduled for children, for the daytime home audience generally, and at weekends. In 1996 the main German networks were showing 245 hours per week of Hollywood 'fiction'; this did not include 'factual' imports.

While Hollywood was losing its grip on European TV prime time and failing to achieve the highest level of TV audiences, Hollywood was perhaps also tightening its grip on much of 'fringe' and daytime on numerous European networks. Moreover, by focusing their production money on prime time, the European networks were forced to fix very low budgets for programming scheduled at other times. This can easily mean that in daytime, at 5 p.m., or at 11 p.m., a Hollywood series which originally was produced for $1 million per hour (or a multi-million dollar film) is competing in the same time slot with programming whose production cost only a few per cent of this sum.

European governments and Brussels officials were aware of these problems; but it was only a few large companies which were seriously confronting them. 'Bouquet' is, of course, a French word coined for use in the brave new world of multi-channel TV companies. Canal Plus—whatever the weaknesses of its film strategy—was nevertheless a European leader in being a major force in television, in film, in satellite digital delivery, and in developing its bouquet business across Europe.

A few other European companies were also seeking to compete with the bulked-up vertical Hollywood players. When Polygram Filmed Entertainment was sold by its vertical owner, Philips, in 1998, no other European company stepped forward to carry the torch. Polygram had in effect become a leading 'Independent' film company, but it still had a long way to go to become a 'major' on the Hollywood model; its television activities were still quite modest; it still only had a few film successes (mainly from its Working Title subsidiary in Britain); and, despite its access to Philips/Polygram music offices across the world, it was still well short of a genuinely worldwide distribution organization. PFE had nevertheless lost over $1 billion in getting thus far. It was presumably the prospect of further substantial losses which made the other European companies hold back.

While Polygram Filmed Entertainment was 'not big enough' seriously to take on Hollywood, other big European companies with interests in both film and television may find the competition/monopoly authorities (domestically and in Brussels) thinking them to be too large. We return to this monopoly issue in Chapter 23.

21

Sports Media: Advantage Europe, Game USA

In sports media we find yet another example of Europe's overall performance being less than the sum of its national and local parts. The United States, despite having a fairly weak portfolio of sports in terms of international appeal, has been able to become an international media sports power. Meanwhile Europe—the clear leader in the most global of sports, such as (soccer) football and both the summer and winter Olympics—has squandered its media sporting assets.

Once more also, Britain—the mother country of numerous sports and the mother country of the sporting (British) Commonwealth—has not played an adequate role in Europe. The prevailing picture across the continent is one of sports nationalism. The audience enthusiasm, the finance, and the political concerns have focused heavily on national sports in general and upon each European nation's own top football league in particular.

Television sport developed across Europe in a monopolistic way; typically the national public service broadcaster took its pick of the national sporting treasures and paid little for them. During the 1980s and into the 1990s European TV sport developed more competitively, often with competition between the main public broadcaster and a newer commercial network. This increased the hours of sport available on TV per week and also radically increased the sums of money paid per hour and per annual contract.

The 'competitive' phase was then followed by a new era of all-sports channels competing against traditional broadcast networks. From the mid-1990s onwards a new American era dawned involving DirecTV and its digital satellite to home competitors as well as enhanced cable systems. Europe also launched a number of new satellite and digital sports channels. This new era promised future profusion, with a number of competing sports networks per household as well as a lengthy menu of possible pay-per-event, pay-per-team, pay-per-league, and other sport offerings.

The digital TV sports revolution has involved both new technologies and new industrial strategies. The new technologies make possible not only pay-per-view and multiple digital sports channels but also the combination of these with Internet and other interactive technologies. The Internet is available to provide additional sports back-up material, and ESPN with its Sports

Zone quickly became one of the most visited US Internet sites. The Internet is also available as a system for merchandising sports stars and products, selling tickets, supporting advertisers, consolidating the brand, and much else.

Network strategies have increasingly given a prominent place to sports. The sports network has become a key ingredient in the 'bouquet' or bunch of offerings. To change the metaphor, sports networks and programming can act as 'flagships' of the big media enterprise—the uniquely prestigious and exclusive entertainment programming, contractually denied to competitors.

The superstar sports personality was another element of this sporting revolution. The superstar often became as prominent in advertising endorsements, and in popular culture generally, as in the specific sport. Alongside this 'superstaring' and 'popular culturing' of sport there was the 'human interesting' or, perhaps, 'soap opera-ing' of sport. At least from the 1984 Los Angeles Olympics onwards, American network coverage focused heavily on the selected (American) athlete's personality, family, home town, and early struggles; the actual athletic performance often seemed to take second place. The 1994 on-and-off-the-ice saga of two American contestants in women's figure skating generated astronomical US TV ratings (48 and 44) for the Winter Olympics in Lillehammer, Norway.

Televised sport can indeed uniquely present genuine raw human emotion in live action; while most TV is pre-recorded and/or acted, much sporting TV presents live performance and real emotion. Moreover, much sporting success or failure is 'in the mind'. Viewers can recognize the psychological struggles especially in individual sports like tennis, gymnastics, skating, or golf, but also in team sports. We can empathize with players who 'choke' and with gallant skaters who get up off the ice and finish fourth. There is also the 'soap opera' appeal of watching frequently and knowing this very particular little world, its recurring melodramas, its rags-to-riches story-lines, its sudden incapacitating accidents, its startling plot twists and improbable coincidences, its in close-up stars and villains.

Sport is unusual in the strength of its appeal to certain committed minorities. Many football fans retain a lifelong loyalty to a team they first watched as boys. Both club teams and national teams can also be supported against foreign opponents. All of this translates into a willingness to pay premium rates in order to view live premium sport.

Television executives—confronted by these waves of sporting enthusiasm and potential sporting profit—are naturally keen to rearrange the sports, and especially the scheduling—so as to generate the most emotional appeal and the most cash flow. This means arranging and scheduling sports programming for the highly committed and knowledgeable niche audience. But there is also the wider, more occasional, sports audience, which only views the biggest events, or the final rounds of the Olympics or the Football World Cup.

One of the oddities of TV sport is that the wider, non-expert, audience is often most interested in things which are hardly 'sport' at all as traditionally defined. Some of these are recent innovations such as extreme sports or volley ball. Various kinds of 'motor sport' are super-popular, but not everyone's idea of sport; some popular TV 'sports' are artistic activities such as figure skating and ice-dancing. Other non-sporting sports are the old warhorses, boxing and wrestling. Boxing is not respectable on health and other grounds, which has been a major embarrassment for pay-per-view. Wrestling—long presented as 'entertainment', not sport—has long played a key ratings role for American cable television. At the digital dawn these 400-pound human cartoon characters were among America's most watched sporting stars.

European Sports Strength Dissipated by Sports Nationalism

Sport is another 'cultural' area in which western Europe has chosen to cultivate the local and the national rather than the European. Despite Europe being the leader in most of the world's most popular sports, the US tends to lead in the media presentation of sport. Despite there being many European sporting competitions, the only well-established Europe versus USA sporting encounter is Ryder Cup golf; and even the Ryder Cup was originally a British–USA contest.

Europe is the clear leader in all of the sports events which attract the largest television audiences around the world, namely (soccer) football, the summer and winter Olympics (and other international athletics contests), and Formula One motor racing. The main television presentation of each of these sports has traditionally been in the hands of public service broadcasting organizations. These public broadcasters have combined together in the European Broadcasting Union (EBU) to acquire the rights cheaply; but their television presentation has always stressed the narrow national interest, not the European interest. More recently, most European countries saw a migration of popular sports from public to commercial television, but here again the emphasis was on the domestic national football league and other national contests. In each of the years from 1995 several new all-sports networks appeared in Europe. But they were all *national*, not European, all-sports networks.

In the first three decades after 1945, western Europe had a united front in terms of media sports. Until about 1975 the EBU (and its public service members) largely prevailed. But from the mid-1970s onwards divisions appeared, especially between a still public service northern Europe and a more Berlusconi-Latin-commercially inclined southern Europe.

Until the mid-1970s the EBU approach prevailed not only in Europe, but broadly across all major international sporting contests. The United States networks also paid what were, by later standards, only token sums for both domestic and international sports rights. Until the 1970s the Americans and the British played prominent leadership roles. These two countries were seen as leaders in all aspects of television and not least of sports TV. The 1948 Olympic Games took place in London, meaning that the BBC (with this unique 1948 television experience) then provided television advice for the 1952 summer Olympics in Helsinki;[1] the 1956 Olympics were in Melbourne, thus continuing the Anglo theme. Americans and Britons (often of advanced ages) played leading administrative roles.

Britain also had a prominent role in the world football body, FIFA. Two Englishmen (Arthur Drewry, and then Stanley Rous) were presidents of FIFA for eighteen years, 1956–74; both believed in a very public service and BBC conception of football as a game first and a business only second.

There was a radical change, however, in FIFA when the Brazilian, João Havelange, took over as FIFA President (and stayed for twenty-four years, 1974–98). In contrast to Stanley Rous, who had a schoolteaching background, Havelange was a wealthy Brazilian newspaper owner, who had also acquired a Brazilian television station. Under Havelange international football and the football World Cup took advantage of the possibilities provided by satellite technology to create a worldwide live audience. From the 1970s, the sums of money involved in TV rights, sponsorship, advertising, and related merchandising rose rapidly. An even more rapid revolution occurred in athletics and many other previously amateur sports in the Olympic games.

Although the German Adidas company was a leader in the merchandising side of these revolutions, northern Europe in general, the public broadcasters, and not least the BBC, looked on aghast at these commercial developments. Increasingly huge swathes of international sport seemed to many northern eyes to be presided over by a gerontocracy of Latin millionaires.

The fascist past of Spain's Antonio Samaranch, president of the International Olympic Committee, has been well documented. . . . other objects of Anglo-Saxon suspicion are Primo Nebiolo, a Milanese construction magnate who has been head of the International Amateur Athletics Federation for almost two decades, and Joao Havelange, a Brazilian millionaire. . . . who has been president since 1974 of FIFA, the governing body for world soccer. Such men, say their critics, have simply put their sports up for sale to the highest bidder—and grown powerful in the process.'[2]

One recurring accusation was that these sports administrators had tolerated

[1] Briggs, Sound and Vision, 270–4, 495–6, 846–7.
[2] 'The World of Sport', The Economist, 6 June 1998.

large-scale drug abuse by East German (and other) athletics and swimming teams, despite the artificially bulked-up bodies being clearly visible to TV viewers. Money, merchandising, marketing—and television rights, sponsorship, and advertising—seemed to have prevailed over honesty, good sense, and good health. There were also accusations (many subsequently documented) that cities bidding for future Olympics were systematically bribing selected International Olympic Committee (IOC) decision-makers.

These developments split Europe between north and south both in the Olympics and especially in football. The TV commercialization of football—including the buying up of Latin American talent—moved most rapidly in Italy and alongside (and as part of) the Berlusconi revolution in television from the late 1970s onwards.

Gradually the rest of western Europe followed the Italian and Spanish lead in football. Britain through the 1980s continued to be the most traditional of the larger countries. In the 1990s the commercial and pay television revolutions advanced rapidly first in France and Britain, and then across Europe. But the media presentation of some European sports still fell awkwardly between the public service bargain and the super-expensive pay operation. The United States has, of course, maintained a much more consistent commercial emphasis. But, paradoxically, while European countries saw live football and other live sport migrating to 'pay TV', in the USA the expensively acquired live sports still mainly appeared on 'free TV'; recognizing the popularity of expensive sport on free TV, many Washington politicians wanted to retain as much free TV sport as possible, even in the digital era.

Football (soccer) is clearly the world's most played and most popular game and equally clearly it is dominated by Europe and Latin America. Most of the world's best players—including the South Americans, East Europeans, and Africans—play for West European clubs. Meanwhile the traditional European pattern of national football leagues—with several superimposed European cup competitions—was seen by many as requiring major reforms, including some kind of European football super-league.

Once more, much of the impetus for 'reform' or further 'commercialization' came from Italy in general and from Milan in particular. Italy already had an established tradition of 'vertical' connections between big companies, big media, and big football. Fiat owned Juventus as well as newspapers; Silvio Berlusconi was the owner of AC Milan as well as of most Italian commercial television. The movie mogul Vittorio Cechi Gori owned the Florence team, Fiorentina. Now in 1996, as the digital age dawned, the Milan-based Media Partners negotiated Europe's first pay-per-view football contract for the Italian league. In 1998 four top Italian football clubs (AC Milan, Inter Milan, Juventus, and Napoli) made an exclusive pay-TV deal with Canal Plus. It was also the Milan trio of Media Partners and the two big

Milan football clubs (plus Juventus) which took the lead in a proposed European football league that would include three teams from each of the big countries.

European countries together collect most of the medals in the summer Olympics, while European countries dominate the Winter Olympics.[3] But Europe—using its combined public service buying power (EBU)—gets the Olympics coverage quite cheaply. Thus a single high-bidding United States network (NBC) paid 55 per cent of the Sydney 2000 Olympics TV revenue; while the EBU paid only 27 per cent. The imagery of the Olympics is given a further strong American gloss by the dominance of US multi-nationals, such as Coca-Cola, McDonald's, and Kodak among the 'global sponsors'. The centrality of American TV, sponsorship, and advertising finance in the Olympic Games meant that of six Summer Olympics in the 1976–96 period three took place in the USA and Canada (Montreal 1976; Los Angeles 1984; Atlanta 1996). Even the inclusion of new Olympic sports was straight out of *USA Today*; the Atlanta games saw volley ball, softball, women's soccer, and mountain biking included for the first time.

Formula One motor racing claims to attract the biggest world audiences after the Olympics and World Cup football. The seventeen races per year are seen by huge audiences, but the cars, the drivers, and the race locations are predominantly European. This is one interesting exception to the rule that the big international sports TV finance tends to be American. Formula One has—perhaps more than any other 'sport'—been redesigned around the purpose of embedding its advertising (trackside, on-car, and on-driver) into the TV programming. The urge to slow down the cars for safety purposes has been combined with the commercial desirability of slowing down the cars for advertising purposes; numerous additional sharp bends have been introduced which just happen to show off the advertising to maximum effect.

Cycling is another sport in which Europe leads. The Tour de France, as the premier cycling event, is widely regarded as one of the world's most physic-ally demanding contests as well as the world's most televisually pleasing sporting contests. Yet this gem of the European sporting calendar has not escaped from its close association with the idiosyncratic Amaury (*L'Équipe*) newspaper group and French advertising; drug abuse seems to have been positively encouraged by the advertising-driven major cycling teams. The drug revelations of the 1998 Tour painted a distinctly negative picture of this supposedly super-fit and super-healthy sport. Meanwhile Coca-Cola, main sponsor of the Tour de France, somehow escaped without significant criticism.

In terms of international sports leadership, the main American-led sports

[3] The 1998 Winter Olympics medal table was led by 1. Germany 2. Norway 3. Russia 4. Canada 5. United States 6. Holland 7. Japan 8. Austria.

have been American Football, baseball, basketball, and boxing. The National
Football League (NFL) has—with the assistance of various sponsors and TV
interests—attempted to make an end run around the massed defences of
European soccer and rugby. Despite much newspaper and some TV coverage, it has failed to get much past novelty status. For most Europeans,
American Football lacks continuous action and is too slow, too cluttered
with on-screen quantification, and too spliced up by advertising breaks.

Basketball is the one big weapon of potential world hegemony for US
sport. Basketball has universal appeal. It is played indoors, as well as in the
street and the suburban driveway. The smallish playing area means that
individuals loom large on the TV screen, thus allowing the audience to
identify with star players and their clothing. With these bland and
innocuous materials, the NBA has set out in relentless pursuit of world
domination.

Battered Britain: A Euro-Sports Loss

> Sport absolutely overpowers film and everything else in the entertain-
> ment genre . . . . Football, of all sports, is number one. Look at what we
> have done in Britain with our Premier League soccer, and now with
> rugby union and rugby league in the United Kingdom as well. We
> expect the next three World Cups will have a significant place on our
> platforms. Sport will remain very important and we will be investing in
> and acquiring long-term rights . . . .
>
> [There is] one development which is very pleasing in our sports
> programming in India, which was beginning to get very expensive . . .
> We have now formed a partnership with our former sports program-
> ming competition, ESPN of the United States.
>
> We have the long-term rights in most countries to major sporting
> events and we will be doing in Asia what we intend to do elsewhere in
> the world, that is, use sports as a 'battering ram' and a lead offering in
> all our pay television operations.'
>
> Rupert Murdoch, 15 October 1996 (speaking at the annual meeting
> of News Corporation, in Adelaide, Australia)

In sport we can see another example of Britain's twin roles; in some
respects Britain is a big player on the international media sports scene, but
in other respects Britain has a colonial status in the wide world of sporting
action. True, Britain has made some sports contribution to—and does
obtain some sports advantages from—Europe; but United States interests in
general outdo European interests in the deployment of British sporting
assets.

Britain is certainly one of the leading European sporting nations. It has a
unique tradition, because so many of the major sports were born in Britain.
BBC radio, beginning in the 1920s and 1930s played a big role in orchestrat-

ing a distinctive annual calendar of sporting events including football, rugby, cricket, golf, Wimbledon tennis, horse racing on the flat and over jumps, and Henley rowing. In the 1990s British televised sport went through its own revolution. BSkyB played a part in this, although even Premier League football obtained less than 20 per cent of its income from TV. The football revolution of the 1990s was also greatly assisted by Britain's strong national press and its now much fatter newspapers. Both the *Sun* and *The Times* and also the two Murdoch Sundays gave added space to sport in the 1990s; all other British nationals deployed their colour-picture ability and extra pages also to provide added coverage to sports, whose live coverage on Murdoch BSkyB was thus helpfully promoted.

Also significant was British government subsidy for stadium renovation and a broader in-flow of finance from new entrepreneurs and from the stock market public flotation of twenty top clubs. The added excitement generated by these combined factors allowed huge increases in season ticket prices, which in turn financed an in-flow of star football players from across Europe and around the world. The anticipation of further (digital) financial growth led to increasing numbers of players earning £1 million annually, and to an even larger number earning $1 million annually.

Formula One motor racing is largely based in Europe. But much of the entrepreneurial drive comes from Britain; a common or predominant pattern has been of British-built cars powered by engines supplied by major European car manufacturers. The construction of racing cars has become largely a British-based business.

In two other sports of worldwide appeal—namely rugby and cricket—Britain is potentially a huge asset to Europe. Both of these sports are more internationally popular (outside their home country) than are the loose American equivalents of American Football and baseball. Rugby Union is played in seventy countries and is quite widely played in Europe; the leading European contest is the Six (previously five) Nations (France, Italy, England, Scotland, Wales, Ireland). The northern tier of world rugby nations also includes Canada and Japan; the formidable southern tier includes Argentina, South Africa, Australia, and New Zealand. But the main entrepreneurial thrust (in both Rugby League and Rugby Union) comes from Australia (and its competitive TV system), while there is little or no Europe-wide attempt to develop this European sporting asset.

Cricket is another British originated sport which has a significant following, mainly in Australia, India, New Zealand, Pakistan, South Africa, Sri Lanka, and the West Indies, as well as in Britain. The finals of the cricket World Cup (played in England in 1999) involved twelve countries whose combined populations were nearly one-quarter of the world total. Television and sponsorship income has risen dramatically in recent years.

But while Britain can regard itself as the proud mother of—and still active leader within—several internationally important sports, there is equal substance in the opposite image of Britain as sports colony, and especially as television sports colony. While Europe takes little interest in rugby and cricket, these European-born sports have been revolutionized by Australian and American commercial enterprise.

Cricket was revolutionized by the repackaging of the one-day, quickie, version of the game; this repackaging was largely done by the Australian media mogul Kerry Packer, and was the by-product of a dispute between his Channel Nine television and the Australian public broadcaster, ABC. Australian disputes also played a major role in a revolution within Rugby League. British Rugby League teams agreed—in return for generous BSkyB funding—to switch their, mainly north of England, game from winter to summer. This had the advantage (for BSkyB) of strengthening its summer sports schedule (while relieving the heavily footballed winter). Rugby Union underwent its own revolution, also heavily driven by BSkyB finance. The previously amateur (and gentlemanly) game of Rugby Union suddenly accepted the Sky money and entered a professional era of commercial turbulence, initial chaos, and much soul-searching about British inadequacies.

The newly colonial status of Britain's (and Europe's) sport is neatly encapsulated in such America-via-Australia renaming of British Rugby League teams as the London Broncos and the Bradford Bulls. English one-day cricket demonstrates its colonial status in its switch from the elegant Victorian all-white to the jarring colours and crumpled look of the day-before-yesterday's track suit.

Some of the most British of sporting occasions are sold around the world by the American International Management Group (IMG) and its sports subsidiary, Trans World Sports (TWI). IMG's founder, Mark McCormack, began handling the television coverage of Wimbledon tennis and Saint Andrew's golf back in the 1970s. London became a key location in IMG's international chain of offices. IMG was contracted in 1988 to produce an entire sports channel for BSB; subsequently after the merger with Sky, IMG/TWI became a major supplier to BSkyB. TWI supplied the first live coverage of the England cricket tour in the West Indies for Sky in 1990. In 1996 TWI combined with Associated Press to run a worldwide sports news agency service, SNTV, which despatched seven sports TV news bulletins each day from London to customers around the world. TWI also sold TV coverage of English Premier League football around the world (in partnership with Canal Plus).

Why were these services supplied by an American? Because Mark McCormack, who began by representing Arnold Palmer and other golf and tennis stars, was operating in a United States environment in which stars were paid more, and more quickly (than in Europe) became major television personalities. McCormack also saw the possibility of bringing together several previously separate elements. IMG and TWI represented sports players, acquired the TV rights to major sporting events, produced sports coverage, created fresh events for television, and tapped huge new sources of funds such as advertising endorsement and pay television. These entrepreneurial activities were based on the domestic US market; the internationalization of these activities—involving over twenty offices around the world—depended heavily upon the London operations. In particular McCormack had shown that he could deliver what the All England Tennis and Croquet Club (Wimbledon) and the Royal and Ancient Golf Club (Saint Andrews) most wanted—namely American TV network money.

Sport as Network Flagship, and Bouquet Ingredient

Television networks are willing to pay more for sports rights than seems to be justified by the audience numbers reached or the extra advertising sold. This is because top sports programming has been given a flagship role. Fox was not the first American network to employ football in a flagship role. ABC had done this when it launched *Monday Night Football* in 1970, one of a number of innovations which did, indeed, confirm ABC as the third TV network. When Rupert Murdoch acquired the National Conference (half) of the NFL for 1994–8, the intention was to confirm Fox as the fourth network, and as such the expensive purchase subsequently looked like a success. Murdoch, like others, recognized that a broad range of benefits could be obtained by the football-as-flagship strategy. The football programming itself attracted a large audience; it impressed the newspaper and advertising worlds and helped Fox to raise its advertising rates; the football programming also attracted youthful and affluent 'demographics' and allowed Fox to promote its other programming to this young target audience. The football and other sports acquisitions helped to deny a similar sports strategy to rivals (including the would-be fifth networks) over an extended period. The acquisition of top football, baseball, and ice hockey rights enabled Fox to attract a stronger line-up of affiliated stations into its Fox network. The rising tide of Fox ratings also raised the value of the Fox network's then (1993) nine owned-and-operated stations, thus helping it to buy others.

The culmination of this 1990s network competition was the mammoth sum of $17.6 billion, which four networks agreed to pay for eight years (ending in 2006) of NFL football. Over half of this was accounted for by the ESPN/ABC (Disney) combination, contracting to pay $9.2 billion for eight years of Sunday and Monday night football.

In Europe also all-sports offerings have been cast into leading roles. In Britain the exclusive sports offerings were crucial to the rapidly escalating profits of BSkyB, and the strategy was built on a pay window supplied with massive live coverage of football and other sports. Europe's other leading pay-TV success of the 1990s was Canal Plus which (along with movies) targeted sports. Canal Plus and its competitors, both in France and across Europe, also cast sport into an even more prominent role in the launch of their bouquets of digital channels. Moreover the quick success of American digital satellite offerings, such as DirecTV, depended significantly on an attractive array of sport programming, including à la carte offerings of one specific match, or a 'season ticket' to a bundle of games.

Sport matched neatly with the requirement of cable channels (and especially new ones) for large quantities of cheap material. Several of the first wave of successful American cable networks and 'superstations' carried large proportions of sport, and the increasingly popular sport of basketball was ideal. Basketball (including college basketball) came in attractively large quantities; it had a long season (unlike American football) and, initially, the basketball rights were very cheap. In 1979 the USA cable net paid only $500,000 for NBA basketball and even in 1984 the price paid for cable rights by WTBS was only $10 million. But in 1984 ABC bought ESPN and Michael Jordan joined the Chicago Bulls. The NBA subsequently used the massive cable coverage to expand basketball's ability to sell merchandise, and thus to fund superstar earnings. Increasingly basketball continued its marketing campaigns onto foreign cable systems; marketing tactics used in the USA were then deployed internationally by Nike, Reebok, and their contracted stars. The National Basketball Association also established an international chain of NBA offices, dedicated to transforming this All-American sport into an All-World sport.

The channel multiplication revolution in media sport has also led to greatly heightened competition and conflict over the share-out of the financial spoils. Well into the 1980s, it was the American local cable operators who were the main beneficiaries of channel multiplication. The large multiple system operators (MSOs) were in the most powerful position, not only in relation to new movie offerings (such as HBO) but also in relation to sport. As late as 1984 the rights holders of an attractive sport like basketball (the NBA) were being paid only a nominal fee; the local system operators were paying only a few cents per subscriber per month to show huge blocks of this popular programming. The local MSOs were exploiting their monopoly position. Since 1984, however, there has been a fierce struggle between the three vertical levels—first the sports rights holders, second the networks of various kinds, and third those (including local cable operators) who deliver the sports programming to consumers and households.

Since 1984 the top sports rights holders have hugely increased the sums they obtain from selling TV rights. The NBA sold its combined broadcasting and cable rights for $44m in 1984 and for $660m in 1998. Similarly huge increases in a number of countries led to major conflicts between different sports associations, and between leading team owners and the associations.

There were also conflicts involving the highly paid leading players, such as the strike of American professional baseball players in 1994, and the lockout of the basketball players in 1998–9.

At the network level there were bidding contests which often saw networks—with flagship, machismo, or other motivation—paying more than the apparent value of the rights. In some cases this was competition between similar networks. In other cases the struggle over rights was between different media technologies—terrestrial networks versus direct-to-home versus cable. Especially in the United States this kind of contest typically led to a splitting of the rights in one sport (such as NFL football) between more than one network. In some cases—such as British co-habitation between the BBC and BSkyB—there was a degree of governmental approval or even blessing. In other cases, such as Spain, a national government openly and belligerently supported one cohabiting sports partnership against another (politically opposed) partnership.

Competition at the final consuming household level also increased. The arrival of successful satellite-to-home systems in the 1990s started to weaken the position of cable operators; this competition was heightened by digital technology in satellite (and other) services. In the USA—and in some European countries, such as Spain—there was also competition from strong local broadcast TV stations; this led to national TV vs. local TV vs. satellite vs. cable competition, plus the crucial added complexity of digital services.

The strength of the satellite-to-home operator emphasizes the leverage gained by an operator who can both deliver a bundle of networks and can cut out the local operator by delivering direct-to-home. Such vertical strength is especially significant in a sports environment where large blocks of the most commercially attractive programming are effectively auctioned off in multi-year contracts to the highest bidder. The sports revolution of recent years has meant that there is no conventional or 'normal' price level; outcomes are determined by bargaining machismo, and by the fear of being denied key sporting assets.

The most commercially successful player in the US TV sport business has been the highly vertical Disney-ABC-ESPN combination. Next most successful have been other leading vertical players such as News/Fox and Time-Warner-Turner. In the USA these vertical players themselves owned key sports rights; Ted Turner's media empire was significantly dependent on his early ownership of sports teams and rights in Atlanta. Both Disney and News/Fox were major owners of sports franchises and rights in Los Angeles. A number of large American cable companies also owned major sports franchises. When Rupert Murdoch failed in 1998 to acquire Manchester United for over $600m, he was hoping to bring to Britain an American linkage already common in Italy and France and elsewhere in Europe.

World Sports Rights Cartel: ESPN, Fox, Eurosport

ESPN International, part of the Disney-ABC corporate empire, is the leader in televised sport on the world scene. ESPNI is also the leader of what amounts to cartel control of international sports rights. In Europe, ESPN is allied with (and a part owner of) Eurosport; Eurosport-ESPN is the only significant Europe-wide sports cable offering. In Asia ESPN is allied with the News Corporation (Murdoch) controlled Star company; this ESPN-Star combination is the only significant sports offering which spans across India, China, and the rest of Asia.

Consequently, ESPN only competes directly, outside the USA, with News Corporation (Fox-Sky) in Latin America and Africa, both of which are relatively insignificant in terms of sports TV revenues. The broad picture here is the familiar global-local one in which two or three world players compete against, and cooperate with, each other around the world; these world players then supply partly localized variants of the service within specific language markets and world regions.

Europe is not fully using its assets, while American players—behaving in a more commercial and more entrepreneurial style—are exercising more control, extracting more profit, and are more successfully recycling their domestic product through international windows onto the world's screens.

Another familiar element is Britain's historical importance—and continuing significance—as a stepping stone and additional resource deployed by American companies in shaping their world strategies. Britain has played a significant role in relation to all three world TV sports players. First, ESPN initially came to Europe (in 1984) by acquiring an interest in the British based sports-cable service, Screensport. Second, the Sky Sports offerings in Britain played a key role in the Murdoch attempt to rival ESPN with a News/Fox/Sky/Star international sports offering; the British Sky sports contribution to the global Murdoch sports enterprise involved both attractive programming and attractive profits. Third, Britain made a significant but ambiguous contribution to Eurosport (see below).

Like MTV and CNN, the ESPN network was successful at home in the US cable market before it ventured out onto the world scene. ESPN launched in 1980 with the then common combination of sports and entertainment. After the usual early struggles, ESPN became the American market leader in sports cable; it was acquired (80 per cent) by ABC in 1984 and became part of Disney-ABC in 1995. ESPN developed, within the bigger Disney network bouquet, its own mini-bouquet of sports offerings: ESPN One, ESPN Two (specializing in extreme and youth-oriented sport), ESPNews, and the Classic Sports Network; also building the ESPN mini-bouquet were the ESPN website, *ESPN* magazine, and ESPN's significant radio networking effort.

ESPN International began with a few one-off sales in 1983 and grew rapidly. The international spread of ESPNI paralleled that of CNNI; Bristol (Connecticut) came to play for ESPNI the role of Atlanta in the CNN story. The ESPNI roll-out on to the world scene was made possible by satellite technology, first across the Atlantic, then across the world. Initially ESPNI mainly syndicated specific sports events and blocks of programming to networks in other countries; syndication onto terrestrial and other networks continued to be important in building up commercial relationships and consumer appeal. Increasingly ESPNI offered itself as an entire network of overwhelmingly American sport. Subsequently the key move was made into two elements of regionalization. One element was the supply of commentaries in different languages; much of this language commentary effort involved sports specialists looking at a screen in Bristol, Connecticut, and doing commentary in Portuguese, Spanish, and other languages. The second regional effort was ESPNI's strategy of purchasing some key local sports rights, such as cricket for South Asia and Argentine rugby for Argentina. This locally popular programming was then presented as the prime-time sports material.

After the acquisition of sports rights, ESPNI also moved on to acquire slices of local sports networks. ESPNI acquired a slice of Eurosport in 1993, a third of the Canadian TSN sports network in 1995 and the whole of Telesport in Argentina in 1996. By 1998 ESPNI claimed to own, in whole or in part, twenty-one foreign networks.

Consequently ESPNI was able to offer around the world some very popular local sport. It also offered sport from afar which had a local interest; for example, there is a big Latin American interest in Spanish football because many Latin American players are attracted, by the higher salaries, to play for Spanish clubs. ESPNI could then fill up much of the lower audience times on its local networks with United States ESPN material.

With NBC and CBS deciding to limit their sports output mainly to their terrestrial TV networks, the Murdoch sports interests (News, Fox, Sky, Star) could claim increasingly by the later 1990s to be rivalling ESPN as the second significant world player. The Murdoch strategy was to build a world sports offering not only from the USA outwards, but also from Britain, Australia, and Hong Kong inwards into the United States. Inside the USA the News/ Murdoch sports effort also had several strands. First there was the Fox network acquisition of major football, baseball, and hockey contracts. Second there was the Fox cable network which (in line with an earlier cable tradition) offered a combination of sport and entertainment. Third there was the high-profile strategy of combining national and local sports offerings through a 1997 three-way merger of Fox Sports/Liberty Media/ Cablevision. This Fox focus on local sports was designed to combine the home-town appeal of local sports for the sports fan, with a national brand appeal to national advertisers.

Another possible reward of local sports lay in its attractions in pay-per-view formats. Murdoch's sporting enterprises in Britain and Australia may have made him especially aware of this point. Other Hollywood/Network companies may have been more cautious because of PPV's quite heavy previous dependence on sleazy pornography and sleazy heavyweight boxing.

These News Corporation sporting plans carried the trademark Murdoch combination of the high-risk venture supported by the cash cow back-up. As News Corporation made its high-profile risky shift into local US sport, it had already nailed down some strong US major contracts; it also had a strong position in Australia and a very strong sports rights position in Britain (with no direct ESPN competition). Moreover in Asia in 1996 the News/Star company made a 50/50 deal with ESPN to combine their still separate networks under common ownership, common management, and combined bidding for rights. Also in Latin America News Corporation had agreements with the two largest national TV companies, Televisa (Mexico) and Globo (Brazil).

The term 'cartel' seemed justified by the current world leadership position in TV sports rights. In first place is ESPN; perhaps about second equal are Eurosport and News/Fox/Sky/Star. But ESPN has a comfortable deal with the main potential competitor in Europe and another comfortable deal with the main potential competitor in Asia.

Meanwhile European sport, which could be a key ingredient of Europe's internal common culture (and also worldwide cultural exports) is less than the sum of its parts. In terms of sports TV networks and sports TV rights, Europe is split three ways. While there is some Europe–Europe cooperation, the most active cooperation is Euro-American (Eurosport–ESPN) and Anglo-American (BSkyB–Fox).

Eurosport: The Rise and Fall of a Major Pan-European Television Network

Eurosport is yet another example of a European media enterprise which lacked European support. Indeed without both British and American support this most widely watched across Europe of all television channels might never have been born, or, if born, survived.

Britain played a significant role in the early days of both Eurosport and the competitor which it eventually absorbed, Screensport. The first of the two was Screensport and it began in 1983–4 under the unlikely ownership of W. H. Smith, the UK retailer. Screensport lasted almost a decade and in its last days was owned by ESPN, the American network.

Eurosport itself was launched in partnership with the EBU as part of the initial Murdoch Sky offer to British households in 1989. Many early references actually called it 'Rupert Murdoch's Eurosport'. One (minor) reason for Murdoch's decision to drop Eurosport in 1991 was that this Murdoch-run and London-based network was accused of being anti-competitive; the main accusers were the (British-born) Screensport and the equally British European Commissioner Leon Brittan.

The History of Eurosport

Eurosport was launched in 1989.

Up to 1989: The Screensport Era
Screensport was a British cable sports channel which launched on Swindon Cable in October 1984. Screensport's majority owner was W. H. Smith (the UK retail chain) with ESPN a minority owner which supplied much American sports programming. Screensport had few UK cable customers, but it became available by Astra satellite (see Table 19.1 above).

The Murdoch-Eurosport Era: February 1989–May 1991
Following the unsuccessful Eurikon and Europa experiments, both the European Commission and the European Broadcasting Union wanted to launch a Europe-wide TV sports channel. The EBU's public service broadcasters had a lot of sports programming, but no risk capital; the EBU looked for a commercial partner and chose Rupert Murdoch, because of his previous experience with the lone (Europe-oriented) Sky channel and because he needed a sports channel for his new four-channel Sky offer focused, this time, on the British public. A partnership agreement between the EBU (16 members, 14 countries) and News International was signed in December 1988. Eurosport initially offered six hours a day of sport, mainly from EBU members; separate sound was provided initially in English (for Sky) and in German and Dutch. Eurosport's production location for these two years was at Sky's premises in Isleworth, West London. The News–EBU agreement specified that Murdoch could not escape until News International had lost £40 million. By early 1991 the losses had passed this amount. Moreover Murdoch, following the BSB-Sky merger of late 1990 had acquired all of BSB's channels, including 'The Sports Channel' which was now converted into the Sky Sports channel. The EBU, having been forced into an odd marriage with its worst enemy, was now deserted.

Eurosport versus Screensport and Brussels, 1991–3
For two weeks (6–22 May) in 1991 Eurosport disappeared from TV screens. It then reopened in Paris. The EBU's new commercial partner was TFI, the French ratings leader. For two years TFI and Eurosport

struggled against adversity. The move to Paris and the blank screens had lost about half of Eurosport's previously 28 million households. Eurosport was still competing against Screensport, which had complained to Brussels about Eurosport's monopolistic access to the public service broadcasters' sporting properties across Europe. The competition directorate (DG4) in Brussels was headed by the British Commissioner Leon Brittan, who had set up the 1985–6 Peacock Committee and who supported commercial competition in broadcasting. As seen by people within Eurosport, this amounted to a European channel being perversely persecuted by the European Commission, while the American (ESPN) Screensport was encouraged as a valiant competitor.

Eurosport's Franco-American Alliance, 1993–9
In 1993 Eurosport's fortunes improved; Leon Brittan ceased to be competition Commissioner and his successor (Van Miert) was more EBU-friendly. Screensport (whose main owners were now the American ESPN and the French Canal Plus) decided to merge with Eurosport. The Eurosport consortium continued to involve selected EBU public service broadcast members in 50/50 combination with commercial broadcasters. Following the 1993 merger the commercial side now involved French TF1 (34 per cent and the chair), French Canal Plus (33 per cent) and American ESPN (33 per cent). This was yet another odd combination because it included not only French and American owners but also two fiercely competing French companies.

Nevertheless despite this peculiar *ménage à trois*, Eurosport prospered. By winter 1998–9 it passed the 80 million homes mark (with cable homes outnumbering satellite homes by about two to one). Germany accounted for a third of all Eurosport homes; the network had a significant presence in thirty-eight countries from Portugal to Russia, and from Iceland to Turkey.

Consequently certain British politicians and TV executives can be accused of having abandoned a gallant, and hard-pressed Eurosport. True, enough. However—another common pattern—other European countries (and their politicians and governments) were probably more guilty in this regard. The major sporting associations across Europe—from whom international rights had to be acquired—were not outstandingly helpful. Nor were European advertisers eager to help the struggling infant network; much of the early (rather sparse) advertising came from Japanese and other Asian companies eager to establish their brands across Europe.

The European cable operators also were far from generous. Nearly all of them used their bargaining strength in the early days to ensure that Eurosport paid the companies to obtain access to their local cable systems. This was (and is) a standard hazard for new cable networks, but nobody— cable operators, regulators, politicians—saw the need for an exemption from these harsh practices of the cable business. Eventually most cable systems did pay Eurosport small sums of money; this, together with increasing advertising revenue, enabled Eurosport to prosper. But the most powerful, largest, and most monopolistic cable operator—the German Telekom— continued, even a decade after Eurosport's birth, to demand payment in return for allowing Eurosport access to German households.

By 1998–9 Eurosport's greatest days were probably already behind it. Whereas it had in most countries been the only available all-sports network, increasing numbers of countries were following the Sky Sports lead. Moreover increasingly the pattern was of not just one sports net but (like Sky's and ESPN's several sports nets) a number of sports nets within each country.

Eurosport itself had stuck mainly to a standard offering across Europe; this involved identical pictures but fourteen separate language commentaries. There was some differentiation for Scandinavia and France (two hours a day). In 1999 the English-language service (for UK and Ireland) was awarded English-speaking on-screen personalities and titles for the entire output. With these countries receiving some separate treatment, Germany loomed ever larger in the mainstream Eurovision output and advertising.

The EBU still had the rights to the Olympics down to 2006, but it had already lost the World Football Cup finals to Kirch of Germany. The prospect for Eurosport was that it would probably continue to appear in many countries' total offerings of sports channels. But in each European country there would be at least one national sports network, and in the larger countries several sports networks, which would have under contract those sporting contests most treasured in that particular country. From having been the leading sports channel, Eurosport will become a lesser back-up to the main national sports channels.

In 1999 Europe already had over 250 networks, most of them carrying some sport. The digital revolution was already ensuring that Sports Associations sold their rights in several different packages—live matches, entire tournament, recorded highlights, and so on—to different broadcasters. The prospect was thus for sport appearing on several levels of networks, both analogue and digital:

- The All Sport 'pay' networks offering live events and pay-per-view to sports fans.
- The big traditional broadcasters still seeking to show some live sport and some highlights to big general audiences.

- The big little networks perhaps focusing on just one or two sports suitable for their specific audience and useful as a network branding device.
- Small digital networks offering specialized packages (such as golf only, or tennis only) or one locality, or one team.

Without some radical change in funding, Eurosport's long-term prospects—for contracts and for audiences—do not look good against such opposition. ESPN and Fox/Sky/Star, with their growing sports bouquets, appear to be much better prepared for the future.

22
Smaller Countries: Media Nationalism Multiplied

THE smaller nations of western Europe face a more severe form of the media policy dilemmas which confront the large countries. Each country follows its own idiosyncratic set of policies. Even countries like Norway and Iceland insist on making their own feature films, financed predominantly by subsidy.

Western Europe has two neatly defined divisions in population size. The five 'large' countries (Germany, France, Britain, Italy, Spain) have an average of about 60 million people each; this contrasts with an average of about 9 million in a group of 'small' countries (Austria, Belgium, Denmark, Finland, Greece, Ireland, Netherlands, Norway, Portugal, Sweden, and Switzerland). These eleven are the most heavily cabled group of countries in the world; however their 'leadership' role is somewhat ambiguous, because the major impetus to cable growth was cable's ability to bring in TV channels from other countries.

This chapter will try to indicate some common points, which unite and also divide, the media of these eleven countries. In particular:

- These small countries and their media industries have to look in three directions; the small nation has to face not only the Anglo-American media, but often also the inescapable presence of a next door 'big brother', a larger west European nation, which speaks the same language. These small nations' media often also have internal dilemmas; Belgium—with its French- and Dutch-speaking 'communities'—is not alone, amongst these small nation states in containing more than one 'nation'.

- In these smaller countries 'everything changed' with the arrival of multiple new commercial TV channels. Nevertheless 'everything stayed the same' because the main new winner, commercial terrestrial television, was an offshoot of the press and the old public service system.

- Behind the many new on-screen offerings, the ancient forces of telecommunications and press remained potent. In several countries the old telecommunications monopoly provider acquired a commanding presence in some or all of cable, satellite provision, and Internet services.

- The press in these small countries (as in the large countries) continued to wield the most political influence. Press influence was evident in the low rates of Value Added Tax as well as the subsidies available for newspapers in most of these eleven smaller countries. The level of newspaper sales-per-population was four or five times higher in Scandinavia than in such southern countries as Portugal and Greece. However the potency of the newspaper press seemed not to depend upon sales penetration, but upon the continuing centrality of newspapers within national politics. This national political power enabled the newspapers in a number of smaller countries to acquire the additional privilege of owning (in whole or in part) new commercial television networks.

Media nationalism is far from dead, in either eastern or western Europe. National, local, and international media will continue to coexist; this coexistent mix will, however, take a different form within each country. National media will continue to be nationally idiosyncratic.

Small Nations' Media Confront Big Brother, Hollywood, and Britain

These smaller countries' media systems were transformed—especially by the launch of strong new commercial channels in the late 1980s and early 1990s. But although there was some genuinely radical change towards channel multiplication and commercial television, much also stayed much the same. In less than a decade most of the national public service systems had dropped from a 100 per cent audience share to below 50 per cent. Most of these countries by the late 1990s had one dominant commercial channel while some had two. But this typically meant that just three (or four) national networks (involving a public and private mix) still had the huge bulk of the audience.

However, these few dominant domestic channels had been hugely influenced by various foreign channels:

- *Additional channels from neighbouring countries available on cable* were increasingly popular; in the Netherlands and Belgium, for instance, cable systems offered increasing numbers of channels from France, Germany, and Britain. Initially most of these were public channels, although commercial channels (especially from Luxembourg) became more salient during the 1980s.
- *European versions of American channels* also started to appear; CNNI began in Europe in 1985, while MTV's European launch was in 1987. These channels led many people to think (incorrectly) that numerous all-American channels would acquire big audiences across Europe.

- *Own language channels from abroad* were the most popular, a pattern of viewing which had existed since the early days of television. Channels from France had been viewed across the border especially in Belgium and Switzerland; channels from Germany had been followed in Austria, Switzerland, and the German-speaking corner of Belgium. This phenomenon—noted in the earliest *TV without Frontiers* documents—steadily expanded with the growth of cable systems, not least in the 'little three' of the original European Six, namely Belgium, the Netherlands, and Luxembourg.

In the 1990s it became increasingly difficult to categorize some of these channels as either domestic or foreign. 'Foreign' owned channels were often highly local and national in other respects; meanwhile many 'national' TV channels involved foreign ownership of 25 per cent or some other substantial minority slice.

Let us now consider briefly three separate sets of foreign forces—Big Brother, American and British—which most smaller countries had to face.

Big brothers were typically neighbouring larger countries speaking the same language. Austria's big brother was Germany, while Ireland's big brother was Britain; French Belgium's big brother was France. Each of these connections had its own lengthy history; in recent years it typically meant that about one-third of TV viewing in the smaller country involved programming (on both domestic and imported networks) from the larger country.

However some of these relationships are even more complex, while the big brother's television presence is even more dominant. Portugal, for example, is geographically dominated by a much larger neighbour, Spain. But in media terms it is the Brazilian presence which exerts an extraordinary dominance. Brazilian *telenovelas*, strong in many export markets, have an overwhelming presence in same-language Portugal.

Switzerland also suffers under huge big-brother dominance of a quite different kind. It is the fate of Switzerland to adjoin, not one, but three big brothers—Germany, France, and Italy. Foreign material from the three big brothers dominates not only the Swiss cable systems but also the domestic Swiss channels. Paradoxically the democratic need in a small-population country to produce domestic programming in three separate languages merely exacerbates Switzerland's problem of overwhelming import levels.

Other countries have yet different big-brother difficulties. In Scandinavia, for example, Sweden's population is less than double the population of each of its three cousins, Denmark, Norway, and Finland. These Scandinavian national mass media systems do overlap, with each country's largest media company active in the other countries. But Sweden—as the largest country—does somewhat more in terms of foreign ownership, and the export of programming and channels onto local cable systems. While there is genuine cooperation, especially between the language-similar trio of Sweden, Norway, and Denmark, there is some suspicion of some big brotherly Swedish tendencies.

Hollywood was already a massive supplier of films and a substantial supplier of television programming to all of these countries well before 1985. After 1985 there was an increase in percentage share and a huge increase in, for example, the number of Hollywood films shown on the small country's now expanded number of TV channels. By the mid-1990s the four leading channels in a typical smaller country were each showing over 300 films a year; the majority of these 1,200 films shown in each smaller country were from Hollywood.

The Hollywood presence also took several other forms, in particular the importing of prime-time American series. Where strong big-brother relationships existed, the smaller country would typically be importing the Hollywood product only after it had been dubbed in the big-brother country; for example German-Swiss and Austrians would be viewing Hollywood products dubbed into German by German actors. If the series had not been dubbed in the big-brother country, then the small country would probably have had to accept a (cheaper) subtitled version. In addition to importing of Hollywood products either on cable channels from big-brothers, or direct onto domestic networks, there was all the usual buying and copying of game show and other genre formats.

Britain was traditionally a possible alternative source of programming. Mary Kelly found that in 1985–6 seven small northern markets (Belgium/ Flanders, Netherlands, Ireland, Sweden, Finland, Denmark, Norway) devoted 15 per cent of all TV time to American, and 9 per cent to British, programming—as against 8 per cent from the rest of Europe.[1] With the channel multiplication after 1986, the proportion of US programming undoubtedly increased and the British proportion declined. But the British influence on national media policies and national media systems across the smaller European countries continued to be important. These countries continued to look towards Britain, (and Germany and France) for appropriate models. But Britain's attempted combination of traditional 'public service' plus Thatcherite 'privatization' in the 1980s (and subsequently) was perhaps more directly influential than was Washington-style deregulation of a massive US media system, which was clearly so different from that of a smaller European country:

- The privatization of British Telecom was of great interest in Scandinavia which already possessed Europe's most efficient telephone systems.

[1] Mary Kelly, 'National, European or American Programmes: Trends in European Television', *Journal of the Institute of Public Administration of Ireland*, 36 (1988), 9–24.

Sweden and Finland also became increasingly important exporters of telecoms equipment.

- The early and mid-1980s satellite efforts (such as Sky and Superchannel) launched from Britain had their biggest impact in Scandinavia and the Netherlands, where large proportions of young people could understand the English language and where the public broadcasting offerings were especially restricted and old-fashioned.
- London was used as the location for 'own-language channels' from abroad by such companies as Kinnevik, which launched TV-3 channels into Sweden, Norway, and Denmark. Kinnevik deliberately tried to model these channels on Britain's BSkyB.
- The BBC's 1990s strategy of reshaping itself into a more market-oriented and competitive force influenced other public broadcasters such as YLE in Finland.[2]

Britain's commitment to both the public system and Thatcherite deregulation may sound paradoxical. But, of course, some Scandinavian policy-makers saw themselves as needing to catch up with Britain's 1955 launch of ITV as a 100 per cent advertising-funded channel. Moreover the biggest single change in northern Europe by the mid-1990s was, indeed, the establishment of mainstream commercial terrestrial channels, similar to the British ITV or the French TF1.

Many politicians and policy-makers in northern Europe hesitated to adopt such all-American approaches as 'deregulation'. But British 'privatization', and the 1982 launch of Channel Four as a second advertising-financed channel, could appeal in northern Europe as a more moderate, less American, and more British-familiar mode of modest change.

Consequently the 'special relationship' between the media of northern Europe and Britain did not disappear. While in some obvious respects the relationship with the US media has grown closer, in other respects the relationship with Britain has also grown closer. In terms of sports programming, comedy, and (in recent years) game shows, some Scandinavians feel closer to the British media than to the American media. Moreover some major Dutch media players (Reed Elsevier and Polygram films) have had major British participation.

A significant British element was also noticeable in the channels made available to multi-channel subscribers in northern Europe. For example Norway's leading cable company in 1997–8 was offering seventeen foreign channels on all of its local systems (plus others in certain localities). Five of the foreign channels were Swedish, and one was Eurosport. Eleven of the seventeen were Anglo-American, with American channels outnumbering

---

[2] Gregory Ferrell Lowe and Ari Alm, 'Public Service Broadcasting as Cultural Industry: Value Transformation in the Finnish Market-place', *European Journal of Communication*, 12.2 (June 1997), 169–91.

British by seven and a half to three and a half. The three fully British channels were BBC World, BBC Prime, and Sky News. Several of the American channels in this Norwegian offering—CNNI, Discovery, MTVE—also included British elements.[3]

And the Winner is . . . National Commercial Television

> . . . media policy in Austria is one of the areas where corporatist structures predominate over market forces. The 'iron triumvirate', consisting of the political parties, the ORF and the Publishers' Association, has kept all developments under its firm control for decades.
>
> Josef Trappel (1997)[4]

In Austria the political parties, the public broadcaster, and the newspaper publishers still kept their iron grip on media policy well into the 1990s. But across the rest of western Europe, most equivalent 'Iron Triumvirates' experienced some meltdown. Even in the four main Scandinavian countries the average public broadcaster audience share fell from nearly 100 per cent in the mid-1980s to 73 per cent in 1990, and by 1998 to about 40 per cent. Across Europe much of this change occurred in a few years in the late 1980s and early 1990s. In the Netherlands, for example, it took only two years (1989–91) for a new commercial offering (RTL4) to win the ratings lead.

The three traditional forces—parties, press, and public broadcasters—did indeed shift their positions. The political parties withdrew at least some of their support from public broadcasting. Across Scandinavia, and across Europe generally, there was a swing to the political right, which often included a switch to more market driven media and more deregulatory policies. The newspaper owners decided that, since they would not be able to stop commercial television, they must acquire slices of it.

The third grouping in the policy threesome, the public service broadcasters, were forced into radical change by the other two. In the early 1980s Italy and Britain were two countries which devoted a substantial proportion of advertising expenditure to television. But across Europe the main reliance was still on the licence fee; in 1984 only 10 per cent of German and 15 per cent of French advertising expenditure went into TV (while in the next decade both of these proportions doubled). In Sweden, Norway, and Denmark there was still no TV advertising in 1984. Thus there was a realistic expectation that more *advertising* finance could fund more channels, while expanded *subscription* revenue could generate expanded cable channel offerings.

A decade after channel multiplication and commercialization began in

---

[3] 'Cable Norway: Trial by Jury', *Cable and Satellite Europe* (Feb. 1998), 37–9.
[4] Euromedia Research Group, *The Media in Western Europe* (London: Sage, 1997), 12.

these smaller countries, the typical late 1990s picture was of a country with the following television channels and audience percentage shares:

A commercial channel. . . .	40
A commercial or public channel	20
A public channel	20
These three, combined	= 80
Numerous other small audience offerings	20
Grand total	100

The dividing line between 'public' and 'commercial' channels became less clear. Commercial channels may now be domestically regulated, or a spill-over from a next-door country, or a channel specially beamed from Luxembourg or London into a specific country, or a 'Pan-European' (often American) commercial channel. There are also pay (subscription) channels. Meanwhile channels can change from one category to another; for example, the Swedish TV4 began as a foreign satellite offering, before becoming an 'official' Swedish terrestrial channel. Increasingly channels became available via satellite and cable and also by terrestrial transmission in different localities.

The larger countries typically had two or three newly dominant groupings—and hence significant competition to dominate in the digital era. However most of the smaller population west European countries had acquired, by the mid-1990s, just one dominant new channel (while others had two such channels).

This one leading commercial channel (with a 30–45 per cent audience share) became the dominant force within a number of the smaller countries. Because the newspapers typically had an ownership interest in the leading commercial channels, this constituted a rearrangement of the old 'iron triumvirate'. The public broadcasters were still there (with a 40 per cent audience share), while the political parties and the press had brought their close friends into the club in the form of commercial broadcasters.

The leading one or two commercial channels were typically even more important than their large audience share at first suggested. If the licence fee-funded public channels still had a 35 per cent share, a single commercial channel with a 35–40 per cent audience share would have substantially more advertising revenue than all of the other smaller channels combined. The leading commercial channel would be a 'must' for many advertisers and could charge premium rates per thousand viewers.

The leading commercial TV channels in Scandinavia tend to have complex interlocking ownership patterns. But a number of newspaper (and magazine) groups became leading TV owners including Bonnier (Sweden), Schibsted (Norway), and Egmont (Denmark). Egmont, for example, began as a printing business in 1878 and became a major Scandinavian publisher of magazines, books, and comics; in 1992 it acquired Nordisk Film and TV and became a leading producer of TV programming and films, as well as a co-owner of channels across Scandinavia. In 1997–8 Egmont's annual revenue passed $1 billion, weighted 60/40 between print and electronic media.[5]

Not only the press, but another industry with roots in the nineteenth century, telecommunications, played a major role in these small countries. Cable grew rapidly across northern Europe in the 1980s and 1990s and much of this growth was funded by the state telephone operators, before they themselves had to face significant competition. In all four of the major Scandinavian countries the big telephone operators were heavily involved in cable. In some cases the telecoms-cable connection was (as in Germany) part of public planning and strategy. In Switzerland the dominant cable company was controlled by Swisscom (formerly the state telephone operator), by Vebacom (Germany's second largest telecoms company), and by Siemens (the German equipment manufacturer).

This prominent position of telecoms interests in cable was important because it gave the ancient telephone interests a privileged path into the Internet and other future interactive media. More broadly, much (but not everything) remained the same, because the big new player (commercial TV) had roots in the press. In most small European countries an old trinity of the press, telephone, and a slimmed-down public broadcasting effort was still in place. All of these communications players not only had roots in the past but had roots in the national past, national media, and national concerns of the particular small nation.

Media Nationalism Continues

Despite the huge changes of recent times, the smaller countries of western Europe continue on their traditional paths which emphasize (1) idiosyncratic media nationalism; (2) imports of both policies and programming from the Anglo-Americans; and only (3) some modest interest in, and deference towards, the European continent.

To take these in reverse order: German and French media ownership involvement did substantially increase in the 1990s. RTL (CLT) was the most important foreign broadcaster. After the merger of this Luxembourg company with Bertelsmann-UFA of Germany, RTL had about one-quarter of the Dutch TV audience, and a slightly larger share of the south (French) Belgian audience.

France was also an important foreign owner in European television enterprises. This occurred initially when the success of Canal Plus in France led on to related pay-television channels in other countries. Subsequently

---

[5] Debra Johnson, 'Solid Foundation', *Television Business International* (June 1998), 28–31.

Canal Plus acquired, from Nethold, several small national pay-television operations (including Filmnet, originally launched by Esselte of Sweden). In the nature of pay-TV channels these operations had small audience shares, with a bigger slice of revenue. But a French-owned 'Canal Digital' offering may carry remarkably little French content. For example Canal Digital's 'Nordic Digital Bouquet', launched in 1997, carried three free Scandinavian channels; the next basic tier offered nineteen channels of which fourteen were American. In addition there were several Canal Plus and other movie offers, heavily dependent, inevitably, on Hollywood.[6]

In eastern Europe there were newer and more chaotic versions of the western Europe small country picture. In eastern Europe the single leading television channel usually had an even more dominant market share than its western equivalent. Dependence on American imports could also be on a bigger scale. East European networks were typically paying semi-token amounts such as $1,000 or $2,000 per hour for expensively made Hollywood TV fiction.

This massive east European dependence on Hollywood was predictably even greater in the cinema. There was a strong urge across eastern and central Europe to break away from past restrictions and to sample the offerings of the outside, western world. This sampling in practice depended on massive quantities of Hollywood product. Increasingly during the 1990s there was also resentment at this American dominance or dumping. But the subsequent swing was usually not towards more imports of French films; the popular demand was typically for more national entertainment in our own national language.

[6] 'Digital Television 2: Nordic Shuffling . . .' *Screen Digest* (Dec. 1977), 273–5. 'Nordic Region', *Screen Digest* (May 1998), 105–10.

PART V

Conclusions

23

A Win for US Media, not USA

At first sight the Anglo-American media connection appears to have no disadvantage for the USA, while it has several obvious advantages. Historically Britain was the leading media power, but Britain gradually gave up the leadership role to the USA. Since this changeover early in the twentieth century, the US media have relied upon Britain in several ways. Britain itself has been a key and open market for the US media. Britain has been an entry gate into two important clubs—the British Empire/Commonwealth and Europe. We will argue (in the next chapter) that Britain has probably been misled into believing that the Anglo-American media connection provides it with any real benefits.

Meanwhile we can anticipate that the US media will continue to grow rapidly in the twenty-first century. Much of the rapid change in American media companies and policies has been driven by the telecommunications and computer industries, as well as by Washington. Big investment in communications capacity—including multiple satellite systems and under-ocean cable capacity—will ensure huge continuing change.

The *vertical* urge in large American companies will continue. Hollywood/TV network/cable combinations will add various Internet and other digital extras. The telephone/cable/computer companies will also continue to stretch into nearby businesses so as to offer one-stop-shopping to business and domestic customers.

Meanwhile Washington will maintain some *anti-trust* limits to the vertical imperative. There may be more anti-trust focus on monopoly pricing, because vertical corporations, such as the Hollywood networkers—while squeezed in certain areas—will seek to charge monopoly prices in niche markets where they are dominant. As costs fall sharply in some telecoms-computer-interactive areas, monopoly pricing can consist simply of holding prices steady.

The United States in both the 1980s and 1990s produced a steady flow of fresh *media moguls* and this is likely to continue. Moguls have several major impacts on the American scene. Some moguls (such as John Malone at TCI, Craig McCaw in mobile telephony, and Paul Allen, co-founder of Microsoft) sell their shares; the resulting cash billions are then available to provide big funding for fresh start-up companies. Some moguls adopt a mogul-to-mogul entrepreneurial style. John Malone, while building the cable giant

TCI, also acquired minority stakes in other companies; these minority stakes were, in effect, John Malone placing bets on the success of other entrepreneurs and moguls. Some of Malone's bets were placed on small moguls, while other bets were placed on larger moguls, such as Rupert Murdoch.

The media or communications mogul specializes in the big deal, the merger, the acquisition of a promising small company. Some chief executives (who are not owner-operator moguls) also specialize in big deals. All of these American business approaches seem likely to continue to make for huge uncertainty. The need to acquire anti-trust clearance, and the length of time the Department of Justice can take to reach a decision, will continue to mean that—at any one time—there are big decisions hanging fire. Once the merger is allowed and takes place, there are typically major 'disposals' which cut loose significant businesses and involve substantial finance. Sometimes as many as ten separate companies (perhaps five American and five European or Japanese) are in effect involved in a 'disposal auction'. Competition in these acquisition auctions and competition to acquire slices of—and to place bets on—insurgent entrepreneurs and companies, becomes as important as competition to sell services to consumers.

Meanwhile American communications companies will continue to assume that digitalization, 'the abolition of distance' and 'the weightless economy' ensure that media and communications will become ever more 'global' businesses. Moreover anti-trust policy is not the only US approach which also spills out onto the global playing field. The vertical imperative also, of course, combines with a horizontal and territorial element. The mogul-to-mogul element has its strong international aspect. The American media mogul finds that an effective foreign strategy is to seek out fellow moguls in Britain, Germany, and Japan for some mogul-to-mogul discussions and joint ventures.

Internet: The Last All-American New Medium?

The Internet first achieved mass consumer levels of acceptance in the USA in 1994–5; it was the latest in a long tradition of 'new media' which—over the previous 100 years—had assumed American mass market characteristics, before being exported into, and copied by, the rest of the world. The Internet also exemplified a number of post-1995 US media and communications industry characteristics.

- The *vertical* element was quickly evident as three industries—mass media, telecommunications, and computing—tried to add Internet activities to their existing businesses. Very quickly leading players in the Internet game included Microsoft, the major phone companies, and the vertical media companies. Disney and Time Warner wanted to add

Internet offerings to their already bulging bouquets; the Internet was useful for cross-promotion, for merchandising, and for 'building the brand'.

- *Anti-trust* activity focused especially on the Internet ambitions of Microsoft. As in the equivalent stage of the young cable TV industry, it was being predicted that the chaotic jungle of small companies would soon be dominated by about four 'Portal' companies.
- The Internet very quickly generated its own *moguls*. Steve Case (America Online), Marc Andresson (Netscape), Jeff Bezos (Amazon.com), and others became instant moguls, and in some cases instant billionaires, with rags (or MBA) to riches stories to delight a mass media system, ever more focused on youth and wealth.
- The *deal* was also an important feature of the Internet. The buying and selling of whole companies quickly reached a level of frenzy similar to the frenzied buying and selling of shares in Internet companies.
- *Uncertainty* was also present in full measure. The Internet was a miracle, but a miracle for what? If the Internet had so many wonderful uses, why were so many users young males checking the latest sports scores and pornography?
- *Hype* was an especially prominent feature. Many Internet offerings were promoted as the richest, biggest, or fastest growing in the world. Behind the hype there was sometimes, well, not very much. Amazon.com might be 'the world's largest bookstore' by number of titles listed. But Amazon.com was really just a newer version of the old mail order system. It was also a service which traditional book retailers could replicate.

Like previous born (or at least brought up) in the USA 'new media', the Internet, when it went out into the wider world, went still dressed in distinctively American clothes and reflecting American life, geography, and competing services. Like other new media, it arrived at a time when suitable technologies (packet switching and massive telecoms overcapacity) were already available. The Internet married telephone lines with big and small computers, reflecting conditions in an America where 'local phone calls are free' and where personal computers were widely available. Internet commerce depended upon heavy American use of credit cards and familiarity with distance shopping (from both mail order and cable TV shopping channels).

Could the Internet be the last of the all-singing, all-dancing, and all-American new mass media? Some features of the Internet may not be repeated, for instance, its initial funding and subsidy by the Department of Defense in Washington. Probably no future 'new medium' will be quite so American-controlled as the Internet was in its early years. The system of governance and control—including, for instance, the control of addresses—was dominated by obscure offices near Washington and in California, and by large American companies. It seems unlikely that the European Union will ever again agree to accept such a subordinate role in such an important new medium.

Disadvantages of Being Media Number One

It may be that both United States foreign policy-makers and the US media industry depend upon British support more than they are willing to acknowledge. President Reagan might not have ordered the 1987 assault on Libya and President Bush might not have ordered the 1991 assault on Iraq, had there not been vigorous encouragement from Britain.

The US media industry has come to regard some British media organizations as not really foreign, just as British films do not qualify as 'foreign' films at the Academy Awards. Reuters, the London news agency, is often referred to as an American news agency; nor does the BBC seem really foreign to US viewers of PBS and other up-market networks.

But just as the British media industry is used by Hollywood for its purposes, so also Hollywood is used by its Copyright Alliance partners for their purposes. Because of the peculiar economics of the media, Hollywood and the rest of the US media are able to earn extra revenues through massive exports; but the sums of money earned are (with the exception of movies) quite small in relation to the number of hours of viewing. A typical citizen of a European country views (and listens to) US audio-visual material for about one hour per day; but the US media only receive about $20 a year for this, or about five or six cents an hour. The companies which do make bigger amounts from exports are computer companies and others in the Copyright Alliance.

Meanwhile the export success of the US media industry increases its prestige and political influence at home. The movie and television industries and the print and publishing media—like the computer, telecoms, and Internet companies—have a powerful presence in Washington. Export prestige exists alongside the raw political (and electoral) power of the broadcasters and the newspapers. This prestige and power enabled Hollywood in effect to reassemble a bigger and more vertical cartel than the one which was declared illegal in 1948. By allowing foreign owners to purchase American media companies and by allowing in token amounts of foreign (mainly British) creative material, the Hollywood-network vertical combine has successfully frozen out all other media (except those for language minorities).

Consequently the American domestic media are not only extremely powerful, but also extremely parochial; the citizens of a world power (and world media power) see the world largely through the cameras of the domestic US media. These powerful-parochial media are involved in two paradoxes:

- The media are extremely powerful in Washington but seem ineffective at persuading US citizens to participate even in the democratic ritual of voting at elections.
- The media seem to encourage a belligerent foreign policy stance, while at the same time threatening to give massive negative coverage to the deaths of even a small number of 'our boys' on foreign service. Consequently US presidents prefer to conduct diplomacy by cruise missile, which itself looks more like weakness than strength.

Against this background it can be argued that the extravagant media export successes of the USA in Europe in general, and in Britain in particular, are not helpful to the long-term interests of the United States.

24

Britain's Anglo-American Media Mirage

BRITAIN prides itself on being a world power in the media. True, it has been, and still is, a significant number two within the Anglo-American media on the world scene. Britain is a serious player in, and serious exporter of, facts, data, and news. But Britain is a net importer of media entertainment, fiction, and dreams.

Whereas Washington does have a general policy for the media and has encouraged an ever more commercial (and exporting) thrust, Britain has no such general policy. Like most other European countries, Britain has no overall media policy, no integrated film-and-TV industry, and no real strategy for confronting Hollywood. Britain's most successful media exporter has been the music industry for which no public policy exists. There is no general media policy because, under British conditions, politicians-in-power find it easier to handle (and to divide and rule) a scattered and fragmented media industry which operates under several old and new, explicit and implicit, different policy regimes.

The politicians are naturally most interested in the factual and news media, where Britain does best. British politicians, when making visits abroad, are pleased to be able both to hear and to see BBC news services. Politicians are less concerned with entertainment and the massive volumes of Hollywood fiction available on British TV screens.

If Britain's media policy stance had been closely to follow the French, not the American, lead, European media history might have been somewhat different. Britain, then, would have penalized the video-cassette medium (and its inevitable Hollywood movies). Britain would have heavily subsidized its film industry in direct opposition to Hollywood. If Britain had followed France, there would presumably have been no BSkyB, but a state subsidy (and the fifth British terrestrial TV channel) would have been awarded to British Satellite Broadcasting (BSB) in the mid-1980s.

Instead, of course, Britain loosely followed the United States in several key respects. Britain 'privatized' its telephone operator and introduced competition. This led to satellite channels based in Britain but directed at Europe, which in turn contributed to the Brussels Television without

Frontiers policy, with its (unanticipated but predictable) pro-Hollywood consequences.

From an American media industry viewpoint, Britain was astonishingly, indeed irrationally, supportive. Britain allowed itself to be used as Hollywood's springboard into Europe. Only a few people in Britain questioned precisely what benefits Britain actually obtained from this beautiful relationship. Only a few people pointed out some of the obvious disadvantages; for example, if Hollywood-in-London exported more programming and channels into Europe, this would probably lead to fewer British exports.

1875–2025: Anglo-American News, Facts, and Data

By the 1870s the Associated Press was the strongest national news agency, and Reuters the strongest international news agency, in the world. These two are still the leading agencies and they seem likely to continue as dominant duopolists.

In documentary and natural history television also the Anglo-American lead seems likely to continue, with the Discovery-Flextech-BBC combination as a market leader. There will also be other European players in this field as well as American companies such as Time Warner.

In data-on-screens there are inevitable predictions of a future duopoly, not least because the large investment banks now generate their own internal (but worldwide) fast data-on-screens networks. Reuters dominated this market during the 1985–95 decade. Thereafter Reuters' 50 per cent share of the world market began to decline, mainly due to strong competition from Bloomberg. But of the four world leaders, Reuters was British and the other three—Dow Jones, Bloomberg, and Bridge—were American. All four major companies, then, were Anglo-American, as were most of the successful vendors of more specialized niche financial data services. Thus, if and when the business does boil down to a duopoly, both survivors are likely to be Anglo-American.

It is upon this narrow, but politically and financially potent, platform, that Britain's claim to a number two world media position is mainly based. All of the British organizations involved are quite frail in their different ways. Reuters' greatest days are probably behind it (in the era of floating European exchange rates and before the birth of the Euro currency). The BBC will continue to struggle valiantly against increasingly difficult conditions. The *Financial Times* looks to have a secure future, especially in Europe. British outfits such as ITN (in the driving seat at Euronews) and *The Economist* are successful, but really only niche players on the world scene.

Thus, while there will continue to be some substance to the 'Britain as World Media Number Two' image, it is based on a handful of (by world standards) only medium-sized players. There is an element of the British media industry seeking—and receiving—reassurance that it is indeed a big player on the big world media scene. Yes that's what they are saying out there in the world. The 'they' who are saying it, however, are those same Anglo-American news/factual/data services where Britain (somewhat atypically of the media overall) is indeed a world leader.

Entertainment: The Los Angeles, New York, Miami, London Axis

In the next two or three decades the American entertainment industry will focus more strongly on Latin America, for three reasons. First, Latin America looks to be a promising territory for Hollywood exports and for satellite networks (many of them jointly operated by North and South American partners); the focus will be especially on Brazil, Argentina, and Mexico. Second, Spanish-language programming (and probably mixed English/Hispanic programming) will become increasingly important inside the USA as the huge predicted Hispanic population growth takes place. Cable systems in relevant areas of Los Angeles, Miami, New York, and other big cities will each be carrying scores of Hispanic channels. Third, US-produced and US-distributed Spanish-language entertainment will be significant also in Spain. Miami will be increasingly important in a triangular media trade between North and South America and Spain. Since Los Angeles and New York also have big Hispanic populations, the American entertainment industry will without difficulty come to see itself as strategically placed to exploit, not just the English language, but also a second world language, Spanish.

This Spanish and Latin American strategy will fit quite neatly with the main American entertainment export focus on Europe, a Europe stretching now from Madrid to Moscow. The US–Europe entertainment relationship will be Hollywood's main foreign relationship and there is likely to be further consolidation, or meshing together, of the US and European entertainment industries.

London's (and Britain's) go-between role is likely to be more—not less—important in the future. This in turn raises many further questions. For example will Britain, at long last, develop a significant film industry? The answer may be that Yes, Britain will at last develop a significant film industry. However that 'British' film industry may (like the British car industry) be largely owned by American, French, German, Italian, and Japanese companies.

Addressing Britain's Media Dilemmas

No British government or government-appointed committee has ever considered Britain's media relationship with the United States; nor has any investigation ever been conducted across the broad range of British media and policy. British media policy has always been fragmented and full of bizarre internal contradiction.

In the past there was a custom of setting up several specialized committees to report at the same time. For example, in the year 1977 three major committees all reported—one on Broadcasting, one on the Press, and one on Telecommunications (and the Post Office). However in 1979 Mrs Thatcher came to power and the Maggie and Rupert nod-waive-and-grunt policy-making mode came into its own. Of course the short-term political convenience of governments has always been a factor in setting media policy in Britain, as elsewhere. What was different about the 1979–90 Thatcher era was first the brazen (and dubiously legal) way in which these deals were done; second the novel bartering of massively valuable regulatory favours for tabloid newspaper electoral support; third, while media policy was retreating to such primitive levels the media industries were racing forward in terms of international, technical, political, and social complexity. Both John Major and Tony Blair subsequently continued with media policy-making which was still deeply fragmented and, hence, transparently flawed.

Even though the media have not 'converged' to the extent claimed, convergence has gone far enough to make the old fragmented policy approaches look antiquated. The whole of British media policy needs to be considered against the background of both United States and European media policy. Topics which need attention include the following:

- Britain and Europe need to reconsider public broadcasting, including radical rethinking of its finances.
- The whole BSkyB situation, including BSkyB's monopolistic control of both satellite and cable programming, and in particular BSkyB's exclusive Hollywood and sports contracts, require attention.
- American control of BSkyB and two of the three main cable companies needs to be reconsidered.
- The big financial bite which the Treasury takes from ITV needs to be assessed as part of British media finance.
- The British government's (Foreign Office) direct financing of BBC world service radio seems anachronistic, especially in the post-Communist era.
- The feeding of lottery funds through the government 'Arts' bureaucracy into the British 'Film' industry has been tacked onto the pre-existing audio-visual system without adequate thought.
- Most serious newspapers sold in Britain are foreign owned; this is unique across the world. The situation became grotesque in the 1990s, when two foreign owners (Murdoch and Black) campaigned to bend

British foreign policy in line with their own financial interests and ideological whims.

- Britain's role in Eutelsat needs to be considered in the light of broad media policy.

These are difficult questions, but they won't go away. Indeed some of them will probably still be here in 2025. In the meanwhile, policy-makers in both Washington and Brussels should perhaps also be reassessing their trans-Atlantic media strategies and the part Britain may play in such strategies.

25

Towards Euro- and Anglo-American Media

THE year 1995 saw the dawning of the 'Digital Age', marked by Internet-mania in the American media and telephone industries and on Wall Street. The digital dawn was also marked by the successful launch of digital satellite television both in the USA and in Europe.

The digital era was widely seen as at last generating fundamental 'convergence'—in which voice, vision, sound, entertainment, and data would all merge into a single stream of material available on the same single domestic screen. Convergence onto that single screen may be slow to reach universal acceptance, not least because there will also be divergence onto additional screens designed for specialist tasks and combinations of tasks.

Another kind of 'convergence'—between the media of the United States and Europe—did seem to be proceeding quite rapidly in the years after 1990. In the 1990s there were marked increases of European ownership within selected American media. American involvement in European media also, of course, increased.

Other major changes were happening on the world media scene. By 1996 mainland China already had more 'television households' (containing at least one TV set) than western Europe and the United States combined.[1] It looked highly probable that both China and India would follow Japan in becoming largely self-contained media powers, doing relatively little import-ing. Meanwhile both the USA and Europe will attempt to export to the rest of the world—especially to Latin America, Africa, and to the smaller population countries of Asia.

Against this background, old arguments about 'media imperialism' need to be fundamentally reconsidered.

Common Euro-American Competition Policy for the Digital Era

In the mid and late 1980s European media policy copied earlier American moves towards TV network competition; meanwhile Brussels maintained

[1] *Screen Digest* (May 1998), 111.

the vague (and unarticulated) hope that it could somehow avoid the obvious and logical consequence of more imports from Hollywood.

But a decade later European media policy was taking a very different direction, because it was increasingly driven by an aggressive anti-monopoly policy in the form of decisions from the Competition Directorate (DG4) and its Commissioner, the Belgian politician Karel Van Miert. The DG4 Competition decisions for communications were only one part of a much bigger flow of competition decisions affecting car production, international airlines, and numerous other industries. The DG4 communications decisions involved mergers and joint ventures in such new technology areas as digital television and the Internet. Also important were decisions about telephone deregulation and the proposed involvement of dominant telephone operators in satellite TV and cable TV ventures:

- Several *digital television* proposals in 1997–8 involved national consortia which incorporated previously competitive TV players, plus the major telecoms operator. These proposals involved Britain (Carlton, Granada, and British Telecom), Germany (Bertelsmann, Kirch, Deutsche Telekom), Italy (Mediaset, RAI, and Telecom Italia), and Spain (Canal Plus España and Telefónica).
- DG4 was also involved with DG13 (Telecommunications) in developing a major policy for *telecommunications deregulation and competition*, which came into effect in January 1998. In addition, the EU decided that where the main telecoms operator had a dominant position in cable TV (as in Germany and several other countries) cable should be separated from such dominance (Cable Directive, 1995).
- Other interventions involved *international sports* and its newly buoyant media finances. One issue was the German proposal that professional football could be exempted from general monopoly law. Another issue was the control of Formula One grand prix car racing, mainly by British businessmen via French-based 'world' bodies.
- *Dominant position in specialist journal publishing* was also challenged in a proposed merger between the British-Dutch Reed Elsevier and the Dutch Wolters Kluwer company.

Two cases involving the spread of the Internet into Europe were especially important in leading towards similar European and American communications policies. One case concerned the proposed merger of two US long-distance telephone companies, WorldCom and MCI; Van Miert and DG4 decided that this merger of two US companies would lead to a combined American company with excessive dominance in the Internet connection business in Europe. DG4 and the EU required that the relevant parts of MCI should be excluded from the merger, and these were sold to Cable and Wireless of Britain.

Another case in 1998 found DG4 objecting to the dominant position of Microsoft and its Explorer software on the Internet in western Europe. Microsoft was required to 'loosen' its contracts with twenty-five Internet service suppliers across Europe (including major players, such as France Telecom).

An amicable, indeed highly cooperative, relationship developed between Karel Van Miert at DG4 and Joel Klein, the anti-trust chief at the Department of Justice in Washington. Quite soon, some informal division of labour evolved. Van Miert in Brussels, despite having a small staff, was required to move quickly and thus tended to take the initiative in Euro-American cases. Joel Klein in Washington, with the larger DOJ tended to take on more complex cases, including cases involving taxation and high-technology issues; perhaps most complex of all was the Microsoft case initiated by the DOJ in 1998, which had obvious implications for Europe.

Despite some strong elements of 'convergence', European and American policies remained separate even on specific competition and anti-monopoly issues. For example, both the EU and the US were focusing on telecommunications competition. But the EU was still introducing deregulation and competition to most of its member countries. In the United States, however, there were mergers and proposed mergers between several of the seven regional Bell companies which had been created in the DOJ break-up of AT&T back in 1982–4.

One common criticism of the Van Miert DG4 competition policies was that the EU was focusing on maintaining phone competition, and keeping digital TV access open, within each separate European country. This—the critics said—ensured a European market fragmented into numerous small country markets, and into even more numerous small companies, but without adequate common standardization in the new digital fields. However the United States' performance in terms of digital standards was also fairly chaotic; and DG4 argued that competition—and open access—within national markets precisely provided the opportunity for trans-European companies.

Competition and technical standards issues will remain contested and controversial. But these contests and controversies are likely to take place within a loosely coordinated American-European set of common decisions and understandings. Europe will no longer dabble in vague nostrums about Television without Frontiers or Americans. In the future it will be a matter of Policies across the Atlantic, usually with Euro-American coordination.

Europe at Last Getting its Media Act Together?

The year 1995, in Europe as in the USA, marked the beginning of the digital television era. In October 1995 Europe's first digital satellite (Astra 1E) was successfully placed into orbit.

It could still be argued, however, that in several respects the United States was about to extend still further its media leadership, and to emphasize still further the backward condition of media Europe. While the US digital launch was chaotic, it was perhaps less chaotic than Europe's separate fragmented national efforts. Hollywood still seemed to be riding high; big movies, big TV series, and US popular culture (including African-American and Hispanic-American popular culture) were still very big indeed in Europe. Hollywood cartoons, and other kidvid product, were still taking up ever more billions of hours of European children's viewing.

Nevertheless there were, and are, more numerous reasons to suggest that Europe was gradually getting its media act together. Conflicts between national regulators (such as the German Cartel Authority) and Brussels regulators are quoted as evidence of chaos, indecision, and fragmentation. But conflict—and cooperation—between national and Brussels regulators also help to highlight and to dramatize the issues.

Karel Van Miert, from around 1995 onwards, became the leading personality in the establishment of media competition policy across Europe. Such personalization again helps to dramatize complex issues; it also provides a necessary balance to the focus upon owner-moguls and could help to shed more light upon media mogul-to-mogul personal relationships.

European national media variety is taking an increasingly positive (and less fragmented) form as different countries start to cultivate distinctive national styles and niche markets. Germany and France are between them developing three or four major vertical press-television companies. There are the German Bertelsmann-UFA-CLT and Kirch-Springer combinations. In France there is a separate pattern of companies moving out from French state protection to become major vertical players; this includes Hachette-Filipacchi and, most notably, Havas (a child of the 1830s) which controls Canal Plus and is controlled by the Vivendi water-and-media grouping, prompting *Variety*'s September 1997 headline, 'There's no business like Eaux business'.

Europe has a substantial portfolio of Euro-media entities and, at least some of these may become bigger players in the future. Eurovision is known for its famously bland annual song contest and its important daily exchange of television news. Euronews (born 1993) is an all-news channel, which in its early years[2] used European public broadcaster material under French leadership; when in 1998 the British ITN took over the French role (and 49 per cent ownership) plans were announced for expansion beyond the single video feed with five separate language soundtracks. Eurosport (with one-third Disney-ESPN ownership) has long been Europe's single most popular channel, although it faces ever stronger national competition. Eutelsat was

[2] Marcel Machill, 'Euronews: the first European news channel ... ' *Media, Culture and Society*, 20 July 1998, pp. 427–50.

the satellite child of the European telecommunications monopolists; Eutel-sat has been transformed by telecoms deregulation and as a commercial company is an increasingly aggressive competitor to the SES-Astra commercial satellite system. Another interesting satellite organization, Inmarsat, was originally a marine satellite service for the world; but Inmarsat has also moved in a commercial direction (and into other services) and it is a London-based organization with European ownership elements in the lead. As all of these entities have moved in a more commercial direction, they have also increasingly shown the wide possibilities for a more assertive European media presence on the world scene.

Sport continues to have much potential for strengthening European consciousness. Just as the battle of Waterloo (1815) was proverbially won on the playing fields of Eton, so the battle of European consciousness may be won on the football fields (and sports channels) of Europe.

Europe's lack of Venture Capital is said to explain her lack of a California Silicon Valley, or a New York Silicon Alley, with their resulting explosions of start-up companies, baby moguls, and general entrepreneurial dynamism. However, a small insurgent company like Nokia, of Finland, was able to compete rather effectively in the world mobile phone business with America's finest (especially Motorola). The case of Finland suggests that we may need a new concept such as the 'Venture Economy'. Finland's great leap forward into its status as perhaps the world's most advanced Information Society involved major government support against a background of unemployment and declining traditional industries.[3]

Europe is now in a phase of greatly heightened competition. Europe has major competition between commercial and ('subsidized') public channels; cable in Europe faced earlier competition from direct-to-home satellite TV (in 28 million European homes in 1997) than did cable in the USA. Telecommunications deregulation in Europe ensures increasingly sharp competition for many years to come.

What happens to public broadcasting will be important for the European future. But so long as Europe retains some public broadcasting funded by licence fee, it has another long-term advantage over the USA. Europe will not only have advertising finance and subscription revenue for its television, it will also have the third financial source of the licence fee.

European newspapers in their huge variety and number constitute another continuing advantage. The almost complete lack of local American newspaper competition (outside New York City) is a disadvantage. Newspapers can look towards partnerships of various kinds with electronic media and interactive services. Europe should also be able to learn from Norway, Finland, and Sweden, which led the entire world in the early use of Internet

[3] Helena Trapper (University of Helsinki), 'Information Society Strategy. . . . The Case of Finland', paper presented at IAMCR Conference, Glasgow, July 1998.

and mobile phones, whilst also sharing with Japan the world's highest levels of daily newspaper purchase.

Euro-American Ownership

Table 25.1 shows the different strengths of Europe and the USA in terms of their numbers of large television companies. Europe had the most, 42 per cent of the world total. But the biggest American strength lay in having seven of the ten largest TV organizations in the world. This again emphasizes 'vertical' strength within all levels of television and cable (the Table does not include additional vertical strength in movies, print, and other media). The seven (out of the top ten) companies predictably included such Hollywood-and-network (TV and/or cable) outfits as Time Warner, Disney, and Viacom.

These latter companies are prominent among the group of six or seven companies which account for most of Europe's huge audio-visual trade deficit with the United States.

The most visible parts of this US trade surplus are in movies and TV series. But there are some other less glitzy, and Hollywood glamorous, fields in which the transatlantic trade advantage already lies in Europe. These include:

- *Magazines*—five of the twenty largest American magazine companies (by revenue) are foreign-owned. These companies are the British-Dutch Reed Elsevier; the Canadian Thomson company; the French Hachette-Filipacchi; the German Gruner and Jahr (Bertelsmann); and the British United News and Media. These companies are mainly

Table 25.1 The world's 100 largest television companies, 1998 (by television revenue only)

	Ten largest companies (1–10)	Next forty largest (11–50)	Next fifty largest (51–100)	Hundred largest (1–100) total
Europe	0	19	23	42
USA	7	9	10	26
Australia/Canada/New Zealand	1	4	6	11
Japan	1	6	1	8
Latin America	1	1	6	8
Other	0	1	4	5
Total	10	40	50	100

Source: Television Business International (July/August 1998)

involved in unglamorous women's magazines (*Woman's Day, Family Circle, McCall's, Parents, Elle*, and *Woman's World* are all European owned). Reed Elsevier (through its Cahners subsidiary) also owns a lot of leading trade publications including *Variety* and *Broadcasting and Cable.*

- In *book publishing* Bertelsmann claims to be the largest publisher inside the USA. Bertelsmann, the British Pearson, and other European book publishers own a large slice of this American industry.
- In the provision of *on-line data or data-on-screens*, foreign companies play leading roles in the domestic US market. In scientific publishing, the Anglo-Dutch Reed Elsevier with its 1,200 scientific journals is the largest science publisher in the USA, both on paper and on-line. In American legal publishing the Canadian Thomson company and Reed Elsevier (Lexis-Nexis) occupy leading positions.

It is becoming increasingly difficult to decide whether certain companies are American or European. Large minority holdings—such as 30 per cent— are common in France, Germany, the USA and elsewhere. This may well become still more common.

We anticipate that in the future the American and European media industries will increasingly merge into a single giant industry. There will also be other participation, especially perhaps by Sony, which already is a leading Hollywood company and spreads its business activities increasingly evenly across Japan, the USA, Europe, and the rest of the world.

Under these more co-owned and cooperative Euro-American media conditions of the future, there seems likely to be an increasingly common and cooperative regulatory regime, with the Competition/Monopoly authorities in both Brussels and Washington playing the joint lead roles. It will be interesting to see what the Washington regulators have to say in the future about European government intervention and public subsidy of the media. It will also be interesting to see whether the Brussels authorities are willing to go for the Hollywood jugular by accusing it of being a cartel of about six movie/TV/cable vertical companies which conspire to exclude Europeans from the movie, TV, and cable businesses.

Select Bibliography

ALGER, DEAN, *Megamedia* (Lanham, Md.: Rowan and Littlefield, 1998).

ALLEN, ROBERT C. (ed.), *To Be Continued. . . Soap Operas around the World* (London: Routledge, 1995).

ALLEYNE, MARK D., *News Revolution* (New York: Saint Martin's Press, 1997).

ANDERSON, CHRISTOPHER, *Hollywood TV: The Studio System in the Fifties* (Austin: University of Texas Press, 1994).

AULETTA, KEN, *Three Blind Mice: How the Networks Lost their Way* (New York: Vintage, 1992 edition).

—— *The Highwaymen* (New York: Random House, 1997).

BARNES, JAMES L., *Authors, Publishers and Politicians* (London: Routledge, 1974).

BARNET, RICHARD J., AND CAVANAGH, JOHN, *Global Dreams: Imperial Corporations and the New World Order* (New York: Touchstone/Simon and Schuster, 1994).

BLAIN, NEIL, and CERE, RINELLA, 'Dangerous Television: The TV a luci rosse Phenomenon', *Media, Culture and Society*, 17 (July 1995), 483–98.

BLOOMBERG, MICHAEL, *Bloomberg by Bloomberg* (New York: John Wiley, 1997).

BODDY, WILLIAM F., 'Launching Television: RCA, the FCC and the Battle for Frequency Allocations, 1940–1947', *Historical Journal of Film, Radio and Television*, 9, (1989), 45–57.

BONDEBJERG, IB, and BONO, FRANCESCO (eds.), *Television in Scandinavia* (Luton: University of Luton Press, 1996).

BORDEN, DIANE L., and HARVEY, KERRIC (eds.), *The Electronic Grapevine* (Mahwah, NJ: Lawrence Erlbaum, 1998).

BOYD-BARRETT, OLIVER, and RANTANEN, TEHRI (eds.), *The Globalization of News* (London: Sage, 1998).

BRAESTRUP, PETER, *The Big Story*, 2 vols. (Boulder, Colo.: Westview Press, 1977).

BRAGG, MELVYN, *Rich: The Life of Richard Burton* (London: Coronet Books, 1989).

BRIGGS, ASA, *Sound and Vision* (Oxford: Oxford University Press, 1979).

—— *Competition, 1955–1974* (Oxford: Oxford University Press, 1995).

BUONANNO, MILLY (ed.), *Imaginary Dreamscapes: Television Fiction in Europe* (Luton: University of Luton Press, 1998).

CANTOR, MURIEL G., and PINGREE, SUZANNE, *The Soap Opera* (Beverly Hills, Calif.: Sage, 1983).

CHALABY, JEAN K., 'Journalism as an Anglo-American Invention', *European Journal of Communication*, 11 (Sept. 1996), 303–26.

CHRISTIE, IAN, *Arrows of Desire: The Films of Michael Powell and Emeric Pressburger* (London: Faber and Faber, 1994).

COHEN, AKIBA, LEVY, MARK, GUREVITCH, MICHAEL, and ROEH, ITZAK, *Global Newsrooms, Local Audiences* (London: John Libbey, 1996).

COLERIDGE, NICHOLAS, *Paper Tigers* (London: Mandarin, 1994).

COLLINS, RICHARD, *Broadcasting and Audio-Visual Policy in the Single European Market* (London: John Libbey, 1994).

—— *From Satellite to Single Market* (London: Routledge, 1998).

—— and MURRONI, CRISTINA, *New Media, New Policies* (Oxford: Polity Press, 1996).

COOPER, KENT, *Barriers Down* (New York: Farrar and Rinehart, 1942).

CORNER, JOHN and HARVEY, SYLVIA (eds.), *Television Times* (London: Arnold, 1996).

CRANDALL, ROBERT W., and FURCHTGOTT-ROTH, HAROLD, *Cable TV: Regulation or Competition* (Washington: The Brookings Institution, 1996).

CRYSTAL, DAVID, *English as a Global Language* (Cambridge: Cambridge University Press, 1997).

CULL, NICHOLAS JOHN, *Selling War: The British Propaganda Campaign against American 'Neutrality' in World War II* (New York: Oxford University Press, 1995).

CURWEN, PETER, *The World Book Industry* (London: Euromonitor, 1986).

DALE, MARTIN, *The Movie Game* (London: Cassell, 1997).

DEGEORGE, GAIL, *The Making of a Blockbuster* (New York: John Wiley, 1996).

Department of National Heritage, *The Future of the BBC* (London: HMSO, 1994).

EBERTS, JAKE, and ILOTT, TERRY, *My Indecision is Final: The Rise and Fall of Goldcrest Films* (London: Faber and Faber, 1992 edition).

Euromedia Research Group, *The Media in Western Europe* (London: Sage, 1997).

Film Policy Review Group, *A Bigger Picture* (London: Department of Culture, Media and Sport, 1998).

FINNEY, ANGUS, *The Egos Have Landed: The Rise and Fall of Palace Pictures* (London: Mandarin, 1997).

FLOURNOY, DON M., and STEWART, ROBERT K., *CNN: Making News in the Global Market* (Luton: John Libbey/University of Luton Press, 1997).

Fortune, The Editors of, *The Amazing Advertising Business* (New York: Simon and Schuster, 1957).

FRIEDLAND, LEWIS A., *Covering the World: The International Television News Services* (New York: Twentieth Century Fund, 1992).

GOODWIN, PETER, *Television under the Tories: Broadcasting Policy, 1979–1997* (London: British Film Institute, 1998).

GRAHAM, ANDREW, and DAVIES, GAVYN, *Broadcasting, Society and Policy in the Multimedia Age* (Luton: University of Luton Press, 1997).

—— et al., *Public Purposes in Broadcasting: Funding the BBC* (Luton: University of Luton Press, 1999).

GRECO, ALBERT N., *The Book Publishing Industry* (Boston: Allyn and Bacon, 1997).

GUBACK, THOMAS, *The International Film Industry* (Bloomington: Indiana University Press, 1969).

IOSIFIDES, PETROS, 'Media Concentration Policy in the European Union and the Public Interest', unpublished Ph.D. dissertation, University of Westminster (London), 1996.

HALBERSTAM, DAVID, *The Making of a Quagmire* (London: Bodley Head, 1965).

HESS, STEPHEN, *International News and Foreign Correspondents* (Washington: The Brookings Institution, 1996).

HILMES, MICHELE, *Hollywood and Broadcasting* (Chicago: University of Illinois Press, 1990).

HOLLAND, STEVE, *The Mushroom Jungle: A History of Postwar Paperback Publishing* (Westbury: Zeon Books, 1993).

Home Office, *Direct Broadcasting by Satellite* (London: HMSO, 1981).

HORRIE, CHRIS, and CLARKE, STEVE, *Fuzzy Monsters: Fear and Loathing at the BBC* (London: Heinemann, 1994).

HORSMAN, MATHEW, *Sky High* (London: Orion Business Books, 1997).

House of Commons, National Heritage Committee, *The British Film Industry*, vol. i, Session 1994–5 (London: HMSO, 1995), 57–I.

HUMPHREYS, PETER J., *Media and Media Policy in Germany: The Press and Broadcasting since 1945* (Oxford: Berg, 1994 edition).

HUNT, LORD (chairman), *Report of the Inquiry into Cable Expansion and Broadcasting Policy* (London: HMSO, 1982).

JANKOWSKI, GENE, and FUCHS, DAVID C., *Television Today and Tomorrow* (New York: Oxford University Press, 1995).

JARVIK, LAWRENCE, *PBS: Behind the Screen* (Rocklin, Calif.: Prima, Forum, 1997).

KELLY, MARY, 'National, European or American Programmes: Trends in European Television', *Journal of the Institute of Public Administration of Ireland*, 36 (1988), 9–24.

KYNASTON, DAVID, *The Financial Times* (London: Viking, 1988).

LANDY, MARCIA, *British Genres: Cinema and Society, 1930–60* (Princeton: Princeton University Press, 1991).

LEVY, EMMANUEL, *And the Winner Is . . . .* (New York: Frederick Ungar/Continuum, 1990).

LITTLETON, SUELLEN, *The Wapping Dispute* (Aldershot: Avebury, 1992).

McANANY, EMILE G., and WILKINSON, KENTON T. (eds.), *Mass Media and Free Trade* (Austin: University of Texas Press, 1996).

MACBRIDE, SEAN (chairman), *Many Voices, One World* (London: Kogan Page/ Unesco, 1980).

MACHILL, MARCEL, 'Euronews: The First European News Channel. . .', *Media, Culture and Society*. 20 (July 1998), 427–50.

MACNAB, GEOFFREY, *J. Arthur Rank and the British Film Industry* (London: Routledge, 1993).

McQUAIL, DENIS, and SIUNE, KAREN (eds.), *Media Policy: Convergence, Concentration and Commerce* (London: Sage, 1998).

MAIER, THOMAS, *Newhouse* (Boulder, Colo.: Johnson Books, 1997).

MAYER, MARTIN, *Madison Avenue, USA* (London: Bodley Head, 1958).

MELVERN, LINDA, *The End of the Street* (London: Methuen, 1986).

MEYERSON, MICHAEL I., 'Ideas of the Marketplace: A Guide to the 1996 Telecommunications Act', *Federal Communications Law Journal*, 49 (Feb. 1997), 251–88.

MIDDLETON, SIR PETER (chairman), *The Advisory Committee on Film Finance: Report to the Secretary of State for National Heritage* (London, 1996).

Monopolies and Mergers Commission, *Films: A Report on the Supply of Films for Exhibition in Cinemas in the UK* (London: HMSO, 1994, Cm. 2673).

MORAN, ALBERT (ed.), *Film Policy: International, National and Regional Perspectives* (London: Routledge, 1996).

—— *Copycat TV: Globalization, Program Formats and Cultural Identity* (Luton: University of Luton Press, 1998).

MULGAN, GEOFF, and PATERSON, RICHARD (eds.), *Hollywood of Europe?* (London: British Film Institute, 1993).

MURPHY, ROBERT, *Realism and Tinsel: Cinema and British Society, 1939–48* (London: Routledge, 1989).

NEGUS, KEITH, *Producing Pop* (London: Edward Arnold, 1992).

NEIL, ANDREW, *Full Disclosure* (London: Macmillan, 1996).

NOAM, ELI, *Television in Europe* (New York: Oxford University Press, 1991).

NOWELL-SMITH, GEOFFREY, and STEVEN RICCI (eds.), *Hollywood and Europe* (London: British Film Institute, 1998).

O'DONNELL, HUGH, *Good Times, Bad Times: Soap Operas and Society in Western Europe.* (London: Leicester University Press, 1999).

PALMER, MICHAEL, 'The Political Economy of News Flow within Europe: News Agencies, Foreign Exchange Dealing and the European Monetary Crisis of September 1992', in Farrell Corcoran and Paschal Preston (eds.), *Democracy and Communication in the New Europe.* (Cresskill, NJ: Hampton Press, 1995), 143–55.

—— and TUNSTALL, JEREMY, *Liberating Communications: Policy-Making in France and Britain* (Oxford: Blackwell, 1990).

PARKER, RICHARD, *Mixed Signals: The Prospects for Global Television News* (New York: Twentieth Century Fund Press, 1995).

PANDIT, S. A., *From Making to Music: The History of Thorn EMI* (London: Hodder and Stoughton, 1996).

PEACOCK, ALAN (chairman), *Report of the Committee on Financing the BBC* (London: HMSO, 1986).

PUTTNAM, DAVID, *The Undeclared War: The Struggle for Control of the World's Film Industry* (London: HarperCollins, 1997).

READ, DONALD, *The Power of News: The History of Reuters* (Oxford: Oxford University Press, 1992).

RIFFENBURGH, BEAU, T*he Myth of the Explorer: The Press, Sensationalism and Geographical Discovery* (Oxford: Oxford University Press, 1993).

ROSE, FRANK, *The Agency: William Morris and the Hidden History of Showbusiness* (New York: HarperCollins, 1995).

ROSENBERG, JERRY, *Inside the Wall Street Journal* (New York: Macmillan, 1982).

ROSTEN, LEO, *Hollywood: The Movie Colony, the Movie Makers* (New York: Harcourt Brace, 1941).

SHAWCROSS, WILLIAM, *Rupert Murdoch* (London: Chatto and Windus, 1992).

SIKLOS, RICHARD, *Shades of Black: Conrad Black* (London: Heinemann, 1995).

SINCLAIR, JOHN, JACKA, ELIZABETH, and CUNNINGHAM, STUART, *New Patterns in Global Television* (Oxford: Oxford University Press, 1996).

SIUNE, KAREN, and TRUETZSCHLER, WOLFGANG, *Dynamics of Media Politics* (London: Sage, 1992).

SLATER, ROBERT, *Ovitz* (New York: McGraw Hill, 1997).

SOILA, TYTTI, WIDDING, ASTRID SÖDERBERGH, and IVERSON, GUNNAR, *Nordic National Cinemas* (London: Routledge, 1998).

STEEMERS, JEANETTE (ed.), *Changing Channels: The Prospects for Television in a Digital World* (London: John Libbey/University of Luton, 1998).

STERLING, CHRISTOPHER H., and KITTROSS, JOHN M., *Stay Tuned: A Concise History of American Broadcasting* (Belmont, Calif.: Wadsworth, 1990).

STERLING, CHRISTOPHER, 'Changing American Telecommunications Law: Assessing the 1996 Amendments', *Telecommunications and Space Journal*, 3 (1996), 1–25.

TEBBEL, JOHN, *The Media in America* (New York: Thames Y. Crowell, 1974).

THOMPSON, KRISTIN, *Exporting Entertainment: America in the World Film Market, 1907–1934* (London: British Film Institute, 1985).

Tracey, Michael, *The Decline and Fall of Public Service Broadcasting* (Oxford: Oxford University Press, 1998).

Tunstall, Jeremy, *The Advertising Man* (London: Chapman and Hall, 1964).

—— *The Media are American: Anglo-American Media in the World* (London: Constable; New York: Columbia University Press, 1977).

—— *The Media in Britain* (London: Constable, 1983).

—— *Communications Deregulation* (Oxford: Basil Blackwell, 1986).

—— *Television Producers* (London: Routledge, 1993).

—— *Newspaper Power* (Oxford: Oxford University Press, 1996).

—— 'Europe as World News Leader', *Journal of Communication*, 42 (Summer 1992), 84–99.

—— and Palmer, Michael, *Media Moguls* (London: Routledge, 1991).

—— and Walker, David, *Media Made in California* (New York: Oxford University Press, 1981).

Van Hemel, Hans Mommaas, and Smithuijsen, Cas (eds.), *Trading Culture: GATT, European Cultural Policies and the Transatlantic Market* (Amsterdam: Boekman Foundation, 1996).

Walker, Alexander, *Hollywood, England: The British Film Industry in the Sixties* (London: Michael Joseph, 1974).

Walker, Andrew, *A Skyful of Freedom: 60 Years of the BBC World Service* (London: Broadside Books, 1992).

Wasko, Janet, *Hollywood in the Information Age* (Oxford: Polity Press, 1994).

Wendt, Lloyd, *The Wall Street Journal* (Chicago: Rand, McNally, 1982).

Willett, Ralph, *The Americanization of Germany, 1945–1949* (London: Routledge, 1989).

Young, Hugo, *One of Us* (London: Pan, 1993).

Yule, Andrew, *Enigma: David Puttnam, the Story so Far* (Edinburgh: Mainstream Publishing, 1988).

Index